From Leila Philip's

THE ROAD THROUGH MIYAMA

"I hold my right hand up to the light and look at it slowly. The skin is cracked in places, wrinkled and dry from daily contact with clay, the nails filed down past the fleshy tip. It looks more like a tool than a hand. I flex the fingers, watching the tendons pull over the knuckles in long lines. What did this hand look like a year ago! The fingers are thinner now; the muscles at the base of the thumb are thick and flexible. A long band of muscle running from my wrist up my forearm bulges slightly. Fall spent on teacups, winter repeating rice bowls, then spring concentrating on plates, and finally summer months of small-necked bottles and flower holders—my hands have been molded too."

THE ROAD THROUGH MIYAMA

THE ROAD

THROUGH MIYAMA

LEILA PHILIP

Vintage Books   A Division of Random House, Inc.   New York

VINTAGE DEPARTURES

FIRST VINTAGE DEPARTURES EDITION, February 1991

Copyright © 1989 by Leila Philip
Cartography copyright © 1989 by Anita Karl

Library of Congress Cataloging-in-Publication Data
Philip, Leila.
The road through Miyama / Leila Philip.—1st Vintage departures ed.
p. cm.—(Vintage departures)
Reprint. Originally published: New York: Random House, 1989.
ISBN 0-679-72501-6
1. Higashiichiki-chō (Japan)—Social life and customs.
2. Pottery—Japan—Higashiichiki-chō. 3. Satsuma pottery.
4. Philip, Leila. I. Title.
[DS897.H4249P48 1990]
738′.092—dc20
[B] 90-50149 CIP

Author photograph copyright © 1989 by Jim Kalett

Manufactured in the United States of America
10 9 8 7 6 5 4 3 2 1

FOR MY TEACHER AND HIS WIFE,
KAZU AND REIKO NAGAYOSHI

It is not every truth
that recommends itself
to the common sense.

—Thoreau,
"Walking"

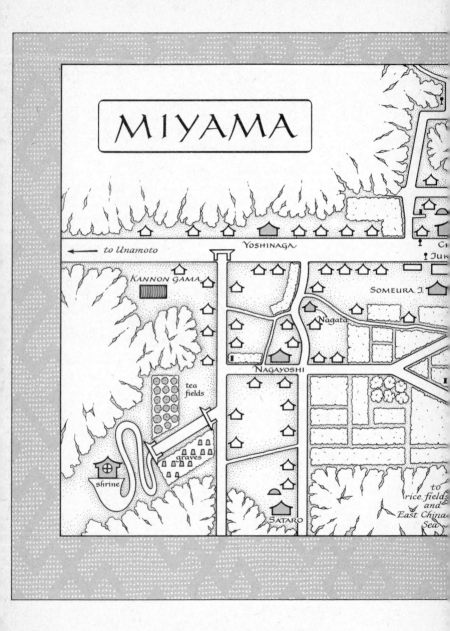

MIYAMA

← to Unamoto

YOSHINAGA

KANNON GAMA

SOMEURA J.

Nagata

NAGAYOSHI

tea
fields

graves

shrine

SATARO

to
rice fields
and
East China
Sea

JUK

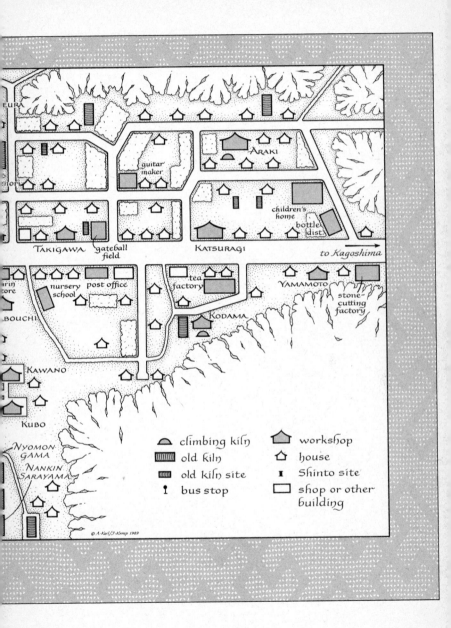

EUR

guitar
maker

ARAKI

children's
home

bottle
dist.

TAKIGAWA   gateball
field

KATSURAGI

to Kagoshima

arin
ore

nursery   post office
school

tea
factory

YAMAMOTO

stone-
cutting
factory

BOUCHI

KODAMA

KAWANO

KUBO

NYOMON-
GAMA
NANKIN
SARAYAMA

⌒ climbing kiln   ⬠ workshop

▥ old kiln   ⌂ house

▭ old kiln site   ᛁ Shinto site

⏺ bus stop   ▢ shop or other
                            building

© A.Karl/J.Kemp 1989

I AM INDEBTED to the people of Miyama, whose kindness and generosity made it possible for me to learn so much about their lives. In the pottery workshops, over tea, or in the rice fields, my numerous inquiries were met with patience and good humor. Many friends in Kagoshima deserve special thanks, most of all my teacher, Kazu Nagayoshi, and his wife, Reiko, to whom this work is dedicated. Although all facts about the village and the pottery industry stand as printed, certain names have been changed to respect the privacy of individuals.

I would like to thank Louise Cort, from whom I learned of Miyama and who guided my research from start to end; also William Howarth, who provided valued counsel and feedback on the early incarnation of this book. John McPhee and Toshiko Takaezu were two teachers who gave me the inspiration to begin. Professors Mary Elizabeth Berry and Thomas R. Havens read the manuscript and offered advice on historical matters. Finally, the interest and dedication of my editor, Becky Saletan, shows on every page. For their friendship and support, I would also like to thank my parents, Julia and Van Ness Philip, my extended family, many friends, and Dave, who was there in countless ways during the writing of this book.

Travel/study grants from the East Asian Studies department and the Woodrow Wilson School at Princeton in 1983 made my initial journey possible; Professors Marius Jansen and Earl Miner helped me to obtain funding. For my return to Japan in 1986 I am grateful to the U.S.-Japan Culture Center, in Washington, D.C.

The illustrations that open each chapter are from the *Sangoku Meisho Zue (Illustrations of Famous Places from Three Countries)*, a sixty-volume set of travel books published in Japan in 1834. My thanks to the East Asiatic Library at the University of California, Berkeley, for giving me access to them.

A
C
K
N
O
W
L
E
D
G
M
E
N
T
S

CONTENTS

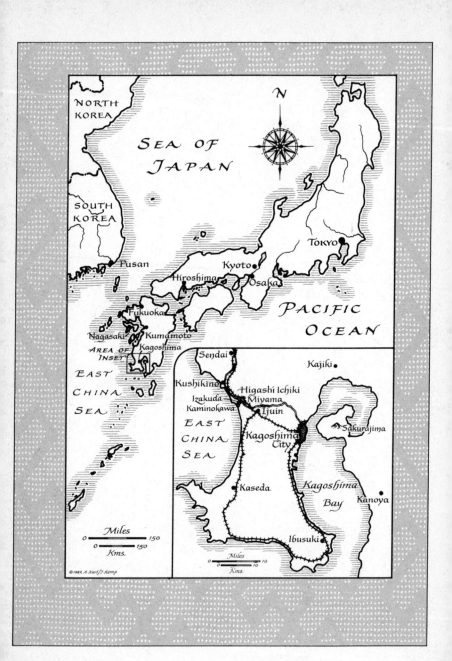

THE ROAD THROUGH MIYAMA

A cross within a circle, lord Shimazu
the road crossing time
and everywhere kuromon

IN THE SPRING OF 1640 SHIMAZU MITSU-
hisa, the nineteenth feudal lord of Satsuma, marched toward the small
mountain village of Naeshirogawa in
southern Kyushu. He was on his bian-
nual journey to the capital in Edo.
Throughout the Edo period, *sankin-
kōtai*, the "attendance by turns" system,
mandated that all *daimyō*—landholding
military lords—render annual or bian-
nual service to the shōgun. Naeshirogawa was not exactly on Lord
Shimazu's way. The direct route to the
capital led north from his castle residence, which lay just across the bay
from the smoking volcano Sakurajima
and what is now Kagoshima City. The
bamboo groves of Naeshirogawa were
a daylong side trip of twenty-eight kilometers over the mountains to the

northwest. But Shimazu ordered that his procession go by way of the village, and its main road came to be called sankin-kōtai ro—"road to the capital."

Shimazu's retinue marched from the east through the hills to the village. Gradually the stands of cedar gave way to tall thickets of bamboo, a flat plain crossed by a low river and flooded squares of green rice paddies. On the rise of a long hill, single-story thatched mud-walled houses and low-roofed pottery workshops appeared on either side. A low stone wall followed the road, marking off the yards and walled-in gardens of the dwellings. At the entrance to some of the larger houses the stone walls led into roofed gates indicating rural samurai status. Houses extended back from the road in a network of dirt pathways and cluttered yards, intersected by strips of garden and stands of bamboo. Not far from the workshops, long climbing kilns lined the hillside. Thick-walled, sturdy brown and black storage pots, tall and short, swelling outward and stiffly upright, stood everywhere, leaning in groups by the wells or tumbled in the grass, sitting idle by the smoking fires of outdoor kitchens.

At the head and rear of Shimazu's entourage marched domain officials, favored vassals and ranks of servants. At the center, wearing bright native costumes and playing the Ro-jigaku music of their southern Ryukyu Islands, trooped the Ryukyuan subjects brought along to enliven the journey. Villagers, knee-deep in the mud of newly planted rice or busy in the outlying fields of buckwheat and Satsuma potatoes, looked up from beneath low-brimmed hats at a safe distance. They knew at once that these colorful troops were those of their feudal lord, "devil Shimazu." A large white banner emblazoned with the crest of the house of Shimazu led the way. Every piece of equipment, from armor and horse harnesses down to the tiniest sake cup, bore the same simple mark: a perfect 90-degree crossroad trapped within a circle.

Forty-two years earlier Shimazu's grandfather, Yoshihiro, at the warlord Hideyoshi's command, had marched into Korea and sailed back with seventy potters in tow. Yi, Pak, Shin, Ke—twenty-one family names in all—they were brought from southern Korea, from Cholla and Kyong-sang provinces, the fallen fortresses of Namwon and Kimhae, carrying a few possessions and bags full of white clay. No one knows how many voluntarily enlisted and how many were "kidnapped" along the way. From then on they were the property of Lord Shimazu, and the ware they produced, the beginnings of Satsuma pottery.

As word of the daimyō's arrival spread, villagers rushed to finish preparations. Along the road white banners with the black Shimazu crest were hung. Dancers prepared their brilliant high-waisted robes. The best pottery was assembled for inspection. Shimazu Mitsuhisa's procession headed straight for the tallest stand of bamboo. Here at the central point in the village stood Sakurababa, his temporary residence, where later that evening he watched the slow dances of the Koreans before retiring for the night.

Before leaving the next day Lord Shimazu singled out two potters. He ordered them to put on their most extravagant Korean dress and took them along to Edo. In the capital his new "vassals" were paraded before envious daimyō from other domains. Word would reach the shōgun. Some might even believe that this swaggering Kyushu lord had indeed captured Korea.

I follow Lord Shimazu's route on my lime-green bicycle. Autumn sun bounces off the cedar tops, slipping down through the groves of slim bamboo. A truck roars by. At the crossroads of the sankin-kōtai route and the smaller road to the western coast is a small store. I go there to buy tōfu. Across from the narrow bamboo-lined road that I follow onto the main street, a tidy garden bursts out gold and red—all that is left of Sakurababa. The village elders maintain this place; they also care for the Shintō shrine, sweeping away the dead leaves each month and attending the monthly service. One-story wooden houses line the road now, each with its clutter of tools, bags of rice and seed potatoes, stacks of branches and firewood, old buckets, assorted boots and sandals. Everywhere in the weeds are ancient black pots. Bits of black pottery crunch underfoot on all the pathways; the earth itself is potsherds.

Only two thatched houses remain along the road. Abandoned, they are crumbling like dry cake, sagging between beams and timbers, almost completely obscured by bushes and tall grass. Zealous sprouts of bamboo, seizing a chance to grow unmolested, shoot up through the swaybacked roofs. In a couple of weeks they will grow ten, fifteen, even twenty feet high. The main street is paved, a two-lane road that leads onto highway 3, which runs throughout southern Kyushu. Trucks roar through, heading for a lumber mill below the hill in Higashi-Ichiki, or over to the stonecutting factory near Ijuin, some five kilometers to the southeast. Trucks and cars alike stop at the many vending machines lined up along the road. One can buy hot or cold canned coffee, cigarettes, juices, soft drinks, ice cream bars and five kinds of beer. None has ever been vandalized. Nearby are also two food stores, a liquor store, a small cigarette and gum concession, and a post office.

The morning bus pulls in across the street. Pottery workers

dressed in work pants and faded smocks step down. Stout old women carrying baskets and plastic sacks step up, as do two young women in fashionable high heels and skirts, who commute to work in the large Yamakataya *depaato*—"department store"—in Kagoshima City. Almost every hour throughout the day this bus stops in the village. On Saturdays I ride it east an hour and a quarter to Kagoshima City. The capital of Kagoshima prefecture, it is a sprawling metropolis of 520,000 people.

In the one-street village of Miyama, the only industry is pottery, and the population has remained at a constant of about six hundred for the past fifteen years. Through almost three hundred years of successive daimyō rulers, through the 1871 abolition of feudal clans and domains in the new Meiji period, when Naeshirogawa was renamed Miyama—"Beautiful Mountain"—through World War I and World War II and the increased modernization that followed, the village has endured. But unlike better-known Japanese pottery communities, such as Mashiko, Shigaraki, Onta, or Bizen, which now support restaurants, inns, gift shops, and, in the case of Mashiko, scores of potters, the number of Miyama potteries has dwindled. The village is hard to reach—it takes all day by train from Tokyo. Consequently, it was not significantly affected by the postwar *mingei* (folkcraft) boom, which produced a commercial explosion in areas closer to Tokyo and Kyoto. In Miyama there is no restaurant or visitor center, just fourteen potteries and pottery painting workshops along the road.

Today, a small wheelbarrow full of freshly dug *daikon* stands waiting at the entrance to the small store, owned by Kirin Obāsan. No one is outside, but the sliding glass doors are open. The *obāsan*—literally, "grandmother"—is always about. Usually she sits on a *tatami* (mat) platform behind the counter, which forms an entryway into her house, waiting for customers. To travelers and truck drivers her store is the local 7-11. They rush in, leaving their motors running, to grab soda and cakes, potato chips, seaweed candies and hard rice crackers. Young housewives with children in hand or strapped to their backs wander in to fill last-minute needs from shelves cluttered with containers of *miso*, packages of instant *ramen*, cans of sweetened fish and pickled *daikon*, and numerous teatime sweets, from Twinkies and butter cookies to traditional Satsuma *manju*, a cake made of steamed flour and bean paste.

Squinting but alert, Kirin Obāsan peers out from behind an old pair of glasses with brown plastic frames. Her gray hair, pulled back into a loose bun, reveals a wide, kind face. She wears the faded blue work apron of a shopkeeper and equally faded blue *mompei*, loose, shapeless work pants of tough cotton gathered with elastic at the ankles. Durable and soft, mompei were once the standard dress of village women, and you could tell the wearer's background from the pattern of the cloth. The older women who work in the fields and construction sites along the roads still wear checked blue-and-white mompei, but now all patterns and colors are sold at the huge Daimaru supermarket in the nearby town of Ijuin. My mompei are black, with a generic white, red, and green design.

Perched amid papers and a box of eggs from the chicken farm on the hill, Obāsan sits remarkably still, upright. Sixty-five years in the rice paddies have stooped her shoulders markedly, although not as severely as those of many older village women who walk hunched over from osteoporosis and years of field labor. She sits *seiza*, legs folded under her at the knees, the only polite and correct way for a Japanese woman to sit—especially in Kagoshima, famous for the expression *Danson johi*, "Men in front, women last." Here one still sees men's and women's laundry hung on separate lines, and wives address their husbands as *goshujin*, or *danna-sama*, "honorable master."

"*Konnichiwa*," I call at the entrance, parking my bicycle to one side of the wheelbarrow. Kirin Obāsan looks up and smiles. "Hello, hello. How are you? Good weather, isn't it? Tōfu, right? It's fresh made this morning, you know. Still warm." She rises slowly, pushing aside various works in progress. The abacus drops, its black wooden beads rattling. Newspapers rustle. Pulling up her sleeve, she reaches into a tin can filled with cold water and chunks of quivering snowy tōfu. With a generous slosh of water she pours a half-pound square into my bag. "Good tōfu today!" she exclaims. On the shelves behind her are tall bottles of sake and *shōchū*, the locally made potato liquor, wrapped in paper, each one bearing the ancient Shimazu crest.

"Hey, did you hear Sakurajima this morning? What a noise! Ash all over. Where did you go yesterday? I saw you on your bicycle. What are you making now? More teacups? Your teacher works you hard, doesn't he? That's good, you know. Do you really like Japan that much, eating tōfu and making pots? Don't you miss your mother and father? They miss you, I tell you. . . . Do you write them letters enough? Why don't you just find a nice Japanese man and live here? It's time for you to marry." Her voice becomes wistful, the swift cascade of Kagoshima *ben*, the hearty undulating regional dialect, drifts away. She forgets to tie the bag of tōfu, and water drips down the counter along the wooden frame and into the rows of hard candies. "*Aigato gowashtah*. Thank you," I call hastily in dialect and place ninety yen (about forty U.S. cents) on the counter.

Carefully balancing the tōfu, I slip for the door. She doesn't seem to notice. Another obāsan, owner of the wheelbarrow, pokes an unsmiling weathered face in the doorway. Her mompei are caked with dried mud, as are her feet in their cleft-toe rubber work shoes. One arm hangs limp at her side. I recognize her as the sharp-eyed obāsan I often see in the fields. She once told me that her arm was injured by a bomb during the war. "*Konnichiwa!*" she says gruffly, stamping the mud off her feet and stepping into the store. She turns to Kirin Obāsan and the bargaining begins.

"Hey, I've got some good daikon today. One hundred yen."

"One hundred yen . . . Hmm . . . they're a little small."

"Small? They're nice and fresh, a real bargain."

With a fierce look she lifts two of the largest radishes from the pile and shakes them vigorously. Small clods of dirt spatter across the floor.

"Look at that," she says, turning to me.

"Nice," I answer quickly.

"See, one hundred yen!"

Still unsure of the role of a blond foreigner in such situations, I grab my bag of tōfu and make a hasty exit. Besides, it is a quarter to eight. They may bargain over the price all morning, breaking for tea at ten o'clock. I am a potter's apprentice, and work begins at eight sharp.

The clay won't center. On the surface of the spinning wheel head, five pounds of gray-brown clay lurch and weave in lopsided circles. A distinct spiral marks where my hands have cut in too sharply. Uneven pressure has offset the entire mass.

Wetting my hands, I try once more, arms locked at the shoulders, my whole body straining to gain control of the clay. A steady forward pressure with the right hand, balanced by the pulling of the left, should force the clay into a rising cone, and pushing it down should leave the clay spinning in beautiful symmetric circles. Once on center, the entire mass should spin without wavering, smooth and even as a fine-gaited horse. I have worked in clay since high school, long enough to feel myself more than a beginner. But here in Japan even the wheel spins in the opposite direction from wheels at home. The clay refuses to behave. It bucks and kicks at my touch, like a wild-eyed Shetland pony. Instead of a tall straight cone, I produce a warped and rumpled stocking cap. Gobs of clay and water, or slip, spatter against the windows, filling my lap in cold splashes. Droplets slide down both my elbows, tickling, then disappear inside my rolled-up sleeves. One long strand of hair dances before my eyes.

To my right, perched cross-legged and birdlike atop a faded cushion, Nagayoshi-san is busy trimming rice bowls. He works quickly, silently, seemingly oblivious of his apprentice and her silent war with the clay. His wheel is newer than mine and better behaved. Bowl after bowl moves from board to wheel head, centered for a minute on the spinning chock, then cut with a steel blade. Nagayoshi-san uses the blade of an old rice threshing sickle to trim the large pots and makes tools from bent steel strips for bowls and other small pieces. A line of rice bowls at his left awaits trimming to a uniform width of 4.5 centimeters at the base, then transfer to a similar board on the right. When thirty-six bowls are standing in two rows, I will hoist the board onto the bamboo poles of the drying racks, or, if there are no clouds or rain—or volcanic ash—carry it outside.

When Nagayoshi-san trims rice bowls, the electric wheel moves so fast that sometimes its velocity will flip a bowl off the chock. When that happens, he sucks in air through his teeth and glances out the window. Outside, Sakurajima smokes on the bay, a brooding steam furnace. He takes another of the hard cinnamon candies he consumes while working and reaches for another bowl. Soon bowls are moving quickly again in a steady rhythm.

To Japanese potters the foot of a pot is considered a vital part of the whole, a final statement. Nagayoshi-san touches the inside of each bowl before he places it on the spinning chock. His practiced leathery hands assess the weight and shape of the inside curve. Eggshell-thin, each bowl weighs 175 grams after trimming, no more than several eggs together. To be that thin, the exterior of the bowl must be trimmed to an exact reflection of the inside curve. The proper size of a large rice bowl at the workshop is 12.5 centimeters at the rim, 7 centimeters in total height—just large enough to rest comfortably in the left hand and still hold a hefty grapefruit-sized mound of rice. Marked in the tattered notebook of orders for the next kiln firing are thirty rice bowls, six sets of five bowls each. In Japan rice bowls and teacups alike come in sets of five. Not only is four considered an unlucky number, but the model family is two parents and two children; of course one always prepares for a guest.

Before me on the windowsill is a model for a teacup, an unfired workshop sample with a simple upright form and a slight swell at the base. Sold for 1,000 yen (in 1983, just over four U.S. dollars) *yunomi* are in constant demand, especially at the *kamadashi*, when the month's kiln is unloaded and work is sold on the spot. My assigned work for today is fifty teacups. It is 11:30. I have been working since 8:00 A.M. and my board is empty. "Make your pots from the inside out," Nagayoshi-san told me one evening. Right now *I* feel inside out, as empty as my board.

Deciding that I don't care if all five pounds of clay go flying through the window, I make a sudden grab for the spinning mass. I tackle it from the top, concentrating my entire weight. It works, somehow. The rough stalagmite of clay slowly subsides. I catch my breath, exhausted. Close now to the wheel head, the clay limps a little from my attack, but its revolutions are more exact. It will have to do. I press both hands into the clay until my palms form a small ball at the top. This will be my teacup. I try to recall how it looked in the book Nagayoshi-san gave me on Japanese pottery methods. A still, concentrating potter sat before an electric wheel demonstrating four distinct stages: form a ball; open with the thumb; pull out into a small plate; then push the walls of the plate up into a teacup. The caption read "Easy."

But in the book soft, jellylike slip wasn't spattering everywhere, clay always stayed on center. My attempts to go through the progression only throw the clay back into its old habit of lurching about on the wheel head. A sharp pain shoots up from the base of my spine. I look again at my long-empty board.

In Kyoto, where the potters are famous for speed, a good potter makes two to three hundred teacups in a day. Most potteries work from 8:00 to 5:00, with an hour for lunch and another fifteen minutes for tea at 10:00 and 3:00. That means three hundred pots in seven and a half hours, or forty teacups in an hour. Only ninety seconds to make each piece!

"When you've finished that one, let me show you how I do it. Once." Nagayoshi-san speaks softly, in a muffled scratchy voice, without stopping his wheel or looking up.

Surprised, I discard my latest try at a teacup into a waiting ball of clay. Quickly I sop up as much of the slip as I can with a sponge and rinse my finishing leather, which is also coated in clay.

Nagayoshi-san shifts over to take my place. Like all potters, he has his own style and pace. When he sits down at the wheel, it spins so fast the electric engine hums. Taking a breath, he crouches over the spinning clay with fierce concentration. His hands descend, feeling uneven places. Still lurching and faltering, the mass begins to spread and sink. The tendons in his arms bulge, the wheel spins faster. Pulling and pushing, bringing clay toward him and then away, making it rise into a cone and descend, Nagayoshi-san balances alternating forces. Pushed from the right and pulled from the left, the clay has nowhere to go but up and down, in and out, around and around.

"Centering the clay is not a mastering but a conversation," Nagayoshi-san tells me later. Now he and the clay seem to agree. Within seconds it races on the wheel, spinning smoothly, a planet in orbit. His hands, coated with slip and water, seem permanently stuck to it. They seem not to be in control. Yet beneath his hands the clay visibly relaxes, finds that one still point and spins with the smooth grace of a ballerina, on center.

Next he forms a small ball of clay at the top. Thumbs find the center and press down, opening it into a shallow, thick-walled cup. The form relaxes, spreads out into a smooth, slightly curved plate, then suddenly it rises into a cup form again—only, the walls are thinner and twice as tall. Again his hands seem pulled by the very clay he is shaping. Where did this process begin and end? According to the book, he is suddenly at stage four.

In a quick motion Nagayoshi-san places his entire right hand inside the spinning cup upon the wheel. Supporting the walls with the thumb and fingers of his left hand on the outside, he pulls the clay upward. The cup rises, rippling up and swelling out. Slowing the wheel just a little, he reaches into the water bowl for the finishing leather. He touches it to the rim and again the clay responds, flaring out just a little. Another quick pinch, and he separates the newly risen form from its base of clay. A quick slice under the bottom with a wire, and Nagayoshi-san lifts the pot from the spinning wheel with two fingers. On my board now sits one teacup.

"I'm bad at it, you know. You should watch a real pro sometime. But you'll have to find your own way, one that fits your hands, anyhow. Please practice." He wipes his hands on a towel. "*Hai*," I answer promptly, and settle myself back at my wheel with apparent energy and purpose. Inside I am wilting like old lettuce in Kirin Obāsan's store. The wheel begins to spin. I have forgotten everything.

*A train headed south, Mt. Fuji
journeys across the sea, the first
Miyama potters*

I FIRST SET OUT FOR MIYAMA ON A
cloudy day in early October 1983,
wearing a somber blue dress—I had
been told that Japanese women didn't
wear pants or bright colors. My shoul-
der-length blond hair was braided and
pinned up against my head. The trip
west from Tokyo by Shinkansen, "bullet train," to Fukuoka, and then south
by regular express to Kagoshima,
would take the entire day. Through the
windows the scenery was an incoherent
rushing blur of gray and blue roof
lines, green space, more houses. I
stared instead at the dour-looking
woman in a blue uniform and white
gloves who was pushing a small cart of
snack foods, coffee and green tea down
the aisle. "*Bīru, kō-hi, ikaga desu ka?*"
she called in a dull voice, pushing the

W
E
D
G
I
N
G

heavy cart back and forth through the train. It seemed we would never leave Tokyo's treeless outskirts. But then we sped along a flat green plain, and suddenly Mt. Fuji loomed up on the right. I pressed my face against the glass, straining to get a better look. Above the clouds a sheer white pinnacle lifted into view. Fuji-san. The highest volcanic peak in the Japanese archipelago. After the miles of concrete sprawl, broken only by rice fields and scattered gardens, its beauty was immense, cold, terrifying. Within minutes, the train raced past.

Just the night before I had been sitting with an American friend in a Tokyo beer hall, beneath a life-size poster of Marilyn Monroe. Tokyo, with its skyscrapers, rushing traffic, neon signs and crowded streets, was so like New York City, I had almost been disappointed. But by evening I would be over seven hundred miles from Tokyo, in Kyushu's southernmost prefecture, Kagoshima.

In Miyama I hoped to find a teacher and a full-time apprenticeship in a workshop. Louise Cort, the curator of ceramics at the Freer Gallery of Art in Washington, D.C., had first told me about the village. I had explained to her that I wanted to go to a "folk pottery village" and see some of "old Japan." I had studied Japanese and was not a beginner in clay: I wanted to go somewhere in the country where I could study in a "traditional" workshop. She had listened carefully and then suggested Miyama, naming Nagayoshi Kazu, a potter there who she thought might be able to help.

I looked up everything I could find in English about Miyama, which totaled two articles, dated 1888 and 1921, and immediately wrote to the Nagayoshis in my labored Japanese. Months later I received an open-ended invitation. "If you can put up with our small house, simple food and a Japanese-style toilet, please stay with us. We wish to help you as much as we can." A picture of my hosts and their two college-age children arrived before I left the United States, but my vision of the village was a tabula rasa that I filled with images of wood-fired kilns, potters in indigo-dyed clothing, thatched-roof houses and farmers in wide straw hats.

People had warned me that down south they spoke Kagoshima ben, an impossible local dialect that even most Japanese people couldn't follow. In feudal times crafty Shimazu lords had encouraged the development of this strange tongue to thwart espionage: even if spies from other domains infiltrated, they could not understand what they heard, and likewise, should Shimazu spies be caught abroad, they could not confess clan secrets.

Tokyoites had laughed or looked askance when I said I was going to Kagoshima. They talked about the prefecture with the same condescending tone many New Yorkers use when they speak of the Midwest: it had no *haute culture* and few young people—many had gone to the cities in search of greater opportunities—and the "natives" didn't like outsiders. "Things are different down there," people would say vaguely, "attitudes older—feudalistic." I could count on being the first American most people there would meet.

Eighty-two years earlier my great-aunt Elizabeth Worthington Philip had also traveled to Japan. Aunt Bessie was something of a family legend. Eccentric, wealthy, spoiled, she was an excellent horsewoman, not a bad painter, and an adventuress who often did exactly what she pleased. In 1901, when she was twenty-three, she packed her things, summoned her black maid, Isabella, and set off for Japan to study painting. Taking trunks full of white dresses and volumes of

Lafcadio Hearn, she arrived in Japan by steamer from California.

"When we arrived in Nagasaki," Aunt Bessie wrote in her memoirs, "Isabella and I were the first ashore. I thought the harbor and all the little sampans were lovely. I climbed into a rickshaw and was taken to the only good hotel, where I took a room." With her stark white clothes, her flaming red hair, and her dark-skinned companion, Aunt Bessie was a sensation. On more than one occasion Tokyo policemen arrived to break up the crowds.

Isabella soon became tired of life in Japan and was sent home, but Aunt Bessie stayed in Tokyo for two years. She entertained, traveled and studied painting with a Japanese teacher. She led a stubbornly Western life: could not speak Japanese, and ate peaches and cream for breakfast. But before leaving she would win honorable mention in a Japanese exhibition, walk twenty-five miles around Mt. Fuji, live through a typhoon and, holding her Japanese spaniel, pose for a photograph in her Japanese garden in a long silk kimono.

Aunt Bessie's interest in Japan probably stemmed from her association with the American painter James McNeill Whistler, with whom she had studied in Paris. European art circles had long admired the Japanese woodblock print, and an Oriental influence is strong in Whistler's work. In the United States, Ernest Fenollosa, E. S. Morse and the Detroit industrialist Charles Lang Freer had already assembled the first great collections of Japanese art, the paintings, lacquerware and ceramics that would later fill American museums. No doubt she had also been influenced by the formidable British traveler and author Lady Isabella Bird, who had published *Six Months in the Sandwich Islands*, and *Unbeaten Tracks in*

Japan. By 1901 the writings of Lafcadio Hearn, with their romantic descriptions of Japanese people and customs, had helped shape Western views of the Orient. Japan was still that "little" country, considered strange and "backward" by the West. But U.S.-Japan commerce, opened in 1853 by Commodore Perry's landing with three warships in Tokyo Bay, heralded the start of American fascination with things Japanese. The sushi boom, the managerial boom and the technology boom of my generation were still decades away, but already certain individuals were traveling across the Pacific. "After living in Japan for a few months and reading Lafcadio Hearn and seeing as much of the people as I could," wrote Aunt Bessie, "I still was very much surprised by the lighthearted gaiety of the people on the crowded thoroughfares." She ended her account: "With time I became so fond of the Japanese people I wrote down a few anecdotes about them."

In Fukuoka I changed to a bumpy, blue-cushioned express train for Kagoshima. For eight hours the train chugged through towns and cities and a lush green landscape of hills, rice fields and citrus groves. I began to notice that every time I got up from my seat there were whispers, soft giggles, remarks. The sun began to set, spilling red over a rocky strip of wave-pounded coastline. "Ijuin!" called the conductor, at 6:01 sharp, his white gloves flashing signals down the track. My luggage was already waiting by the door: Ijuin was where I had been instructed to disembark and catch a local bus to Miyama. The train stopped with a lurch. Shouldering a small maroon knapsack, I picked up the blue travel bag heavy with clothing, dictionaries and presents for my new hosts—had I brought enough gifts?—and stepped down onto the empty platform, wondering how I was going to find the bus.

"*Konnichiwa, Ri-ra-san!*" Startled to hear my own name, I turned abruptly and saw a Japanese woman with a wide oval face and a brilliant smile walking toward me in short, energetic strides. Over her blue jeans she wore a black artist's smock with a red-and-gold-patterned scarf around her neck, an equally colorful bandanna holding back her short black hair. She held out a small bouquet of pink roses and small white flowers.

"*Yōkoso . . . Irasshai!* Welcome!" she said simply, in polite Japanese. "*Nagayoshi Reiko desu.*"

The Nagayoshis' house was small and modern, consisting of three rooms separated by wooden doors, a kitchen and an *ofuro*, or hot bath. My bags were put into a gray-carpeted bedroom with a wooden desk, a bookshelf, a large rocking chair, a pile of narrow Japanese futon, carefully folded and covered with a purple cloth, a stereo and a wooden bed in the corner. The room belonged to the Nagayoshis' son and daughter, Keisuke and Eri, who were away in school. Although the Nagayoshis slept on futon, they had assumed that, like their own daughter, I would prefer a Western-style bed. Two long traditional Japanese *koto* (zithers) wrapped in silk brocade leaned against a collapsible wardrobe, and full-length sliding glass doors covered one wall. I was told to sit on a cushion at a low table in the living room, and someone handed me a cup of tea.

The friend who had driven us from the train station stayed for a family-style dinner of *sukiyaki* with his wife and their baby. The couple wore matching red T-shirts and blue jeans, and their baby a bib bearing the words "le bébé." The Nagayoshis were surprised that I could use chopsticks, and laughed to hear that I preferred vegetables and tōfu to red meat. I showed them pictures of my three brothers, my sister and her husband at their wedding, and my parents at their apple farm in upstate New York. The two women barely sat still, running back and forth to the kitchen to bring yet more food, beer and then tea. But as soon as the meal was done they measured me front to back, up and down and sideways—for a kimono, they explained. "You're shorter than you looked in your picture," exclaimed Reiko with evident relief. They were surprised that I didn't wear makeup, and curious that one of my ears was double-pierced. I was asked to sing an American song, and sign the guest book.

I had no trouble understanding the women, who spoke slowly on my behalf, but the men's language was a gruff staccato of vexingly unintelligible words. Mr. Nagayoshi had a habit of half covering his mouth with one hand as he spoke. Each word blended into the next, until I could not tell where one sentence ended and another began. I picked up enough to learn that he and his family had moved to Miyama from Tokyo ten years ago. He had been born and raised in Kagoshima, but several kilometers away, in Sendai. In a sense they were still outsiders to Miyama themselves, although they wanted—dekiru dake, "as much as possible"—to help me.

It was a long evening, my head began to swim. Then finally dinner was over, and I was ushered into the steaming ofuro, handed a pair of pink pajamas, and shown my bed. I dreamt that I was stuck in New York City, trying to catch a train somewhere, I didn't know where. The train was so late, I ran to find a car. I got a car, but it would not work. In a panic I rushed into the street. Suddenly the skyline was gone, New York was gone and I was skating, gliding along miles and miles of gleaming white ice.

By the time I got up the sun was high over the hedge. Reiko had already left for Kagoshima City, where she taught a leatherwork class twice a week, and Nagayoshi-san was out in the workshop. When he heard me moving about in the house, he immediately hurried in and ushered me into the small room lined with tatami that served as his and Reiko's bedroom at night, and the dining room by day. In the center sat a low table, cluttered with breakfast dishes and a rice cooker. Nagayoshi-san pulled a yellow toaster oven out from the closet and, pushing aside the bowls for rice and miso soup dishes from his own breakfast, fixed me two thick slices of white toast. He poured for us both cups of strong black coffee, turned on the TV, and sat down cross-legged at the table while I ate. Eventually I would get used to the ubiquitous presence of the television at all meals and casual meetings. Not only did it replace dinnertime conversation (considered rude in a culture where meals are traditionally eaten in silence), but it took the place of small talk as well. Our first conversation was accomplished only by much gesturing, but by the end Nagayoshi-san had drawn a careful map of places to see in the village.

After breakfast, I headed up the lane to a steep hill, which led up to a low plateau of tea fields and another small hill up to the village shrine. The *jinja* itself was not much to look at, a low, open-walled structure of weathered boards. In front of the shrine was a gong with a thick rope hanging down for visitors to ring before praying. Underneath sat a large rectangular wooden box with slats across the top for offerings. Twisted Van Gogh-esque trees encircled the shrine, a green fur of moss covered the stone foundation, and every inch of hillside rock was a landscape of yellow and rust-brown lichen. Carved into the wooden trim under the roof line, cut into the stone basin for ritual washing and engraved in the markers was the sign of Lord Shimazu: the cross within a circle, staking claim for the daimyō.

As I wandered slowly back down I thought of the first Korean potters, brought to Japan by the warlord Shimazu Yoshihiro. Legend tells of how they climbed a hill above the settlement and, seeing land across the ocean to the west, wept for their lost Korea. The potters must only have seen the East China Sea, and a bend in the Japanese coastline. If one could see land across the waves it would be China, somewhere near Shanghai; Korea lies much farther north.

According to Shimazu chronicles, in the winter of Keicho 3 (1598), separate boatloads of Koreans landed in three places: Shimabira near modern-day Kushikino, Ichiki in Kaminokawa, and Maenohama in Kagoshima City. Of these groups, it was the forty-three men and women who landed near Kushikino who founded Naeshirogawa. Soon after their arrival, however, Lord Shimazu was distracted by other concerns. In 1600 he rushed north to the historic Battle of Sekigahara, fighting on the losing side against Tokugawa Ieyasu. The neglected potters dug clay, built kilns and began to produce their ware. By trading with the neighboring farmers and fishermen they were able to make a scant living. But the local people, jealous of the newcomers' status as Shimazu potters, harassed them, raiding the workshops and breaking the pottery. According to one account, the Koreans finally gathered up their things in 1603 and traveled east. Coming upon the valley below modern-day Miyama, they were so struck by its likeness to Korea that they decided to stay. They named the place Naeshirogawa, *naeshiro*, meaning "rice-seedling bed," and *gawa*, meaning "river," although there is no water nearby.

But another account holds that on returning from the Sekigahara war in 1600, Shimazu heard of the potters' misfortune and quickly ordered them to his castle town of Kagoshima. The Korean potters refused, stating that their dead had to be buried within view of the coast and their homeland across the sea. Again Shimazu was distracted by domain concerns until two years later, when he moved the artisans to the area of modern-day Miyama. In 1604, when peace settlements with the victorious Tokugawa Ieyasu were complete, Shimazu granted the Naeshirogawa potters nine *biru* of land and twenty-five dwellings.

Lord Shimazu was not alone in his vision of establishing a ceramics industry in his domain. By the end of the Korea campaigns, sometimes called the "pottery wars" of the sixteenth century, many participating daimyō, especially those from Kyushu, had brought back Korean artisans to their own areas. In 1617 the Korean potter Li Sam Py'ong discovered kaolin-rich clay in northern Kyushu, thus laying the foundation for Arita ware, Japan's first porcelain.

Yet of all the daimyō who brought Korean artisans to Japan, only the Shimazu feudal lord had visions of establishing not only a pottery enterprise but a mini-Korea in his domain as well. In addition to the potters, Korean laborers and stonemasons were brought to build the castle town of Kagoshima, and by 1641, the skills of Korean farmers had made camphor a major Satsuma export to Holland. Strict Shimazu social codes isolated and controlled the "Naeshirogawa people," as a "pure culture." Leaving the village was prohibited, and while Naeshirogawa men could sometimes take an outside bride with special permission, women were not allowed to marry outside the village. Wooden identification tags marked their status, preventing travel, and native Korean dress was mandatory.

Following the traditions of their homeland, the Koreans began to make two distinct types of pottery. *Kuromon*, literally "black stuff," dark ware for daily use, included spouted pouring pots for liquor or tea called *choka*, swelling *mizugame* (water vats) and tall, urn-shaped *kame* for food storage. Kuromon also included thick plates, small round bowls, teacups and liquor decanters. *Shiromon*, or "white stuff," resembled porcelain, and was for the exclusive use of the daimyō. It included flower vases, modeled figures, incense burners for display in the *tokonoma*, the special viewing alcove, and, most important, teabowls and tea caddies for the tea ceremony.

In sixteenth-century Japan the elite affectation wasn't thoroughbred dogs or horses but teabowls. The Way of Tea, *Chanoyu*—literally, "boiling water for tea"—was a warrior's art, a complex discipline that followed strict principles of form and procedure. According to the esteemed fifteenth-century tea master Shuko, when following the Way of Tea, "one should be reverent, sincere, pure in heart and quiet." Later, Sen no Rikyu, the major tea ceremony master and aesthetic adviser to Toyotomi Hideyoshi (1536–1598), enlarged upon the concept of *wabi*, or "refined poverty." But first one needed teabowls, preferably Korean-made, and in large quantities. Roughly made, even cracked in places, the humble *Ido* bowls from Korea summed up the ideal perfectly.

The Chinese custom of drinking *matcha*, powdered green tea, had been introduced to Japan by Zen Buddhist monks in the twelfth century. Accordingly, the first teabowls and utensils were imported from China. But by the mid-sixteenth century 20 percent of the teabowls used in Japan were imported from Korea. In its native land this simple pottery was considered peasants' ware for daily use, but in the hands of Japanese tea masters it became precious and rare.

The uses of tea ware extended beyond the practical and the spiritual. By 1592 the tea ceremony was one of Hideyoshi's policies of state, and his entertainments and gifts were legendary. In what was considered a vulgar display, he celebrated his victory over the Shimazu family in Kyushu in 1587 by throwing a giant tea party at a Shintō shrine in Kyoto and inviting hundreds of tea ceremony teachers and thousands of guests (the usual wabi tea ceremony involved no more than five). All brought their favorite teabowls and Hideyoshi himself went around sampling their Chanoyu. Teabowls were wrapped in layers of silk and placed in custom-made wooden boxes, given poetic names, even pedigrees that recorded which master had used them and what guests he had entertained. Some teabowls, such as "Kizaemon," now famous as "Japan's Number One Teabowl," were even thought to have supernatural powers.

A nod from Hideyoshi, who became more and more irrational in his waning years, could mean life or death, a grant of hundreds of new rice fields or exile. But daimyō vassals might impress him with a particularly rare or eye-catching teabowl. Loyal vassals might be repaid for services rendered with a teabowl from the lord's collection. Teabowls meant something beyond the world of tea; they were a trophy and a form of currency.

Hideyoshi died in 1598, but the teabowl craze lived on. Throughout the Tokugawa period, gift-giving was a critical weapon of domestic policy. Networks of patronage were formed and enforced by the exchange of military services, hostages and a constant stream of gifts. On arrival in Edo a daimyō's most important task was the presentation of his sankin-kōtai gift to the shōgun. This might be horses, falcons, swords, silk, gold, silver, or fine ceramics. By the end of the Edo period (1600–1868) more than two thousand distinct types of pottery were produced in Japan.

At the bottom of the hill, just above the second of the stone gates leading up to the shrine, I stopped to look down over the village from the tea fields. From above, Miyama seems to have no center at all, it is just a long track through the green—Lord Shimazu's route to Edo. The road through Miyama runs straight and narrow, a slim groove through unruly thickets of bamboo and dark cedar green. For a short stretch, houses and workshops line up along the road, strung like a single strand of beads. But halfway down the scattered length of houses a wide road cuts off to the right and runs past the grade school and terraced rice paddies until it drops through the green hills to the coast on the East China Sea. A smaller road once cut to the left, leading up to Sakurababa. Miyama's surrounding hills reach out in a wide circle of green around the branched road. A cross within a circle: Shimazu domain.

Well into the nineteenth century, travelers to Miyama were struck by its "Korean" flavor. In an article titled "Old Satsuma" in the September 1888 issue of *Harper's Magazine*, the American collector of Japanese ceramics E. S. Morse recounted the observations of a traveler to the village: "They did their hair in a knot on top of their head after the Korean fashion, preserved their ancient dress, which they wore on great ceremonial occasions such as the annual journey of the Prince to Yedo [Edo], when they went forth to salute him as he passed through the village." Up until the late nineteenth century, the village had been the official source of Korean-language interpreters for the Satsuma domain. Shimazu had forbidden residents to take Japanese names, and until recently shrine festivals included Korean songs and chants. But today the only Korean that remains is a few technical pottery terms and all villagers have become naturalized Japanese citizens.

Yet Korean tourists to Miyama still insist that despite Japanese-style houses and workshops the village is somehow "Korean." Even Japanese tourists from nearby Kagoshima City insist that Miyama is a world apart. Visitors from Tokyo escape to its bamboo groves and prewar "old Japan" ambience. In a country one twenty-fifth the size of the United States, with a population density of over three hundred people per square kilometer, the empty back streets of Miyama are a shock. Tourists wearing Pierre Cardin scarves and Gucci shoes walk the streets, but the mompei of Miyama's older women are reminders of wartime scarcity. In many homes small wood fires heat the hot tubs, and the houses have few cooking ovens and no central heating. The few homes that boast a Western-style flush toilet usually have operating instructions carefully pasted on the wall. Many of the country people still fertilize their fields with night soil from the outhouse; many farmers till the rice fields by hand. Ask any of the old people in the village and they will tell you that Japan is a *bimbōna kuni*—"poor country."

To me, the village was neither distinctly Japanese nor Korean, just different from anywhere that I had ever been. On that early October morning the beauty of the hills and surrounding valley was sharp and clear. I scanned the valley. Cold morning air rushed down the hills, as if somewhere trees were turning orange and gold. But I found no signs of a New England fall, not in Miyama, on a latitude of 32 degrees north, directly parallel with Savannah, Georgia. The entire landscape was an ink painting in washes of green. Thickets of gangly yellowing bamboo bent over stout rows of cedar. The few deciduous trees were leafed and full. Only scattered rice paddies broke the green in a quilted pattern of yellow and brown. Where rice harvest had begun, the paddies were ridged with brown stubble. In each field, parallel lines of bound stalks were hung to dry on long bamboo poles, suspended shoulder height by a pair of crossed stakes at each end. Wind swept through the lines of drying rice straw as if through a rack of upended brooms, and a soft rustling filled the valley. South and east, the road leveled out, pushing through the fields toward the busy streets of Ijuin.

Spotting open horizon beyond the trees at the corner of the tea fields, I walked over to the edge of the field and, pushing through some tall grasses, almost fell off the edge of a steep embankment. Across the valley green hills met a silver bay, and in the middle, Sakurajima rose above the waves, a silver plume rising from its far ridge. Over the blue outline of the volcano I watched arcs of sun splinter and divide, rejoin and filter out through drifting clouds of gray ash and rising volcanic steam.

But it was not the smoking volcano, half consumed in its own exhalations of rising smoke and gray volcanic ash, that held me to the spot. It was the shimmering waves, and beyond them a faint touch of coastline. This must be the spot where those first Koreans were said to have looked out over the ocean and thought they saw Korea. I strained to imagine that if I turned my head east, I too could see my own home waiting across seven thousand miles of Pacific.

Back at the house, I excitedly told Nagayoshi-san of my

discovery. He smiled and, drawing a map, pointed out that I had been looking in the wrong direction. The hill where the first Koreans had stood was across the village, facing the opposite way, toward the East China Sea. I had been staring south across Kinko Bay toward Okinawa and, farther still, the Philippines.

In the workshop, teacup practice
clay and silence, riddles
shadows on a silver moon

"ASAGOHAN DESU YO! BREAKFAAAST!"
Reiko calls from the kitchen. Inside I
hear a rattling of pans and opening of
wooden cupboards—Reiko is making
breakfast, and I should help. But my
teacher is working fast. Leaning against
the wall are bags of the grayish-blue
clay that Nagayoshi-san mixes for
throwing his large exhibition pieces,
which I've been waiting since September for him to begin. Glancing at the
clock, I haul a sack of clay up onto the
workbench. When the clay lies in heaps
of measured two-pound squares, I
reach to turn on the pug mill. With a
bang the kitchen door flies open and
Reiko shouts something at Nagayoshi-
san. He rushes in, his longish gray hair
in disarray, tightly belted tan corduroy
pants swinging above his ankles.

F
A
L
L

"It's time for breakfast, do that later," he says quickly, running a hand through his hair with a worried look.

"*Hai*," I answer, hoping he won't begin without me.

Inside the narrow kitchen Reiko juggles a pot of miso soup on the stove top. As she works she sings, seeming younger than her forty-four years, more like a schoolgirl than the mother of two grown children. A brightly patterned scarf holds back her stylishly short hair, accentuating the roundness of her face and her strong, bright smile. Over her blue jeans and black sweater she wears the white frilly apron of the Japanese housewife, or *okusan*—literally, "woman of the interior." On the back burner a kettle of rice steams.

As is customary, I addressed my teacher and other Japanese men by the last name followed by the honorific *san*, and women by their given names plus *san*. The use of given names without the honorific is usually restricted to spouses—and to the privacy of the home as well. For Nagayoshi-san, pronouncing "Ri-ra-san" was preferable to the social awkwardness of a more casual form of address. But progressive-minded Reiko called me simply Ri-ra, and in return had me call her by her given name alone.

"*Ohayō gozaimasu*," we greet each other now. With an inward sigh I reach behind her and pull out the collapsible table.

Usually we sit down to a breakfast that reflects Reiko's cosmopolitan style: *pan*—after the Spanish *pan*, which is actually thick Wonderbread in European guise—freshly ground coffee, fruit, salad and sometimes yogurt. But when he's working hard, Nagayoshi-san quietly asks for a Japanese breakfast. I put out teacups, small plates of purple and green seaweed, and a dish of salted plums. Under my thumb, the rice bowls made by my teacher have paper-thin edges. Rice bowls are the next shape in my practice. When they are mastered I will move on to small plates and eventually small-necked vases.

At the traditional Sataro workshop for kuromon just down the lane, apprentices learn in a similar progression, building up from cups and rounded bowls to plates and finally spouted choka. Nagayoshi-san has said that I must make two hundred copies of each form, of the same size and weight, before I progress to the next. This system of teaching is much faster than that of thirty years ago, when apprentices spent ten years learning their craft. And even today, most Japanese pottery apprentices generally spend three to five years with one teacher. But it feels slower than I could have imagined. Back in the States I made bowls and teapots, vases, any shape I wanted. But though I've made over two hundred teacups, none of them have yet been signed with the kiln mark "Naga." They pile up in a basket by the showroom door and sell for eight hundred yen each (in 1983, about three U.S. dollars), or are simply given away to customers as "service," for free.

Some of my cups are warped, others shrunken by the firing a full size smaller. Once a woman from Tokyo bought a mottled brown cup for the tea ceremony. "Oh, how interesting," she said. Placed too close to the burner in firing, the cup resembled a charred marshmallow. When I handed it out of the kiln, Nagayoshi-san joked that I had reinvented the Shimazu's beloved "dragon-skin" tea ware produced for ceremonial use in nineteenth-century Satsuma kilns. At least my cups had the advantage of novelty. They were *mezurashii mono*—something unexpected and new, like a blond *gaijin* apprentice.

In a few minutes Nagayoshi-san drops his canvas shoes by

the door with a thud and steps in with a newspaper and a clump of daikon left by Suzuki-san's wife. As he does every morning, he pulls out the color advertising section from the paper and hands everyone a page as an impromptu place mat. I receive a full-page travel ad for Australia; my delicate rice bowl rests on the face of a koala. Reiko's sheet proclaims "sexy house" construction. Under his own bowl Nagayoshi-san has placed an ad for women's lingerie. Reiko ladles out golden miso soup, swimming with seaweed and transparent bug-eyed fish. Rice and cups of tea follow.

While we eat no one talks. A small color TV in the corner fills the silence with morning news, a slow-motion playback of Sakurajima's midnight eruption on the screen. From the rim of the volcano shoot streaks of red, followed by clouds of swirling ash and steam. During the course of the night Sakurajima had thrown rocks into windshields, shattered telephone booths, and caused earthquakes as far as Miyama. This morning the schoolchildren pedaled off to school, their yellow safety helmets on tight, through an inch of gritty volcanic ash.

Sakurajima is one of the twenty-three volcanoes, fifteen craters and ten calderas that make up the Kirishima range in southern Kyushu. Thirteen thousand years ago the volcano heaved itself up in the middle of Kinko Bay. Despite its gentle name, "Cherry Island," Sakurajima is a boiling furnace of volcanic energy whose rumbling, ash and nocturnal fireworks are monitored daily. Until the last major eruption, in 1914, the entire volcano was an island. When Sakurajima exploded, it spewed three billion tons of lava into the bay, connecting itself to the mainland.

People continue to live on the thirty-square-mile volcanic

island, refusing to leave their ancestral land although scientists predict another major eruption soon. I once ran in a fifteen-kilometer race around the volcano through angular pumice formations and hardened lava flows. Halfway through the event Sakurajima seemed to disapprove, letting out a great spray of ash and flying rock. Rain began to fall, coating the runners with gritty black ash. TV cameramen ran to cover their lenses, while old women, watching in brown and gray kimonos, calmly brought out umbrellas. The children were delighted. At the finish line, runners resembled mud wrestlers. From yellow tents, the race's sponsor, Avon cosmetics, hastily gave out free towels, pink T-shirts and makeup kits. I won a prize for being the only blond runner: an enormous "Sakurajima daikon" as large as a beach ball.

Last night Reiko, Nagayoshi-san and I had gone to see a movie in Kagoshima City, James Bond with Japanese subtitles—Nagayoshi-san's choice. Afterwards we sat in the Nagayoshis' favorite coffee shop, a European-style café where waiters in black tuxedos served us coffee and pastry. By the time we left, volcanic ash was falling like gray snow, blanketing parked cars. People rushed down the street, holding umbrellas or covering their heads with towels. Nagayoshi-san hailed a taxi, which we took all the way home.

Although all clay, formed by the weathering of rocks and their minerals, particularly granite (formed when magma cools), has its origins in volcanic activity, volcanic ash itself can't be used for glazes like wood ash, because it melts at a much higher temperature than clay. Thus, when ash falls on the pots before firing, uneven spots and discolorations occur. "Ash today," Nagayoshi says absently, looking up from the paper. Today's pottery must be carefully stored inside. On the TV a wind chart shows an unusual westward ash pattern. Air currents usually channel ash away from Kagoshima City and the direction of Miyama in the fall and winter, and bring clouds of ash in the summer months. But today seasonal "yellow winds" have swept across China.

I wait impatiently, as Nagayoshi-san continues to read, glancing at the page of chopstick instructions that regularly appears in the daily paper. Fearing that young Japanese—who often prefer curry rice, spaghetti, hamburgers and fried chicken to traditional fare—will soon lose all sense of culinary heritage, the government has sponsored a national campaign to educate them on chopstick etiquette. *Oshin*, a soap opera, comes on. We have stayed an extra half hour over breakfast. Suddenly Nagayoshi-san grabs his crocheted wool hat and bolts for the door. I pick up as many dishes as I can and hurry into the kitchen. Finally all the dishes are rinsed and put away; time to work. "Hang out your futon, please," Reiko calls from where she watches the television. I barely squeak out an answering "*Hai.*" Will I ever get to the workshop? If I were a male apprentice, would I have all these extra duties? But I know I cannot shout, "I'll do it later."

It is said in Japan that an apprentice's worst obstacle is the okusan of the house. Certainly in feudal times, when the only one lower than the wife in the family pecking order was the *deshi* (apprentice), this would seem to have been so. Even today, for female deshi (a telling contradiction in terms, for *deshi* literally means "younger brother") one might argue that things are little changed. While traveling to other pottery communities and kiln sites in Japan I met several foreign women who were apprentices, and few of them seemed happy. One Australian woman who was apprenticed at a well-known traditional pottery in northern Kyushu finally left because her teacher's wife was so jealous she refused to let her in the house and threw her meals out the door. Similarly, an American woman in Mashiko who could not speak Japanese was ostracized completely after refusing to do housework. She sat in the corner attaching handles to teapots and was not invited in the house at all.

I didn't like having my workshop tasks and schedule interrupted by Reiko's demands. But after visiting other workshops I began to see my role differently. Not only was the pottery a family business, with house and workshop not clearly divided, but as I was fast discovering, the role of apprentice was also that of adopted daughter.

In addition to creating and teaching leatherwork, as okusan Reiko managed the pottery sales and household finances, and, most important, played the critical role of hostess to pottery guests. Nagayoshi-san sometimes joked that Reiko had been his "patron," supporting the family when he was just starting out as a potter. If Reiko needed a sudden errand run, packages carried home from the store, or help when guests arrived for tea, it made sense that as apprentice I pitch in. Being busy with my own affairs was not an acceptable excuse. As a member of the family and workshop, it was simply not expected that I have my own separate plans.

The Nagayoshis fussed about me as if I were their child. If we went somewhere together they insisted on paying my way. At mealtimes Reiko watched how much rice I ate—usually, not enough. If she was nearby, I could not address an envelope without her interrupting to show me "how it should be done." And if I went out with friends it was expected that I call if I was going to return later than 10:00 P.M.

Only if I met with other foreigners in Kagoshima City, which I did once or twice a month, was my curfew extended. Since buses and trains back to the village stopped running at 11:00 P.M., it was arranged that I stay at a friend's place in the city overnight and return to Miyama the next morning. On such nights I was free to do whatever I pleased, and the Nagayoshis made it clear that they simply didn't want to hear about it.

From the start Reiko had been concerned about my wardrobe. My motley assortment of cotton shirts, pants and casual skirts was out of fashion. My mud-spattered running shoes made her shudder. "If you don't take more trouble with how you look, boys won't like you," she sometimes said. When we went to town together she advised me on what to wear, handing me her lipstick to put on so that I would look more "adult."

At first I had been insulted and irritated. But when Eri visited from junior college, I noticed that Reiko offered similar criticism. Eri, who, like most other young Japanese women I knew, was embarrassed by her parents' "old-fashioned ways," fought her mother off tooth and nail. But she herself took great care over her appearance, spending large sums for the latest fashions. And Reiko's worries about me were sometimes warranted. On one of our first outings together I wore a brown wool vest and matching scarf over an apricot-colored long-sleeved shirt that I had just bought because I liked the color and its fine cotton. No one said a word, but later I discovered that my new shirt was a standard article of obāsan lingerie.

Out in the workshop the day's first task is making clay. One by one, chunks of gray and red clay disappear between the rolling gears of the pug mill. I carefully add equal portions of clay for the mixture my teacher uses on large pieces. Hard, unwedged clay goes into the funnel-shaped top and emerges from the side in a smooth cylinder.

Fifty years ago in Miyama, pottery apprentices performed this pre-wedging stage by walking on the clay with bare feet. Throwing down a hump of freshly dug clay, they walked around and around, pushing the clay out with the sides of their feet in an even rhythm. A skilled team of wedgers would leave symmetric circles of clay spread across the floor in a petal pattern. Old Miyama potters Arima Takao, Araki Mikijiro, Yamamoto Tsukasa and Someura Juro remember this process. Like other apprentices, they were sixteen to eighteen years old at the time. Six days a week they walked in circles on slippery red clay in a slow, sullen dance, picking out sticks and stones as they proceeded. "If you think about it now . . . well, it seems just terrible, but we didn't think about it then," Arima-san told me, his mouth spreading into a wide toothless grin. "It couldn't be helped—it was our study!" The new apprentices earned three yen a month—enough money then to buy fifteen pounds of rice. White Satsuma potter Someura Juro, who began as an apprentice at the Jukan workshop during the hard postwar times, had similar memories: "Sure, it was hard," he said softly, "the pay was terrible. But it was a job!"

When a small forest of pug-milled cylinders rises from the wedging table, I take out plastic sheets. Though Nagayoshi-san will use most of this clay today, it must be tightly covered to prevent uneven drying. I lay the cylinders diagonally, like a Japanese shopkeeper wrapping up packages. When I first wrapped clay, I laid it across the middle of the sheet, pulling up the edges as for a Christmas gift. The next day I noticed that every roll was rewrapped Japanese style, the corners bound in tight.

I am ready to wedge. Wedging forces air pockets out of the clay and increases elasticity. The product of thousands of years of weathering—the pounding, cracking and crushing of rocks, then dissolution in water and precipitation as particles—a piece of clay under a microscope resembles a pile of fish scales. During wedging, the tiny plates of clay line up, increasing its elasticity on the wheel and its strength during firing. In America I had learned to wedge by throwing the clay down and letting the force of impact push air bubbles out. In Japan wedging is called *kikumomi*, "chrysanthemum wedging," after the layered, petal-like shape the clay takes on from being rolled over and over on itself like bread dough, and is considered an art form taking years to perfect. Skilled wedgers transform a rough hunk of clay into a smooth rolling ball in minutes with an easy grace, as if pouring tea. The attention paid to clay preparation reflects the traditional concern with process and medium that one sees in many Japanese crafts; hence the unglazed "natural" look and subdued colors of most traditional Japanese ware. Potters readily talk about their work as a process of "letting the clay speak," or "listening to the clay." Wedging was my primary duty as an apprentice. At first it felt like trying to knead a gunnysack full of rocks. My wrists ached; the clay refused to budge.

Today, rolls of smooth gray clay spiral down and out, around and around. In order to roll the mass of clay I stand with my right foot forward and push with my full weight. My teacher comes in with a bucket of water and tools. Three mounds of wedged clay wait by his wheel. Stepping back and catching my breath I ask, "What is the work for today?"

"Please practice . . . anything," he answers, settling down before his wheel.

"But don't you need anything done?"

Nagayoshi-san stops his wheel for a moment and speaks with exaggerated patience. "If I need anything, I'll ask. Please practice."

"*Hai*," I respond quickly, reaching over to pull out a stick of clay.

As I wedge clay for my own practice I concentrate, trying to imagine the swelling teacup form I am to work on. The clay resists, slips to one side, breaking my rhythm. What should be a symmetric pattern of moving clay is a lopsided mound. With a deep breath I pound the clay into a large ball and start over, visualizing the practice form as I begin. Again the clay falters, slipping to the right. My imagined teacup crumples and falls. Suddenly I feel as awkward as the rolling clay, off-balance. Why did my teacher tell me to practice *anything*? I am supposed to practice teacups—has he forgotten? The endless teacups seem pointless. I feel like ripping up that basket of give-aways by the door. The harder I wedge, the more annoyed I feel and roll the clay harder still, until my back aches and my wrists burn. I think back to my early days as an apprentice.

"Make fifty teacups" was all Nagayoshi-san had said before he left the workshop last September. That day I began with vigor, excited with my new tools, the old black kuromon grinding bowl for water, the electric wheel temporarily my own. Autumn sun streamed in through the windows. But after a day alone I felt chilled and uncertain. Why wasn't my teacher working in the shop? Was he annoyed? I had seen both him and Reiko smile in open hospitality to people whom they considered a terrible nuisance.

After three days I began to wonder whether I had made some terrible cultural mistake in asking to become Naga-yoshi-san's apprentice. He must have said yes because at that time I was his guest. But the third day, as if he had never left at all, he quietly reappeared. "Well, I had better get busy," he joked, pouring fresh water into my water bowl, "you'll soon be better than me." I was too relieved to answer. Later that evening, when I sat with him and Reiko watching a John Wayne movie on the TV, he suddenly said, "People who make things don't speak. Please watch and study." I was not to depend on Nagayoshi-san for direction, but to look to the work at hand.

Nagayoshi-san himself came to pottery after twenty years as a painter in Tokyo and Kyoto. After he and Reiko were married, he supported his family by teaching painting in a government school. Every morning he boarded Tokyo's famous rush-hour subway for work. He painted in the evenings, exhibiting in department-store galleries. Often tense and exhausted, he chain-smoked and drank sugared coffee all day.

His decision to become a potter had been abrupt. He quit his job and moved to Kagoshima with his wife and two young children. Reiko says that they had planned for three years of hardship. She began teaching leatherwork in Kagoshima. In America this departure from city life and the financial security of a government job might not have seemed unusual. But in Japan, where lifetime employment and a rigid status system prevail, the move was radical and risky. To the businessmen and bankers who crowd the workshop on Sundays, Naga-yoshi-san represents the dream of freedom. They come dressed in suits, with or without their families, bringing boxes of Japanese cakes and staying for hours over conversation and tea. They leave with a piece of pottery in hand and a promise to be back.

As a *tōgeika* (artist-potter), Nagayoshi-san is a first-generation artisan, creating his own designs, forms and glazes. Unlike *shokunin* (craftsmen), who work for wages in a master's workshop, he runs his own pottery. In cities and new pottery centers like Mashiko, just north of Tokyo, independent workshops are common, but not in small traditional villages like Miyama, where one is either a *Miyama no hito*—"Miyama person"—or a *yoso no hito*—"outsider." Being a Miyama person means having a family grave on the hill, some land, ancestors that were probably potters and, somewhere along the line, a Korean family name. Everyone else—even people from surrounding towns—is a yoso no hito. Only gaijin, real foreigners like myself, can sometimes stretch the rules.

When Nagayoshi-san arrived in Miyama, he was formally introduced to all the workshops. Even then, when the postwar "folkcraft" boom had lifted pottery sales across Japan, no one was pleased with the prospect of new competition. Only Sataro-san, who runs a kuromon workshop, invited Nagayoshi-san to watch in his pottery. During the day Nagayoshi-san ran back and forth to the Sataro workshop, watching the potters throw and then practicing what he had seen. When he talks of the first years in Miyama, Nagayoshi-san shakes his head. "The country is difficult." He admits that neither he nor Reiko expected such resistance. But although they periodically talk about leaving the village and moving closer to Kagoshima City, they have stayed. Despite the hardships, by working in a pottery village Nagayoshi-san connects himself to the long tradition of Satsuma pottery.

Not only are casual visitors and tourists more apt to stop by, but his pottery has a recognizable niche within contemporary ceramics.

Nagayoshi-san's rise as an artist-potter began two years after his arrival, when a large bowl of his was accepted by the Dentō Kōgeiten, the "Traditional Crafts Exhibition." For contemporary artist-potters, acceptance in the annual exhibition is one of the two most prestigious forms of recognition they can aim for. During the twelve days that the show is held, in the Mitsukoshi department store in Tokyo, over one million U.S. dollars' worth of crafts are sold. While the show stays in Tokyo fifteen thousand people visit it daily; then it travels to the provinces. The first time Nagayoshi-san's work was accepted into the show, newspaper reporters from as far away as Fukuoka flocked down to report on this upstart potter who had won entrance into the show only two years after moving to Miyama.

Last year Nagayoshi-san was awarded the title of Honorary Artisan of Kagoshima, by the Kagoshima Prefecture Museum. The award is based on the number of times an artist-potter's work is consistently recognized at the annual art and ceramics exhibitions sponsored by the *Minami Nihon* newspaper and the prefectural art museum. To maintain his title he must submit a new piece of work to both the art and ceramics exhibitions in the spring and fall of each year. He barely has time to throw, design, glaze and fire a piece before the deadline in three weeks. I wedge the clay hard, looking past him, straight-backed at the wheel, and over to my half-finished board of teacups.

"Hey, letters—from America!" a deep voice calls over the hedge. I look up eagerly—it has been days since I got mail.

Brushing ash from his blue uniform, the mailman parks his motorbike by the well and steps inside just as the ten o'clock chimes sound. "Won't you have tea?" calls Nagayoshi-san from his spot at the wheel. "Oh no, I wouldn't want to trouble you," says the mailman, taking a seat. Pocketing the slim envelopes, I nod and head for the kitchen, glad for the excuse to stretch my legs.

Inside, Reiko has already set out a wooden tray with a teapot, cups, plates of rice crackers and a thermos of hot water. I carry it all back into the workshop and pour tea. The first cup, with a wooden saucer underneath, goes to the mailman. I pour my own tea last and sit down to listen.

"Sakurajima again, did you hear? Ash all over," begins the mailman, taking up his cup.

"Anyone hurt?"

"No, but what a noise—shook the windows."

"You don't say."

"Yes, it was terrible. Anyhow, how is business these days?"

"Slow," answers Nagayoshi-san, shaking his head with a smile. "I've been really slacking off."

I look at my teacher in surprise. For the past week he has been working like an engine, throwing so many pots that the overhead racks are full and we have begun storing trimmed pots in the kiln. But when he talks to a guest, work is always *botsu, botsu*—"little by little"—and there is time for tea. In urban Japan such old-fashioned politeness is rare. Tokyoites scoff at "backward" Kagoshima ways, saying that they are too *nombiri*—"soft and easygoing."

Nagayoshi-san laughs, and the conversation veers off to a discussion of the TV show *Columbo*. A few evenings ago Nagayoshi-san, Reiko and I had stayed up late watching a rerun of the show, splitting a beer and bags of dried jellyfish and squid wrapped in American cheese. Most of my friends in Japan loved Columbo, John Wayne and James Bond, and the Nagayoshis were no exception. They had a special feature on their television that allowed them to switch back and forth between the original version and the one dubbed in Japanese. Nagayoshi-san attributed Columbo's popularity to his being *"Nihonjin mitai*—like a Japanese."* He affects great humility, modesty and shyness, and comes across as a slow-witted bumbler, but in the end, by a carefully disguised strategy, he always gets his man. Detective serials like *Columbo* and Westerns are big hits in Japan, and the United States viewed on Japanese TV is a collage of violent clashes. The women are fast and loose and chesty, often blond. The men are burly and drive Ford pickups with gun racks in the back. There is room to argue, fight, run away. This morning, after the local news, we watched Illinois housewives trampling one another at a bargain sale. In the next clip, about a Japanese company in California, slim, blue-uniformed Japanese workers unfolded neat squares of rice next to burly construction workers with rolling potbellies who ate mammoth pepperoni subs. Americans in the media were loud, aggressive, fat and oversexed. They broke every Japanese rule of outward moderation and restraint, and the Japanese loved them.

Even my progressive-minded hosts seemed to have a skewed image of America. On one hand they admired American creativity and innovation; to them the lack of tradition and history meant the freedom to create. Both of them wanted to visit the United States. But when I offered to cook them an American-style meal, Nagayoshi-san immediately shouted, "Cowboy food!" and pantomimed eating beans with a spoon. They thought my tōfu sandwiches were repulsive, and couldn't understand why I did not eat red meat. I was not behaving as an American should. "You're different," they quickly concluded, "not like a *real* American." As indignant as I felt, I had to admit that I found the Nagayoshis themselves so different from what I had expected, I sometimes felt they weren't real Japanese.

The rice crackers disappear as I pour a third round of tea. Glancing at his watch, the mailman abruptly jumps up, bowing and apologizing for his sudden departure. Nagayoshi-san tells me to get on with my own work and carries the tea things into the kitchen. I settle down cross-legged before my wheel. The morning is half gone, but only a thin, wavering line of cups fills my board. I accelerate the wheel until the clay is one even spin.

After lunch the workshop remains as quiet as in the morning. Through the open windows sunlight streams across the dirt floor, and a slight breeze carries in the sharp, sweet smell of chrysanthemums, burning leaves. After only half a day of work my fingers and wrists ache. I dip them in the water bowl and stare at the circling clay.

Some weeks ago one of the Nagayoshi workshop's most frequent customers, a pilot from Tokyo, had driven me home from Kagoshima City. I had been looking forward to the time alone on the bus and hadn't really wanted the ride, but there had been no way to refuse. We drove for a while in silence, his wide black American-made luxury sedan nosing its way through the narrow roads.

"You know, in Japan there is a saying," he began. "Your teacher is a door and you must knock and knock to be let in." I nodded, leaning back in the plush seat.

"If you learn only one thing from Nagayoshi-san while you are here," he continued solemnly, "that is enough."

"What thing?" I asked, suddenly interested.

"*Ikikata* . . . way of life."

Today I am not at all sure of what it is I am learning. I turn to look where, less than three feet away, Nagayoshi-san works silently on a massive, slowly turning bowl. Plastic rain pants protect his legs from flying clay; he wears thick cotton gloves. With tense arms and shoulders he slowly guides the wide rim farther and farther out. Standing up, he arches over the bowl to continue his steady pull. The bowl extends until it seems it must collapse under its own weight, stretched as a bird's wing. Finally he sighs and sits back, looking down at his work. He pushes open the sliding window further to let sunlight fall over the bowl and studies the results of the past twenty minutes.

Without a word he suddenly smashes downward, and the whole form crumples into a folded mess. Every muscle in my back tenses, but I keep my face down and concentrate on my own work. Was there air in the clay? Had I wedged it well enough? Should I offer to take the collapsed bowl away or keep silent? Nagayoshi-san slowly rises from the wheel, his clay-spattered rain pants crackling. "Hmm . . . Did I eat too much?" he says with a laugh, shaking his head. I quickly jump up, hand him another hump of clay and go outside for fresh water.

Around the faucet area a fine layer of ash has collected. Automatically I glance around the yard, checking that no pots sit outside. I linger by the hedge and the fine ash brushes my hands with gray. It is almost time for the vegetable and fish trucks to pass by, their loudspeakers screeching the radio news at full volume. After that a truck advertising eyeglasses makes its rounds. At 5:00 shouts and pounding sneakers will stampede down the lane as children flee from another day at school.

Nagayoshi-san nods a distracted thank-you when I pour fresh water into his bowl full of dark clay slip. He glances at the clock, takes another cinnamon candy and begins again. A second bowl rises from his wheel. I hold my breath, conscious of each spatter from my own spinning clay.

Crash. The silence of the workshop breaks like ice. My hands freeze against the clay, throwing the teacup off center. Nagayoshi-san sucks in air between his teeth. Without a word he pulls the wooden bat off the wheel head, places the crushed bowl to one side, and reaches for another piece of clay. Again I wonder whether I wedged the clay enough. Nagayoshi-san has told me repeatedly never to crush a pot before trimming because you can't see the form. Perhaps my presence is breaking his concentration. I glance at the clock, but it's only 2:00—another hour before I can leave to make tea.

My teacher has begun to rival Sakurajima. Each time a wide bowl rises from the wheel his hands dart out and smash the form to a rumpled mass. Shrinking into my work, I feel like an Alice grown too big for her surroundings. The clock ticks toward 3:00.

"*Konnichiwa . . . Konnichiwa . . . Konnichiwa . . .*" A chorus of voices comes through the hedge. Nagayoshi-san and I jerk our heads up in unison. Three women in high heels and trim skirts enter with a white box of bakery cakes. A flustered robust man in a dark suit and red necktie follows. Nagayoshi-san quickly takes off his hat and jumps down to greet them. I bow my head in greeting and keep working while my teacher leads the group to the house. "*Ocha desu yo!*—teatime!" Reiko calls from the kitchen. I wash up eagerly. Even though I ate a full lunch of cold buckwheat noodles, tea and tangerines, I am hungry.

In the center room the low table is crowded with pottery, wrapping paper and cups for tea. Nagayoshi-san beams and busily wraps purchased rice bowls and teacups in the workshop paper printed in a red, beige and brown geometric design. Reiko pours tea. Though I have met this group many times before at kiln openings, I kneel down at the entrance and bow in a formal greeting. After hours at the wheel it feels good to stretch my back, letting my head fall forward. Seated before tea and small plates of cake, the group bows back. Greetings over, I settle down next to Reiko and reach for tea. As hostess, Reiko talks to the male guest. The three women sit silent. Holding their teacups with both hands, they admire the glaze, shape and color before taking dainty sips.

"Her Japanese is so good," comments one of the women to Nagayoshi-san, looking at me from the corner of her eye. For the most part, I could communicate in standard Japanese and the local dialect without much of a problem. When I first arrived, people had praised my Japanese routinely. "Your Japanese is so good!" they would say, as if in disbelief. At first I had been pleased, but I soon realized that even Westerners who could barely squeak out *Konnichiwa* received the same compliments. Now villagers no longer praised my Japanese; only strangers and pottery guests made it a point of conversation, and there was something about their flattery that made me uneasy.

In Japan, the word for customer, *okyakusama*, is the same word as for guest. And in the Nagayoshi house, *Okyakusama wa kami-sama desu*—the customer is God. Nagayoshi-san pushes cake and a bowl of tangerines in my direction. Despite the encroaching exhibition deadline, he acts as though he is on a picnic. After two rounds of tea have been poured, he grins in my direction and pantomimes the milling of coffee beans. Glad for the excuse to stretch my legs, I rise to fetch hot water, coffee beans and grinder from the kitchen.

In the empty side yard, patterns of light and leaf play through the bamboo and fern. Today the road to the coast will be lit with sun. By 6:00 the long evening light should burn through the rice fields in orange and gold. But I have two more boards of cups to finish. By the time coffee is ground and served, tea break will have lasted another thirty minutes. With sudden annoyance I realize that since guests have come my teacher will work late—will I have time today for a run? "Ri-ra . . . hot water, please." Reiko's voice fills the narrow kitchen. I grab the kettle of boiling water, tuck coffee beans and grinder under my arm and head back into the center room.

Practice is over: two mounds of clay spun, pulled, shaped and cut off the wheel as teacups. I put my washed tools aside and slide open the window in front of my wheel. Cold night air rushes in. I shiver through my light sweater and thin mompei and lean out, looking across the yard and up over the dark line of hedge. Outside the stars gleam fitful, bright, the moon hangs low and to the east. From inside comes the sound of Reiko filling the hot tub with fresh water. I pull my head in and close the window, looking up to the drying racks where three large bowls are perched in the shadows. After tea, Nagayoshi-san had thrown all three without smashing one.

Under the glare of the light bulbs, I examine my three boards of teacups on the bench, but no feelings of satisfaction rise. Instead my shoulders burn with fatigue, my right wrist is numb. The other day my teacher said, "If you make one good pot a day that's enough," then added sternly, "Do you want to make a lot of pots—or a few good ones?"

I had been impatient and I knew it. I was no longer a novice apprentice, and I had read enough about Zen and Japanese culture not to expect praise. I follow my teacher as a member of the workshop, working harder than I ever had in the States, but unrecognized—a shadow potter. Still, the teacups sit like a row of questions. Why doesn't my teacher ever tell me what he wants me to do? Why won't he use any of my cups for the workshop? Sometimes in the kiln-unloading Reiko even mistakes my cups for his. Has he forgotten that after two hundred completed cups I am to graduate to rice bowls? I am fed up with teacups.

Nagayoshi-san's face peers through the open doorway. "Ten o'clock, you know . . ." he says, stepping in.

"Okay, I'm done," I answer, turning off the wheel and opening the door to the drying room. I slide one long board of pots into the racks and reach for another, when I notice that he is holding one of my cups up to the light. The muscles in my jaw tighten. "Getting better," he says quietly. I nod and place the next board in the drying room. "Tomorrow . . . start rice bowls." Without looking up, he replaces the cup on the board. "Don't sign them."

Gripping the edge of the board tightly lest it fall, I slide the batch of teacups into the drying room and flick off the lights. Outside the air is fresh and still, stars shine bright and steady in the wide fabric of the night.

Browning rice, bonnet and scythe
obāsan in the fields
rice harvest

NAGATA-SAN CAME TO MIYAMA AS A
young bride from the coastal town of
Kaminokawa over the hill. But her
husband died early, leaving her with
two children to raise alone. She has
never remarried. A back injury in
youth left her with a crooked rolling
gait, one hip and leg dragging slightly
behind. Now she is in her late sixties,
and her gaunt face, carved by daily exposure to wind and sun, is ridged in a
steady scowl. Even when saying good
morning, she reminds me of an angry
skunk. In order to supplement an income from rice growing, she began
working as grounds and kitchen help at
the Chin Jukan workshop, a job she
has kept for the past twenty-five years.
Most of the older men and women in
Miyama gather daily on the village ex-

R
I
C
E

ercise field to socialize and play gateball, a game similar to croquet, but Nagata-san shuns these events.

After several chance meetings last spring, we have become friends of a sort. My morning walks often take me past her *tambo* (rice paddies), and one day she walked slowly back toward the village with me, telling me of her main trouble. Her unmarried son, who is almost thirty, won't accept any *omiai*, or matchmaking offers. He lives with her, commuting daily to his job in a small company outside of Kagoshima. I met him once. In accordance with rural chic his hair was permed and greased back Elvis Presley style. He wore tight-fitting white jeans, a red shirt and dark sunglasses with Playboy bunnies on the sides.

"He can't find a wife," she complained. "It's terrible. He won't listen to me, I don't know what to do."

"There's still time. Lots of young people don't marry early," I offered. "Maybe he just wants to find someone he likes."

"Life starts at marriage," Reiko often said. By the time she was my age she had already had her first child. According to Nagata-san, at twenty-two I myself was almost past the "suitable age."

"You'd better marry soon yourself," she retorted sharply, shaking her head. "No one wants a bride who's too old, you know!"

One Sunday in the May tea harvest, I stopped to help Nagata-san pick tea leaves from the bushes surrounding her house. She had offered to let me come to the rice planting in June. But weeks later, when I asked about the planting, she had frowned. "A foreigner in a rice field? Impossible!" she answered. "You don't even have the right shoes." She stalked away, one hand steadying her rolling hip.

I gambled that this was more her manner than a direct refusal. Villagers knew Nagata-san as the obāsan with the "bad mouth" and kept out of her way. Her eyes had a habit of slipping to one side as she talked, as if looking for something she'd left behind. Nagayoshi-san said that with her wide brow and high cheekbones, she had one of the few "Korean" faces left in the village. Even after ten years she will not address Reiko or Nagayoshi-san—they are yoso no hito, from Tokyo, and she will have nothing to do with them. I sometimes wonder why she even speaks to me. Perhaps a gaijin is outside village disputes and etiquette. Perhaps she finds my enthusiasm for field work amusing. I don't mind her dark moods or her complaints, half of which I can't understand anyway.

Nagata-san had seeded her nursery beds in April. When the slim blades were six to eight inches tall, a sea of waving green shoots, she had transplanted them into the tambo. In May fast-growing clover spread out over the fields in a thick carpet of purple and white. I would pass her rice paddies on my runs to the coast and think for a moment that I was back in Vermont, staring at a rise of clover-rich pasture. After tilling the clover into the ground with a large-bladed hoe, Nagata-san opened the channel for irrigation.

Each day during the last week in May another field was irrigated, until the entire area was brimming with water, the individual paddies a series of muddy reflecting pools. Across the way, villagers gathered at the Aiko store daily to exchange news and information about the planting.

"Just about time for *otaue*, isn't it?"

"When is your *otaue*?"

"Finished *otaue* yet?"

Miyama farmers, who, like farmers across Japan, are

mostly women, called children home to help and prepared large picnics, making it a festive occasion. Even the Emperor donned his rubber boots and appeared on TV planting a few symbolic seedlings. When Nagata-san's earliest-maturing paddy by the cedar was brimming with brown water, the obāsan of the Aiko store said that she would plant soon. It would probably be on a Sunday, when she had the day off. I simply had to show up at her house on time.

I had looked forward to walking through the wet paddies under a blazing sun like a peasant in a grade B samurai movie. I always enjoyed being with Miyama obāsan. With their weathered hands and faces, and floral-print shirts, their slow way of pouring tea as if time didn't matter, their comforting blend of severity and warmth, they reminded me of my own grandmother, and of a time before the sleek modern life that now dominates Japan. After the concentration the workshop demanded, it felt good to stretch and bend under the open sky. In the fields no one noticed if you spilled your rice or slopped the tea. The obāsan were easy company, and, if only briefly, our lives overlapped in the shared activity of the work at hand.

I slowly slid one foot into the rice paddy, and then the other. Suddenly I was knee-deep in mud that reeked worse than any cattle wallow. The thick bog swirled with threadlike red and black worms, long leeches and multitudes of floating insects. Frogs croaked everywhere at once, like summer crickets. Through my thin rubber-soled boots I felt each twig and stone on the paddy bottom. Hot, rank slime pressed through my thin cotton mompei, covering my calves and knees. In the far corner of the field Nagata-san was busy running a guide string across a deep spot. I watched in horror as the hot mud encased her legs, reaching almost to her hips as she waded across the paddy, and felt grateful for my slight advantage in height.

Ignoring my grimace, Nagata-san showed me how to tuck the spiky green seedlings into the mud, just deep enough to hold them steady.

"Whatever you do, don't run," she said gruffly. "It ruins the mud." I had no intention of running anywhere. The motion of planting wasn't hard, but walking on the slippery bottom was a lesson in balance. The very thought of falling and what I might land on made me freeze in place, storklike, one foot poised in the air.

"Hurry up. The seedlings won't live if you just stand there," barked Nagata-san.

"*Hai*. I'm going," I said quickly, and pushed the seedling down into the paddy, feeling the warm mud slip like a glove up over my wrist. Staring down at my half-submerged arm, I wondered what was living, dying, breeding, spawning, birthing under this teeming slough of mud and water and why I had insisted on coming along.

Just ahead of me Nagai-san and Takara-san plodded slowly through the mud. Talking and laughing as they worked, they were a sharp contrast to my English students in Kagoshima City, who'd been horrified when I'd told them about my weekend plans.

"You, planting rice in the mud," Junko exclaimed. "But, why?"

"I'm curious. We don't grow rice where I live," I said, trying to explain. "And besides, I like working outside." The two sisters shook their heads, delicately covering their mouths with napkins while they giggled.

"Your skin will get brown," said Junko.

"You'll smell," her sister added.

Suddenly I felt depressed, and I finished the lesson in a sour mood.

When I told Reiko that I hoped to help plant the rice that Sunday, she too had wrinkled up her nose in disgust.

"Did you ever work in a rice field?" I had asked.

"Certainly not," she responded stiffly. "My family came from Kobe. We were not farmers." Like most urban Japanese, Reiko would no more consider stepping into a rice paddy than she would wear mompei. Working in the fields was considered lower-class and feudalistic. But before I was to go she reluctantly dug up a sunshade and a pair of gloves for me to wear. Nagayoshi-san, who came from a poor family of rice farmers, thought it amusing that I wanted to help plant and gave me the entire day off.

Although born in Kagoshima, the two sisters whom I taught English conversation weekly knew little about growing rice, and had no desire to learn more. Both of them worked in offices in Kagoshima City. They took English classes, they said, because they wanted to visit the United States someday, and they liked Americans because we were *akarui*—bright, lively. But neither of them ever studied, and our "free conversation" classes always drifted to the topic of American men: at twenty-seven and thirty, their main concern was marriage.

With their perfectly ironed dresses and knee-length skirts, my students looked as if they'd stepped out of *Leave It to Beaver*. Like young Japanese women everywhere, they preferred pastel colors, polka dots and things that were *kawaii*—"cute." They spent their weekends shopping, and a row of pink and white teddy bears lined the rear window of their new white Nissan.

Although intelligent and educated, they affected a cultivated silliness and, around men, assumed the shyness of eleven-year-old girls and soft childlike voices. I was accustomed to hearing this formal women's speech, which to me sounded like baby talk, from the young women who worked in department stores, but it seemed odd to me that it was considered not only polite but seductive. While boy-crazy American girls labor at sophistication, Japanese women of marriageable age tend to act like girls, and are popularly called *burikko*—"pretending kids."

At times burikko, okusan and obāsan acted so differently from one another, it was hard to believe they all belonged to the same culture. With marriage, however, the girlish veneer I saw in my students drops like a wet blanket; as wives and mothers, Japanese women may baby their husbands and spoil their sons, but they rule the icebox, the house, the children and even the family finances with an iron fist. A typical "salary man" may work like a drone, yet see no more of his paycheck than the monthly "allowance" his wife doles out.

At fifty, it is as if another veil drops, revealing the solid steel of the obāsan. In Miyama, census records show that village obāsan have historically outlived their men, and obāsan far outnumber the men in the fields and rice paddies and construction sites along the road. Having reached an age of respect in Japanese society, rural women drop the pro forma female subservience. They are outspoken and frank, and seem to shun the company of older men, preferring their own circles. They till the gardens, mind the stores, sweep the shrine, take care of the grandchildren and know every villager's business. I remembered passing a roof-patching party where two grizzled old men sat in the shade quietly drinking shōchū while three stocky obāsan took turns kneading straw into red-clay mud with their bare feet amid much bantering and laughter.

My students would never gain the bawdy freedom of rural obāsan, who did what they pleased, regardless of protocol, but in Japan, old women everywhere commanded respect. "How could you come here alone?" Junko and her sister had asked incredulously when we first met. "Didn't your father oppose your traveling so far? Weren't you afraid?" No matter how many times I explained that where I came from, college was seen as a transition time away from family, or that I liked traveling alone precisely because of the solitude, they continued to look upon me with a disquieting degree of awe.

But Junko, the elder of the two, had told me of her "secret" plan to move to Tokyo and get a new job of some kind for a year or two, away from her parents. She was attractive, with a soft, reaching smile, but she had been through ten or eleven rounds of omiai without any luck. She liked someone, but he was from Tanegashima, just south of Kagoshima, and her parents had vehemently opposed her marrying one of the southern "islanders" looked down upon by mainland Japanese. She was bored with her office job at a small company, but didn't know what else she wanted to do. I had encouraged her to make a change, to get out of Kagoshima and try something new, until I realized that if she quit her job she would forfeit her chances of finding comparable work on return. Companies preferred young, single women whom they could hire cheaply as "temporary workers" on the expectation that they would quit work when they married. In the end, Junko had given up the idea, saying that once word got around of her *kawatta*—"abnormal"—behavior, her younger sister would have trouble in her own attempts at omiai.

Yet Junko herself seemed ambivalent about marriage, and

she spoke with unconcealed admiration of the single "career women" on the rise in Tokyo. Even in Kagoshima, more opportunities for women were opening up and a growing number of young women were delaying marriage for jobs and careers outside the home. Like most young Japanese women I knew, Junko kept such a busy schedule of "secret" rendezvous and schemes that I never could keep it all straight. Another young working woman I knew, who also lived at home with her parents, had carefully engineered a strategy for maintaining a private social life. She didn't even dare visit her boyfriend's apartment because she was afraid that the neighbors might see her there and tell her parents, but she and two female friends who also lived at home had rented an apartment that they used for parties and trysts.

Other couples, their faces covered, slipped in through the underground entrances of one of the "love hotels" scattered throughout Kagoshima City, especially behind the train station, to rent rooms by the hour. The hotels provided an accepted, if not openly discussed, place for married men to carry on affairs, prostitutes to conduct business, college students to take their dates and young unmarried couples to meet. In a burst of sisterly solicitude, my friend had once told me how to "read" the neon signs outside the hotels. If some of the bulbs were dark, then there were vacancies; if all were lit, the hotel was full.

Once, after teaching my classes and dining in Kagoshima City, I had driven back to the village with Okada-san, an apprentice at the Sataro workshop. When we stopped at a gas station on the way back, the attendant addressed me as Okusan, giving Okada-san a knowing wink. Then I began to notice neon signs bearing such names as Pink Chalet, Castle Romance, and Love Inn appearing with regularity along the road. Apparently we'd found our way onto a love-hotel strip. The whole thing seemed amusing and I was about to say so when I glanced over at Okada-san. Usually calm and collected, he was hunched over the wheel, driving as fast as he could, his face scarlet. Even my sense of humor was closer to that of an obāsan than to my Japanese peers'.

Midmorning, the hot June sun glanced off the rice field in a brown headache glare. I was used to the sewer odors, the constant motion of planting, and ready for tea break. Wedging clay in the cool workshop suddenly seemed inviting. I wouldn't even mind practicing teacups. Already sharp pains ran up and down my back from the constant stooping. I thought of Nagayoshi-san's stories of places where the rice paddies are so deep that farmers push the seedlings about on wooden rafts, half-swimming through the fertile mud.

Suddenly a shriek from the bank made us all start. "Snake!" shouted Nagata-san. Crouching on the bank, she showered rocks and curses upon a large black serpent on the shoreline. No one could see the snake, but Nagata-san, stalking the unseen foe with a large stick in one hand and a flat rock in the other, looked possessed. I froze in place. Glancing at my pale face, Takara-san laughed. "*Ooi, Hebi-san, Hebi-san*— Hey, Mr. Snake, Mr. Snake," she teased, and threw a clump of rice shoots at my feet. Under the deep mud, my toes curled up instinctively.

Soon the thick black snakes became a common sight. They basked in irrigation ditches and along the banks, tongues flicking as they watched us stomp around in their boggy home. The rest of the day was a steady haze of heat, rank slosh and fragile green shoots. When the sun at last sank and cool pink light came over the cedar tops, we headed back to town. Takara-san carried a small glass jar containing three small fishlike salamanders that she had scooped out of the paddy mud and said she would eat for dinner that night. I walked down the road more bent and exhausted than my sixty-year-old friends. Back at the workshop Nagayoshi-san, his hands still coated with clay, was standing by the hedge when I arrived. "Phew, that smells!" Laughing, he called for Reiko, who handed me a towel and a bucket through the back door. "Here, wash off and leave your clothes in the yard. The ofuro is ready, but hurry up, guests are coming for dinner."

Too tired to be modest, I stole a quick glance toward the hedge, peeled off my mud-soaked clothes and darted for the tub. Satisfied that I had carried back no leeches, I sank into the scalding bathwater and stared at the tips of my pink toes; just visible above the steamy bath, they looked vulnerable— bite-sized.

Now in October the rice stands tall, yellow as straw and bent with full heads of ripened grain. Time now for the harvest. Recently a fall harvest festival was held at the village shrine on the hill. The Shintō priest, draped in a snow-white kimono, clapped two sticks together and blessed the twenty or so attending villagers. Old Suzuki-san, the retired school-teacher from across the lane, wore a gray suit for his role as head attendant. Standing stiffly by the entrance, he explained that the ceremony was to celebrate a summer of good weather and a September without typhoons, and to pray for sunny weather in the coming harvest. He recited a low guttural prayer, rising in pitch to the beat of a small drum, then opened the small wooden doors to the shrine's interior and placed the offerings inside next to the hidden rock, Miyama's *kami-sama*.

Villagers had brought long white radishes from their fields, bunches of purple grapes and red-leafed lettuce still wrapped in plastic from the supermarket, bags of rice candies, rice cakes with red-bean filling, and two flasks of shōchū, clear potato liquor, as offerings. When the ceremony was over, the priest opened the doors to the shrine's interior and handed everything back out, spreading a small banquet by the entrance. The men sat cross-legged on the thin tatami inside the open-walled shrine, finishing what remained of the shōchū.

Last week my mother sent a package of eight perfect Lady apples with news of the harvest at home. The potbellied senior postman, arriving with a screech on his green motorbike, had a white box stamped "special delivery" tucked under one arm. He was invited in for tea and Reiko served the fruit, carefully carving one of the small red apples into six slivers and sticking toothpicks into the yellow meat. I showed pictures of the fruit-laden orchards. The size of the gnarled trees, the open fields banked with wildflowers and the tall white pines confirmed the postman's belief that I was the eccentric daughter of a millionaire. I gave up trying to explain that one hundred acres was the average size for an orchard in the Hudson Valley's apple country. After all, I had traveled to and from the village twice, over seven thousand miles each way, while he, like many villagers, had never been as far as Kyoto. The month before, he had asked me for a sample of American money for his eight-year-old son, who already studies English in an after-school program. I gave him what money I had, and the next time I went to the post office he presented me with a small towel and a post office insignia pen. When he finally left, the postman took one small apple for fellow workers, gently cupping it in his palm as if it were an egg.

Chatting about the weather, the latest reports of ash from Sakurajima and the harvest at home came as a welcome relief from teacup practice. Later, when I was seated once again at the wheel, the scent of fresh apples lingered. Even after their long journey, they still smelled of crisp mornings and dew, of falling leaves and orchards thick with grass and the dizzying scent of ripe, falling fruit. Letters from home said that the pick-your-own harvest was in full swing. A lady from Copake had dropped her purse in the portable toilet and it had to be fished out with a stick. A man from the Bronx stayed out picking in a thunderstorm and then swore he'd been hit by lightning—his girlfriend insisted that an ambulance be called at once. Three cars got stuck in the ditch. The gray Shetland pony Bimbo is so fat from kids feeding him apples that he stands all day in the barn, too rotund to move. We won six blue ribbons at the county fair for fruit my sister picked. In the chill autumn weather the maples by the barn are shedding orange, yellow, red across the lawn. And each star-filled night the long-tailed cats creep up closer to the house. By December they will have found a way in through the basement and up into the house, curling in heaps on the armchairs.

I walk down the path to Nagata-san's white house on the corner. The October air smells musty and sweet, not unlike the fall scent of an orchard, but tinged with the sharp odor of distant fire and smoke. Through the tall stands of still bamboo a pale morning light filters down over spreading cinnamon leaf and scattered fern. A quick gray cat leaps across the narrow bamboo-lined pathway, a fish bone dangling from its jaws. Seven-thirty on a Sunday morning. Reiko is busy dyeing leatherwork in the yard, her wide brush leaving trails of scarlet, indigo, magenta, sunflower-yellow and brown. Just inside the glass doors to the living room–gallery Nagayoshi-san sits cross-legged before a pile of wooden boxes, signing each one with steady strokes of his cat-hair brush. Most Miyama households are still sleeping or lingering over breakfast; tourist buses won't start arriving until after nine. Miyama's tailless cats scratch through garbage heaps, compost piles, yards and kitchen doorways for scattered fish bones, their quick eyes bright, watchful. As I walk I scan the fern for broken teapots, chipped plates, old black vats—over three hundred years of pottery history flung into the forest. Pieces of twig and coin-sized potsherds crunch underfoot. My footsteps echo in the still green like the steady fall of hoofbeats on gravel.

Surrounded by a well-swept yard and a low hedge of tea, Nagata-san's house rises on the corner among thick poles of bamboo. Black vats, some of them chest-high, bulge with rainwater, wooden-handled plastic scoops, broken ends of tools, slim bamboo poles, a forgotten plastic sandal, extra gloves and lengths of rope. Others have become planters for stout miniature plum trees. One large kuromon vat leans against the house under a sheet of corrugated metal that covers a Toshiba air conditioner. Built five years ago, the modern stucco house stands on land once occupied by a small wood-firing kiln used by Nagata-san's husband, who died many years ago. In the back, the gray tile-roofed house connects with a low wooden shed that was once his workshop. Inside, waist-high black kame, crocks that once held glaze, still line the walls. But the potter's old kick wheel, split at the base and covered with mold, lies overturned in one corner.

When I arrive, Nagata-san is stepping down from the tiled entrance with a round bundle wrapped in a green-and-blue cloth, the size of a stuffed laundry bag. Concentrating on her load, she mumbles a rough complaining monologue—"Bad weather!"—and shuffles over to a wooden wheelbarrow piled high with similar bundles wrapped in newspaper or faded pastel cloths of red, green and blue. Several pairs of brown chopsticks poke up amid coils of rope, and a clump of bright yellow bananas crowns the precarious load. Part of the payment for laboring in the fields is food; I wonder how many obāsan will help in Nagata-san's field today.

"Good morning, it's Leila," I call across the hedge as loudly as I can without rousing Nagata-san's irritable neighbor, the obāsan with bulging black marble eyes. Nagata-san places the last bag on top with a thump and squints toward the lane. Her face relaxes, then opens into a thin smile.

"Good morning. Early, aren't you?"

"I've come to help with the rice harvest," I say. "Aren't you going to the fields today?"

"Oh yes, but it's hard work. You'd be of no use."

"Look, I've borrowed boots for the rice paddy," I answer quickly, holding up one leg to show off the blue rubber cloven-toe boots that fit tightly around the ankle and pull up over my lower calf, sealing in the bottoms of my baggy mompei. "I have the day off." At the sight of my crab-claw feet Nagata-san's narrow eyes become bright, the lines across her brow quiver, her head shakes. I realize she is laughing at my outfit. Above my mompei, the long sleeves of a black cotton shirt are tucked into white cotton gloves. Dressed for work in the rice fields, I've hidden my yellow hair under a maroon bandanna. Only a pale face and blue gaijin eyes show. I could almost pass for a younger Nagata-san. Her lopsided smile suddenly vanishes, the shaking stops, her whole face tarnishes like copper, twisting into a long frown.

"Come on, then, and be quick, we're already late. Here, carry these." A long-sleeved shirt and a loose apron of sky-blue cover her front, while a white towel tied at the corners forms a loose tentlike sunshade for her head. Her mompei are the plaid design of small blue and white checks with flecks of yellow worn by older farming and pottery women. Like mine, her feet are bound in thin-soled tight-fitting boots that stay on even in the deep gluey mud of the rice fields.

"Yōka! Let's go," she shouts, handing me a green thermos of hot water, a length of straw rope, extra pairs of white cotton gloves, and a short saw-edged sickle over the hedge. Grasping the handles of the wheelbarrow with both gloved hands, Nagata-san bends into the load, half shoving it out of the yard and down the lane. Up the path we stop at a laden persimmon tree to gather some of the soft orange fruit before heading on. Despite her crooked gait, her stride behind the heavy load is light and quick and I have to walk briskly to keep up.

By the moon-shaped mulberry fields at the corner we pass the low stone marker for Ta no kami, the guardian deity of the field, small blue-and-white cups of water or clear shōchū resting on its ledge. The front bears the grinning face of what looks like a hobo under a mushroom-shaped hood. From the back it is shaped to resemble a large phallus. Markers like these line the fields throughout Kagoshima, and in many places a stone or wood phallus is enshrined, adding to the region's reputation for feudal, patriarchal attitudes. While an urban women's movement slowly grows, Kagoshima staunchly preserves its conservative ways. In Miyama, although women work in the potteries, workshop owners are all men, and there are no recognized female "master" craftsmen in the village. Reiko says that when she first moved to Miyama from Tokyo, older women scolded her for not hanging her husband's laundry on separate lines from her own "impure" clothing.

We turn onto the main road to the coast. In the west slim rays of sun slice through the clouds, shining over the waves in streaks of shimmering gold. Across Miyama the sky is a sullen lead-gray.

"Bad weather," grumbles Nagata-san in local slang. Though she can understand my standard Japanese, she speaks the rough, uneven Kagoshima ben. Young people don't learn the dialect, saying that they don't want to sound like hicks, but it is still the common speech of village elders. And although Kobe-born Reiko won't have it spoken in the house, in the workshop Nagayoshi-san talks on the phone to his mother and brother in nearby Sendai, to friends and even to me in the thick dialect. I speak it sometimes. I like the way the sounds roll off the tongue, rising and falling in lazy circles. "*Jiyashtonah*," I answer, Kagoshima slang for "I see," and keep on walking. The rain is worrying. If the rice gets wet it may rot on the stalk. We must finish harvesting her three fields today.

Across from the Aiko food store, the small valley of terraced rice paddies spreads out in a mosaic of green and brown where harvested and unharvested fields meet. Nagata-san pushes the teetering wheelbarrow off the main road and down a narrow grass pathway twisting like a brown snake down the slope. Late-maturing fields still wave wet and green. But most paddies, drained of water and shaved of rice, extend in neat rows of brown stubble. Harvested rice, bound in broom-shaped bundles, hangs chest-high over long bamboo poles suspended by props at each end. Each harvested field is full of identical racks of drying rice, bridging the fields in straight lines.

Though most farmers in Miyama use machines to till, plant and thresh, Nagata-san avoids them. "*Kikai?* Machines? They're terrible," she says. "They tear up the mud, and lose the grain in harvest. No, by hand is much better!" One hundred years ago swaybacked oxen lumbered through the thick mud during planting and harvest. But today the only bovines in Miyama are a herd of white-and-black Holsteins in the small dairy farm on the hill. Some Miyama farmers now use machinery to plant and thresh, but many small farmers like Nagata-san, who plants only three small fields, barter help with friends instead. During the summer she will work alone, weeding, managing the water, and spraying the fields for rice stalk borers, paddy-borers, plant hoppers and rice blight, which, if unattended, would smother the heads of grain in a deadly white film.

We head across the valley where two bent figures make steady progress across the field of waving yellow. Where they pass, the yellow-green rice falls. The rhythmic swishing of sickles cutting through straw grows louder as we approach. Even under the gray sky the arching blades glint silver. I recognize the pair as Takara-san and Nagai-san, the two old women who had helped in the June rice planting.

Ohayō. Ohayō. Ohayō.

We exchange morning greetings. Nagata-san motions for me to join the other women. Sickle in hand, I step down onto the firm mud of the drained paddy. The soil smells rank and sour, a combination of musty old hay and ripe sulfur—

Nagata-san's source of fertilizer is her outhouse. I stand still for a minute, pretending to adjust my gloves while my stomach turns. Dark-eyed Takara-san, the youngest of the three and the most talkative, works toward where I stand. Her upturned face catches my gaze and she flashes a set of gold-filled teeth.

"Well, you're back. Didn't you go back to America to see your parents?" she says quickly. "Did you see Brooke Shields? Did you bring me some Sunkist oranges?"

"Oh, I've been back two weeks now, but my family grows apples, not oranges. Where they live is about as cold as Sapporo."

"I see," answers Takara-san, still smiling. "Well, I've never had an American apple."

I quickly change the subject. I had been back in the States for two weeks. Returning with *omiyage*, travel souvenirs, was a mandatory gesture. For Eri, who was interested in fashion and design, I had brought copies of *Vogue*. For Keisuke, studying photography in Tokyo, I had found a book on Ansel Adams. To my teacher I gave a thick art book about the Mimbres Indian pottery of the Southwest, and for Reiko I had purchased an entire deerhide. Half of my luggage had consisted of boxes of maple sugar candy, soaps, university pins, decals, T-shirts and stationery, New York City mementos, postcards of Niagara Falls and assorted towels and key rings. Even so, the presents ran out. "Just don't tell anyone you ever left," Reiko said firmly. But within days everyone in the village knew that the yellow-haired apprentice had gone on a trip.

I step out onto the rice paddy, following Takara-san and doing my best to imitate her swinging movements.

"That's not too bad. Not even young Japanese girls these

days know how to harvest rice," shouts Takara-san. "Why don't you find a nice Japanese man and settle down here!" She laughs, glancing at me from the corner of her eye as she works. I grunt a noncommittal reply, too busy trying to manage the swinging sickle to converse.

"Yes, what about *omiai*?" a quiet voice pipes up on my right. "It's about time for you to get married, anyway." Working her way up next to me, Nagai-san is not going to miss out on the fun.

"Me, an okusan? *Muri gowandonah*—impossible," I banter back. "I can't make miso soup, and I'm hopeless at tea ceremony. And anyhow, I'm not looking for a husband—I'm too busy."

Nagai-san giggles softly, her long face hidden by her wide sunbonnet. But Takara-san laughs so hard she misses a swing and her sickle gets stuck in the mud. Across the field Nagata-san, busy setting up props and cross poles to hang the rice, hears the laughter and turns with a dark face. "Hurry up, and stop joking around," she scolds. "It's going to rain."

The cutters progress in an even horizontal line across the field, felling several clumps of rice with each sweep of their curved blades. I fall into line with Takara-san, working toward her so that when we meet we finish a row and then move on. Underfoot, the rice paddy feels as slippery as a fresh cow pie. Beneath the dark mud lie streaks of clay and russet iron-rich sand dug for centuries by Miyama potters as the crucial ingredient in the deep black glaze for kuromon. Cutting the straw off evenly to leave a clean two-inch stub is a craft requiring skill, not power. I hack at a clump of rice in frustration. The straw bends like flax, scattering rice grains in the mud. I stoop to pick them up and Takara-san catches sight of me. She comes over and demonstrates how to hook a straw clump with the blade's sharp side and pull upward with a quick tug. A hearty ripping sound, and fallen straw lies flat and even behind her. I try again, and this time, my blade hooks neatly over the base, then cuts through the straw with a loud rip.

Soon three or four rows of straw lie behind us. Takara-san motions me to follow her to the head of the field.

"Well, that's not bad. But two people cutting are enough. Follow behind us now and tie the bundles," she says.

I nod and follow. Already my arms ache from the constant swinging. Taking up a thick armful of scratchy straw, she binds it with three or four strands from the sides. She works quickly, placing a bundle between her knees and twisting the straw deftly despite her thick cotton work gloves.

As a child I loved to braid onion tops, bending and plaiting the rough stems until the whole pile of freshly pulled bulbs hung like a clump of ghostly grapes. This should be easy. I hold up my first effort to have a look: strands of straw stick out from the sides, the whole bundle threatens to collapse. Hung on a pole to dry, this clump would soon be blown across the village. I untie the loose ends, now limp and tangled as wet hair, and start again.

"Pretty bad, huh."

"Watch again," she says, and shows me how to tie the bundle tight, without knocking off grain or breaking the straw.

Imitating her quick movements, I hold the rough rice straw tightly between my own knees and reach around the outside for the straw binders. Tied together, they form a compact sheaf.

"I guess that will do. You're not bad—better than my daughter," jokes Takara-san, pushing back her bonnet. "She's hopeless—won't even come out here!"

"Why not?"

"Her job is studying!" answers Takara-san proudly. Like most children and young people in Miyama, Takara-san's teenage daughter doesn't help in the rice fields or even much at home. Overweight and suffering from acne, she looks as if a day in the sun would do her good. Like Western teenagers, she has a penchant for junk food, especially Coca-Cola and chocolate. The only time I have seen her outside is when she heads off in her blue knee-length uniform to the local high school in Ijuin. For the past month Takara-san has been working an extra night job in order to buy her a red motor scooter so that she won't have to ride the bus to school.

Around where we work many of the tambo lie fallow; the owners are too busy at jobs in Kagoshima City or nearby towns, or, like American wheat farmers, they receive government subsidies not to plant. After one or two weeks of good weather, when the husks and straw are thoroughly dried, Nagata-san will send the rice to a thresher in the next town. Last week I'd seen Suzuki-san sit down in his formal garden before a manual wooden thresher. All morning clouds of dust and a loud clatter came over the hedge. By noon, when Nagayoshi-san and I went to have a look, straw was piled up in the yard next to a heap of ivory rice. Suzuki-san's khaki clothes were white with rice chaff and dust.

Rice straw has been used in Miyama for generations to thatch roofs, insulate walls, fill futons, make tatami and rope, and provide ash for pottery glaze. Inside the roaring kiln the ash melts, fusing with the clay and leaving a shiny silicate surface on the pottery. The first Korean potters in Miyama in the early seventeenth century knew to mix small amounts of wood ash with water and crushed iron-rich rock containing traces of feldspar to make the black glaze for kuromon. Later, potters began mixing wood ash, water and finely ground white clay from Kaseda to make a clear glaze for shiromon. Still later, the potters began to use rice straw ash, which opacifies the glaze and creates a distinct bluish-white finish.

Every fall Nagayoshi-san waits like a farmer for the rice to mature. When the rice is shorn, he returns to his mother's fields and burns great bonfires of straw. The fire rises up orange against the sky, reaching for oxygen to consume the piles of dry stalks. When all that is left is a cool black mound, he gathers it up in bags for the year's supply of glaze. Until recent years Miyama potters farmed during the warm months and potted in the winter or in their spare time.

"*Ocha desu yo!*—Teatime!" Under the gray clouds, Nagata-san calls from the far bank and then bends over her wheelbarrow. We leave our gloves and sickles by the edge of the field and step carefully over the fallen rice for tea. More than half the field is cut, shaved in a neat line. In a far corner, bundles of cut rice form a row. After the entire paddy is cut and bundled, we will tie long bamboo poles onto chest-high stakes and hang the rice straw bundles, grain-end down, to dry. Two more fields await reaping; the harvest will take the whole day.

From her loaded wheelbarrow Nagata-san brings out bags, boxes and a small fat-bellied white Satsuma teapot. Chipped in places, with gilded chrysanthemums drawn across its swelling sides, it is a sample of the cheap, mold-cast souvenir pottery abundant in Miyama workshops. On the lid is a gold cross within a circle—even in the rice fields the ancient crest of Lord Shimazu prevails.

Nagata-san works quickly until four plates are heaped with sugared beans, rice cake, garlic and radish pickles, English cookies ("bisuketto"), seaweed crackers and a banana. The heavy paper plate holds more food than I usually eat for lunch. Food is one form of the day's pay; in addition, Nagata-san will help Nagai-san with her rice and Takara-san with her potato harvest. The two old women pull out faded scarves and wrap up the cakes, eating only the sweetened red beans and yellow-dyed radish pickles between sips of hot tea. I dip my hands in the cold water of a nearby irrigation ditch, keeping one eye out for snakes, and take a seat next to Nagai-san.

A fresh breeze pushes across the field, momentarily relieving the sulfur stench. I take long, burning gulps of the bitter tea and crunch a few pickles. Nagata-san paces like a whiskered terrier, and Takara-san lounges back with her legs extended, her teacup nestled in the grass. But Nagai-san sits upright, shoulders back. She holds her cup lightly with both hands, the proper way for women. Drinking slowly, she finishes her tea in small feminine sips, a gentle half-smile spreading across her face.

Sometimes when I look at Nagata-san I see the wiry old German woman who used to watch our street in Yorkville, always at the same second-floor window, elbows resting on the sill, like some stern, immobile gargoyle. Like Nagata-san, Nagai-san was also an outside bride who married a potter and moved to the village in her early twenties. Although she never talks about him, her husband is a skilled kuromon potter, now retired, who worked at the Jukan workshop from time to time. As an itinerant shokunin, he moved from workshop to workshop, making pots on commission. To supplement this income he and his wife farmed rice and potatoes. Even in postwar Kagoshima, women of Nagai-san's age raised the children, worked in the house and served the men. At mealtimes they ate last, on the road they walked behind. According to Nagai-san, the hardest chore for a young bride was hauling water from the wells, a practice that continued until the late thirties, when the first water lines were installed. *"Benri wa benri desu yo!"* Nagai-san will say quietly when asked about changes in the village. "Convenience is convenience!" Like most villagers she is not nostalgic. When the road was recently widened and repaved, cutting an ugly gash in the hillside and resulting in double the number of trucks roaring down the road, she nodded her head in approval. "It's better-looking." I look down at Nagai-san's hands, still wrapped around the white cup. Although small, they are sturdy and tough like well-worn tools. Hands like those could make a good pot—I wonder what shapes they would form.

"Nagai-san, did you ever try to make pottery?"

"Oh no," she quickly replies. "Women didn't work the wheels."

"But didn't you ever try, just once?"

"It just couldn't be done. It wasn't women's work. How would we have the time?" She shakes her head, holding out her cup for a refill.

"When were you married?"

"Oh, a long time ago. I was younger than you."

"Where did you meet him?"

"Meet him? It was all arranged. My family met him before I did!" she says, laughing at my question. I pick up my own cup of tea and take a long sip, trying to imagine a life without all the choices I've had. I think of Nakada-san's daughter with her baby and no husband, of the young women to whom I teach English. The sky grows black, and I am swimming in a moonless sea. Nagai-san and I seem galaxies, light-years—cultures—apart.

"You young people just don't know. Times were different then," says Nagai-san, her voice firm under her wide bonnet.

"Yes," I say. "Yes, they certainly were."

Like other potters' wives, Nagai-san is skilled in clay and glaze making and full of stories about the firing of the kilns. As a woman she didn't help with the actual firing, but brought trays of food, tea and shōchū for the men. The fertility gods lining the fields are male, but the kiln kami-sama is said to be female, and mortal women make her jealous. At the traditional kuromon workshop run by Sataro-san down the road, there have been female apprentices in recent years, but women still do not help when the *noborigama* (the climbing kiln) is fired, by far the most important and exciting stage of the pottery process. Yet, despite this legacy of hard, often degrading work for Japanese women, the *Kojiki* ("Record of Ancient Matters"), Japan's oldest extant chronicle, holds that the supreme deity, and thus the progenitrix of the Japanese imperial line, is the sun goddess Amaterasu-ō mikami. Even in the Greek pantheon, the sun deity is the male god Apollo. Once this powerful and moody goddess, offended by the misdeeds of her younger brother, Susanoo no Mikoto, hid in a cave, and, like the Greek goddess Demeter, grieving for her lost Persephone, brought darkness and chaos across the land. Eventually Amaterasu sent her grandson Ninigi no Mikoto down to pacify and thus settle the Japanese islands. Holding a sacred mirror, he descended from the heavens onto the pinnacle of Mt. Takachiho, only an hour's drive north from Miyama in the Kirishima mountains.

But today the proud sun goddess has slipped behind a thick blanket of clouds, and we will have to hurry to finish all the fields by dark. I wonder if a typhoon is coming. Typhoons usually batter this southern tip of Kyushu in September, but this year no storms have yet arrived. I set down my cup and glance around the group. No one hurries; it is still time for tea. As if oblivious of the weather, Nagata-san slowly pours another round of the clear green brew. I hand Nagai-san another brimming cupful and take one for myself. I lie back and look across the half-harvested field. When the teapot is finally empty, Nagata-san and the others stretch out on the grass to rest. Under stormy clouds the day slows; their breathing becomes long and steady. Nagata-san begins to snore, a soft droning noise like the rattling of a dried gourd.

By the cedar groves a narrow road twists into the trees and then out of sight. Along this road the clay salesman once brought clay from Izakuda, traveling on his thick-maned bay horse. Sataro-san owns a 16-mm. movie made thirty years ago by a local TV crew that shows the bald old man unloading bags of freshly dug clay in front of the Sataro workshop. When the clay seller died ten years ago, several greedy Miyama potters bulldozed away so much of the hill behind his house to get at the underlying clay that the whole hill collapsed, wiping out the barn, and now the widow, who is called simply Izakuda Obāsan, has forbidden any potter other than Sataro-san to dig clay.

One October day a year before, I had walked out to see my first rice harvest in Miyama. Following a path that led behind the Jukan workshop, I moved quickly in the cool fall breeze, heavy with coming rain and the mineral smells of damp earth. The worn dirt trail soon narrowed and became looped with branches and underbrush and littered with fallen bamboo leaves. Vines caught at my ankles, but the narrow pathway continued steeply down. I walked on, ducking sticky spiderwebs, diving deeper and deeper into patterns of light and leaf. Gradually the thick jungle leveled out and opened onto a compact valley of terraced rice fields, a secret garden surrounded by a thick forest of bamboo and cedar, watered by a carefully constructed system of irrigation.

Spread out like a weaving in deepening hues of yellow and brown, with stripes of green where the pathways ran through, the valley was such a study in texture and design that I didn't notice at first a short figure in light blue work pants and a white housewife's smock. She worked quickly, throwing sheaves of cut and dried rice up onto a bamboo rack that ran the length of a small square paddy. She heaved and pulled at the rack to get it straight and even. When she reached to pick up a large plastic sheet to cover the rice, she saw me.

"*Yōka! Yōka!*" she called with a broad smile, bobbing her head, and then rattled on in Kagoshima dialect.

"*Konnichiwa,*" I answered feebly, nodding and smiling. Having been only a week in Miyama, I understood little of this heated country talk, slowing and speeding, rising and falling, a grinding motor of sounds. But she continued, faster, louder. Suddenly she picked up a nearby sickle and began swinging it in wide circles above her head. I took a step back. Was I trespassing? Did she dislike Americans? Only yesterday the woman who ran the small half-abandoned tōfu shop down the road had come running out shouting "American lady, American lady," and, grabbing my arm, had begun a garbled explanation about how terrible the war had been. "Go back and tell Americans how nice the Japanese are," she had implored, her strong fingers pinching my arm. I had listened in alarm. Only later did I learn that villagers avoided her because she was considered "off" in the head.

From under the tight blue bonnet the old woman's tirade continued. What did she want me to do? I took another step back. Suddenly she stopped and gave me a long disappointed look as if I were hopelessly slow. Then, with a rapid waving of her hand, she motioned for me to come forward. Curious, I stepped carefully along the narrow grass pathway between the rice paddies to where she stood. She waved toward some purple fruit hanging from vines in the cedar and suddenly I understood. I pointed to the fruit, making cutting motions with my hands. She clapped me on the back, handed me a short sickle and calmly went back to work. "*Yōka, yōka!*" she shouted as I brought a clump of the potato-sized fruit down with a crash. Her eyes lit up when I handed her a cluster. She handed me two and then bit into the fruit, chewing the white meat and spitting out mouthfuls of black seeds. I followed suit. The fruit had the sweet musty flavor of a papaya and the consistency of a grape.

"*Yōka! Yōka!*" She wiped her hands on her baggy pants and continued her tussle with the plastic sheet. I grabbed one corner and helped her lift it over the rows of rice. Though in America I am considered short, next to Miyama's old women I become a pale giant. The old woman smiled and jabbered. I recognized occasional words such as *sabishii*—"lonely"—and *tetsudai*—"help."

Once the rice was covered with the plastic sheet and all four corners were tied down, we gathered the sickles, ropes and remaining fruit and walked back up the path to the village. Along the way we finished the fruit, leaving a trail of black seeds. At the hilltop I said good-bye and was just turning away when she grabbed my arm and motioned for me to follow her down the lane. I acquiesced; by this time I liked her rough and eager manner, and the way she kept on talking to me although it was clear how little I actually understood. In front of a rambling wooden house we stopped. She pushed open a sliding wooden door, shouted greetings and stepped in. I waited by the entrance, where bright-eyed finches in a small bamboo cage flitted nervously from perch to perch.

An elderly man in a bright green sweat suit appeared from the back and ushered me into a room floored with tatami. He pointed for me to sit in the lone chair, a large black vinyl armchair with a white doily over the back, then he turned on the large Sony color television and sat down cross-legged before a low table. I leaned back against the cushions and looked around the room. Tacked up on the wall was an oversized calendar, compliments of Kagoshima Bank, bearing an aerial photograph of Sakurajima billowing gray smoke over the brilliant blue bay. On top of the television, next to a large blue-eyed doll in a lime-green taffeta dress, sat three perfect, intricately carved samples of white Satsuma pottery, like those that appear in the museum above the Chin Jukan workshop or in art history books as prewar examples of the white wood-fired pottery. Here, their place of honor was shared with a plastic-wrapped doll one might win at a carnival, their carved designs barely visible through a blanket of dust.

From the back came the sounds of tea preparation—the soft ticking of the gas burners, much rattling and an occasional crash.

"Nice pottery," I said, almost shouting over the blaring TV. "Are they from Miyama?"

"Hey, your Japanese is good!" said the old man brightly in the standard tongue. "Hey, she speaks Japanese!" he shouted in local dialect into the kitchen. He got up stiffly and took one of the pieces from the TV to hand to me. I brushed off the dust and looked it over. It was an ivory-colored incense burner, and the rounded top had been carved into fine latticework, while the whole piece rested on clawlike feet like a miniature Chippendale chair. In my hands it felt as light as blown glass.

"Which workshop?" I asked quickly.

"Oh, that one, over there," he said casually, pointing out the door. "I was once a carver of white Satsuma, but my eyes gave out. No one wanted pottery then, anyhow—it was after the war, wages were low then, you know." He sighed, his words almost lost in the noise of the TV. "There was nothing to eat."

As if on cue, his wife reappeared, bringing a tea tray: plastic dishes loaded with pickles, sweet rice cakes and flat rice crackers, small onionlike bulbs soaked in shōchū, and a simple white cup of green tea. For the old man there was a pot of the clear liquor.

"Do you still carve pots sometimes, in your free time, perhaps for a hobby?" I asked, taking up my teacup. He shook his head, and gave a tight laugh.

"No. I don't work anymore at all. I got sick a few years ago. I don't even work in the fields." He took another sip of shōchū. When he picked up the small cup, I noticed that his hand shook.

We sat quietly for the remainder of the meal. The old man

poured himself another measure of liquor and stared at the television. When my own cup was empty, I thanked them both and, saying good-bye, stepped back out into the lane. I did not think to rush home and take notes, as I did after talks with working potters. Dressed in a sweat suit, a pair of black plastic glasses tipped forward on his nose, he seemed like just another of the many old people who wandered about Miyama's streets. Master potters like Sameshima Sataro wore traditional blue work clothes; they fit my nostalgic image of a pottery village. This old man seemed more like an Oregon rancher than a potter. I enjoyed the tea and conversation; only later did I wish that I had listened better to his story. He was one of the "unknown craftsmen" whom Yanagi Sōetsu, the founder of the Japanese folkcraft movement, exalted as the builders of the Buddhist "kingdom of beauty." A craftsman from prewar Miyama, farming in the warm months, making pots in the winter, his days waxing and waning in the cycles of moon and rice.

Sakurajima, volcano on the bay
rising from the waves
what are you saying?

Across the arched roof of the steel-and-brick glaze kiln, a small New Year's decoration of rice-straw rope and fern rustles in the breeze. Weighted in the center by a dome-shaped *mochi*— rice cake—it resembles the decorations resting on kilns and workshop ledges across the village. Nagayoshi-san is not overtly religious, avoiding even his pottery predecessors' Shintō practice of offering rice, sake and salt to the kiln before each firing. But the day before New Year's we cleaned the entire workshop, washing down the wheels, raking the dirt yard, rinsing the glaze buckets outside, even wiping clean the clay-spattered clock. During the cleaning Nagayoshi-san had quietly made the decoration, which symbolized prosperity in the New Year. New Year's celebrations officially end on January 6, when decorations are taken down and the hard glutinous rice cakes eaten, but this one remains, forgotten on the kiln's edge, where it has collected a fine patina of gray volcanic ash.

In contrast to the Western propensity for merrymaking, New Year's in Japan is a time of reflection and quiet. For the first three days of January, stores in Kagoshima City shut down. The usually quiet Miyama becomes a ghost town. At the Nagayoshi household, preparations for the New Year began with a frenzy of cleaning. When the house, yard and workshop were immaculate, we jumped into the ofuro and scrubbed ourselves as well. The last meal of 1984 was bowls of buckwheat noodles, representing long life, in a soy-sauce broth, with a curled shrimp added for good luck. Nagayoshi-san's eighty-three-year-old mother and his younger brother, who rarely visited, came to stay for several days. While they calmly sat watching television, Eri, home for New Year's vacation from her two-year junior college, wrote ritual *nengajō* (New Year's greetings) and Reiko did last-minute cleaning.

Although Nagayoshi-san entered the kitchen more than most Japanese husbands, fixing lunch and preparing the evening rice when Reiko went to town, he stayed away when she was home; the kitchen was her domain. On New Year's, however, I helped him make pans of mochi, a rice cake traditionally pounded in a wooden mortar, with the electric mochi-maker. He donned a white apron and, with a great opening and shutting of cupboards, pulling out of ingredients and clashing of pans, set to work. By the time we were done, the kitchen was a complete mess. At eleven-thirty, Reiko quickly ran the vacuum cleaner one last time around the living room, and we all sat down to watch live television coverage of New Year's festivals in provinces across Japan. Almost without anyone's noticing, it was midnight. A close-up shot of a giant bronze temple bell being struck one hundred and eight times, once for each of the bad parts of human nature as enumerated by Buddha, flashed across the screen.

The next morning, while everyone slept a little later than usual, I walked up the road to see the New Year's service at the shrine. The Nagayoshis weren't "Miyama people," and never went there, and Eri had also declined, saying she had no intention of waking up early "just to see a bunch of old people."

Over the last *torii* (stone gates) a long rope of twisted rice straw denoting sacred space was looped like a chain and hung with ferns, a tangerine and zigzag strands of folded white paper. The wooden shrine entrance was decorated with white cloth banners printed with a black cross within a circle: even the *jinja* had belonged to Lord Shimazu. For the New Year the priest wore a deep purple robe over his usual white kimono.

Slowly, to the banging of the drum, people arrived. Along with the usual group of old villagers, this morning children and younger adults also knelt down before the priest. When everyone was assembled, the open-walled shrine was almost full. The priest recited long passages in the special language of prayer, adding all our names at the end, then clapped twice and blessed the crowd with his wand of white papers.

Shintō, the indigenous religious tradition of Japan, is a loosely structured set of practices, in which certain places, mountains, trees, rocks and other inanimate objects are worshiped for the *kami*, spirit or spiritual quality felt to reside in them. A religious system based on ritual and nature rather than on dogma or creed, Shintō has no Bible or Ten Commandments. Even prayer is a practical matter. After leaving an offering of food or money, people pray to the kami-sama for good weather, a safe firing, a prosperous year, good health, a son. At the large shrine in Kagoshima City one can buy gilt cloth and paper amulets for everything from health and marital harmony to success on exams and traffic safety. The traffic safety amulets come wrapped in plastic, with a suction cup for easy mounting on your windshield. I once rode in a car so laden with these that one could hardly see out.

On a national level, Shintō also has an important political dimension. According to Japanese mythology, Jimmu-tenno, the first emperor of Japan, descended from the Sun Goddess Amaterasu—the supreme Shintō deity. Although Shintō offers little in the way of written creed or philosophy, the underlying moral of all ten sects is the same: "Follow the impulse of your nature and obey your Emperor."

Throughout history this Shintō aspect of emperor veneration and the mythological supremacy of the Japanese people has been used in Japan by right-wing extremists and militarists to rally a nationalistic spirit. Under the revised 1947 MacArthur constitution, Shintō is no longer the state religion of Japan, but even in Miyama, a wooden plaque painted with a bold red sun hangs on the back wall of the shrine. On national holidays, such as the Emperor's birthday, white flags with the red sun fly from every household. When I saw Nagayoshi-san hanging a Japanese flag on the corner of the kiln shed, he gave me an apologetic look and quickly explained that if he and Reiko didn't join in, neighbors would accuse them of being unpatriotic.

Short and stout, Uchida-san the priest had drooping cheeks that made him look as if he were always on the verge of a yawn. Until he retired sixteen years ago to become a full-time Shintō priest, Uchida-san had been a member of the Izakuda police department. His father had been the Shintō priest for this neighboring hamlet where Uchida-san had been raised, a duty that he had now taken over. But as in many small villages, the congregation of Izakuda had grown so small that over the years he had begun to perform services for several neighboring shrines as well.

I had met him my first October in Miyama. I often slipped out before breakfast to walk a quick circle of the village, starting at the shrine, and I was just coming down the path one warm fall morning when I heard people approaching. Startled, I looked up into the ranks of an oncoming troop of obāsan. A chorus of voices broke out all at once.

"Hey, look who's here."

"What's she doing?"

"Did you come to help clean?"

"Well, I'll be—"

Several women had gone behind the shrine, emerging with armfuls of twig brooms. From bits and pieces of their conversation I understood that they represented the Miyama women's association, the Fujinkai, and that once a month they met to sweep the shrine before the monthly service.

"Grab a broom if you want to help—hurry up, we only have a little time," said one forthright obāsan with short white hair. I began sweeping.

At 8:00 Uchida-san had arrived in a white taxi from Izakuda. Frail to begin with, he was so bundled in his white robes that the taxi driver had to help him disembark, one white-socked foot at a time. Settling his conical black plastic priest's hat atop his balding head, he smiled to everyone before slowly climbing the stairs up into the shrine. At the shrine entrance each of the obāsan took off her shoes, threw a coin into the offerings box, pulled the long rope to sound the gong, and clapped her hands in prayer. Pulled along by the old woman who had given me the broom, I followed, leaving my running shoes at the entrance next to a row of sandals. After the service the women sat in the shrine, talking as they nibbled the cookies and crackers that had been offered to the kami-sama during the service and promptly retrieved afterwards, and Uchida-san welcomed me.

"Shintō is the Japanese heart," he had explained gravely. "If you understand Shintō, then you will understand Japan. And now that you live in Miyama you can pray to Miyama's kami-sama. Do you have any special request? Is anything bothering you?" When I said no, he seemed almost disappointed, but urged me to attend the monthly service. Unlike many small country shrines, Miyama's shrine was well tended by older villagers. The first service of the month was for the women, the fifteenth for the men. As a gaijin I could choose either one.

Once, confusing the dates, I had gone to the men's service. Shiromon potter Someura Juro and old Suzuki-san from across the lane served as attendants. They worked quickly, sweeping the long path and the dirt yard around the shrine, barely talking. I grabbed a broom to help, but one robust old man whom I often met in the post office kept grabbing my arm and introducing me to everyone as his girlfriend. When the service was over I left as quickly as I could. From then on I attended with the chattering obāsan. As an outsider I could enjoy their stories without becoming embroiled in their rapid-fire exchanges of gossip.

First built in 1605, the "Tamayama" jinja was originally a Korean-style building of byo architecture located on a hill just above the present shrine. Miyama residents use its Korean-style name, Gyokuzan. According to village legend, the shrine had been built after the newly arrived Korean potters looked up one night and saw a ball of flame spring over the ocean and land on the tallest hill in the village. They took this to be a sign that Dankun, the Korean creator god, had sent his spirit to protect them in their new home, and they built a shrine on the spot. Here Koregansa was deified as the relative of Dankun; the essence of the god was a large stone.

In 1918, almost fifty years after Shintō was proclaimed the state religion of the new Meiji government, the shrine was rebuilt in the uniform Japanese style and moved down the hill to its present location. Even so, villagers still maintain that the shrine is a Korean place. According to their lore, the outer two stone gates leading up from the main road mark the deification of the indigenous Japanese spirit, but behind the two innermost gates lies the sacred area of Koregansa. Until about 1965 a native Miyama priest had performed the shamanist Korean rituals that the first potters brought from their homeland. Older villagers remember Korean festivals when a pole bearer, called a *hatamodonga* in the local dialect, was elected to communicate with the kami-sama and in a shamanist state bring his message down to the village. At shrine festivals, dancers like those whom Shimazu lords had stopped to watch en route to Edo would sing and dance for the kami-sama. But by 1985 most evidence of the shrine's Korean origin had gone. Draped with New Year's decorations, the shrine could have belonged in any rural province of Japan, a facet of the countryside as familiar as white church spires in New England.

For the first three days of January Miyama's streets had bustled with new faces. During New Year's and *obon*, the

Buddhist festival of the dead in August, Miyama, along with the rest of Japan, experiences mass migration as parents bring their children back to their ancestral home, to visit the grandparents and place incense on the graves. Plane and train tickets for New Year's week are sold out by November. Kirin Obā-san opened her store on January 3, complaining that already she missed her children, who had come to visit from Kumamoto, Osaka and Tokyo. "An old lady like me gets lonely, you know," she had said, wiping the corner of her eye with her blue apron. "They tell me to move to the city, but I was born here, Miyama is my home." She had let me leave only after promising that I would write to my own parents soon.

In the wake of the holiday the yard is empty and still. Today the sky hangs overcast and sullen, even songbirds are silent. Only the bamboo creaks and groans, sharp cracks echoing as the tall spires clash in the wind. Beside the kiln a winter camellia bush blooms brilliant pink. Planted to commemorate Keisuke's graduation from grade school, the bush is over a decade old. Now he studies photography in Tokyo, but the bush is a dwarf, barely knee-high.

Placing my bucket under the tap by the hedge, I bend down and gingerly stretch my back. Righting myself, I still feel as stiff as Kirin Obāsan, her shoulders lifted in a permanent shrug from years of field labor. Today is Friday, the end of a long week. Since last Monday, Nagayoshi-san has been up and out in the workshop by 6:00, working until late to fill New Year's orders, his apprentice limping behind him.

Turning on the tap, I rub my cold palms and wait for the rush of cold water. On top of the clay-recycling vat a heap of unfired pottery piles up, a clutter of smashed clay and ice. Intricate lines of minute ice crystal have pushed up through the surface of the pots in a series of frosted welts. Last night, rushing to catch the last bus to Kagoshima City, Nagayoshi-san forgot to tack protective cloths across the door to the drying room. Drafts seeped in, freezing the freshly thrown pottery still slick with water. The frost was ruthless.

When we opened the door this morning, we gazed at a wreckage of frozen pottery. "*Shimatta na*. Damn," Naga-yoshi-san exclaimed, sucking breath in through his teeth. "How many days' work?" I asked quietly. "Three days, maybe more," he answered, his voice tight, and stepped into the room. Unsure of what to do, I turned back to my own work, setting up for throwing rice bowls. Nagayoshi-san emerged with a full board of withered vases perched on his shoulder and stepped out into the yard. The pottery landed on the clay-recycling vat with a loud crash. Luckily the large exhibition bowls had been slowly drying above the clothes closet in the house.

Taking up the bucket, I walk back into the workshop and fill the rattling kettle on the kerosene stove. We have stuffed gloves and rags between the window panes, but ice-cold wind still seeps in. The only source of heat in the long, uninsulated shed is a kerosene stove. Pulling it any closer only scorches your back and makes the room swim with fumes.

The house, like the rest of the village homes, is not much warmer. Though all Miyama residents seem to own at least one color TV, and most a VCR, I have never visited a home with central heating. For warmth, people build small charcoal fires in ceramic hibachi pots, light kerosene stoves, or huddle around *kotatsu*—low tables with a small electric heater at-tached to the underside and a short curtain around the edges to contain the heat. It is said that the ancient Japanese had to choose between being cool in the summer or warm in the winter. In Miyama, where summer temperatures run from

90 degrees Fahrenheit and up, they undoubtedly chose to endure the brief two months of winter.

Usually I like the forest smells of musty clay and wood and wet earth in the workshop. The rough boards remind me of a creaking New England barn. But today the workshop smells only of kerosene. In the morning chill the towels hang frozen on the rack. Bundled in long winter underwear, sweaters, a frayed camel-colored jacket and his wool cap, Nagayoshi-san hunches over his wheel. To further combat the cold he has slipped an electric heating pad beneath the thin cushions before his wheel. Today he rushes to finish trimming decorative plates that a tea ceremony teacher in Kushikino ordered last month as presents for her students. The wheel hums, and as he works he sings phrases from a popular folk song. After bisque firing he will paint the plates with a design of twisting leaves. Though the order calls for ten plates, Nagayoshi-san has made dozens, to allow for possible cracking and discoloration during the glaze firing.

The tattered green spiral notebook by his side is filled with hurriedly scrawled pottery orders. The new art museum in Sendai, his birthplace, a thirty-minute drive just north and west, has ordered one hundred small-necked vases as gifts to patrons in the opening ceremonies. In addition, the museum wants one of his large decorated exhibition bowls for a display. A group of three flight attendants came in several weeks ago with pooled resources equivalent to two hundred dollars. They asked Nagayoshi-san to make a piece of this value as a wedding gift for their co-worker.

In December the Nagayoshis had held a joint exhibition of their work in the newly renovated Yamakataya department store in Kagoshima City to celebrate their tenth year of joint exhibitions. By the end of the second day almost everything had sold out. Even so, Reiko figured that after subtracting expenses and the gallery's 30 percent commission, they had barely broken even. The point of the exhibition, Nagayoshi-san explained, was to "make new friends," and provide a "service" to old customers. Throughout the week of the department store exhibition Nagayoshi-san's order book filled with requests for rice bowls, tea sets, large jars, plates, coffee cups and numerous custom orders for weddings, graduation gifts and company retirements. The small top-floor gallery was packed. Thirty of my rice bowls, in sets of five, were entered—unsigned, but for sale at 1,500 yen (in 1983, $6.25 U.S. currency) each. Along with almost every other piece of pottery and leatherwork, the bowls sold out by the third day. As a New Year's gift I received all proceeds from the bowls, which I put aside for a trip by ferry to Okinawa.

Trading my mompei for a skirt, I went to the opening day. Sales were handled by efficient blue-uniformed store personnel, but even so we were on our feet all day, greeting guests and serving tea. Reiko and Nagayoshi-san were indefatigable, but by evening I was ready to head home. I had met so many people it felt like my first days in Japan, when all faces, framed in black hair, had blurred together, and names were impossible to remember. That night we celebrated in the only French restaurant in town and returned all the way to Miyama by taxi. Nagayoshi-san and Reiko continued to commute to the show daily, but I stayed in Miyama. Even the cold workshop seemed like home.

In a week we will open the *hatsugama*, the first firing of the year. New Year's has brought a host of "firsts"—the first meal, the first ofuro, the first correspondence—but in Miyama, by far the most important is the first kiln. Even during regular *kamadashi* (kiln unloadings), the workshop teems with people. Kiln preparations take a week. The firing occurs on the first Friday of each month. After a day of cooling it is ready for opening on Sunday. Ceramics enthusiasts and Nagayoshi kiln fans arrive early to get first pick. Sunday strollers amble in throughout the day. The Nagayoshis revel in the partylike atmosphere; everyone who arrives is invited in for tea. But many customers have called up requesting that their orders be included in this first kiln of the New Year. Today we will unload the first pre-fired or bisque kiln, load a second firing and sand the pottery in preparation for the coming week of glazing.

In the center of a small room, the emptied, still-warm kiln heats the air, smelling of musty brick and clay. Surrounding it are piles of kiln shelf and furniture. Pottery for the second firing fills a low table. For the past hour I have been carefully unloading clutches of warm bowls from last night's firing. Racks above and to the right hold long boards of unloaded plates. Reaching up, I take down a plate. Warm and smooth as a pancake, the small disk heats my cheek. I feel the upturned edges. Plates are the next form in my practice.

On New Year's Day, Nagayoshi-san had brought out blocks of hardwood and lengths of bamboo along with a sharp knife. "You might make your own tools, ones that fit your hands. Make the tools you need, whatever you like," he had said simply, as he set about shaping a new set of *tombo*, "grasshopper" measuring sticks, for the workshop. After fashioning some ribs for shaping rice bowls and cups and a sharp paring knife, I was stuck. I wanted to make tools for the upcoming forms I would practice, but would Nagayoshi-san think I was trying to rush ahead as usual?

In the fall, my teacups, small and uneven, had still been

relegated to the basket of give-aways by the door. But after one firing, five cups came out a beautiful, matching blue. My first tea set! I was delighted. No one would notice, I said to myself, if I just set these apart, and put all five under the counter instead of in the basket. But several weeks later, when some guests who had just bought a considerable amount of pottery were leaving, Nagayoshi-san turned to me. "Maybe they would like to take home a sample of your teacups. How about that blue set—you know, the one under the counter?" Speechless, I quickly rose to retrieve them.

Rice bowls had progressed more quickly than teabowls: by November my legs fit comfortably in a cross-legged posture at the wheel. Bending down with equalized pressure, the muscles in my arms tight, hands squeezing, I could guide the clay until it found center, whirling in an even spin. But yesterday when I was trimming, Nagayoshi-san quietly picked up a completed rice bowl and placed it on a small kitchen scale: almost 200 grams. "The shape is good. A nice line. But, *kanji ga chigaimasu*—it doesn't feel right. Your hand would get tired holding a bowl full of rice in this. Please trim it again." Retrimming each rice bowl to the required 150–175 grams took the entire day.

Gently paring the length of the new tool, Nagayoshi-san spoke again: "What did you say you were going to practice next?" I answered cautiously, "I think we said small plates, after rice bowls were done, and maybe more teacups."

"Yes, plates, but you're to draw designs on all of them, right?"

"Should I?"

"Why yes, how else will you get a sense for what shapes you want to make when you start *kabin*?"

"Small vases? What shapes? How many? When? And then *tsubo*?" I was thrilled. Small vases, *kabin*, and the large ornamental *tsubo* were my goals as an apprentice.

"We'll see. Think about what shapes *you* want to make" was all Nagayoshi-san said. Slivers of bamboo fell from his knife; our conversation was over. Picking up the tools, I quickly made a smooth rib for plates, and many long, hooked tools for shaping the insides of small vases.

I put the plate back into the warm kiln and lay my hands over the hot bricks, warming my fingers as I scan the stacks of pottery for the second firing. Loading a bisque kiln requires the skills used in a jigsaw puzzle or a game of sardines. Rice bowls fit over vases and under plates, on or between jars and next to a line of coffee cups. Stacked just high enough to level the layer, salad bowls rattle with clusters of small sake cups. A gingerly stacked layer of small plates covers the heap. At this stage the pottery is bone-dry, "green" and fragile— it chips as easily as soft chalk. In the bisque, or biscuit kiln, the pottery reaches temperatures of 700–900 degrees centigrade. The clay consolidates, partially vitrifying, so that any remaining water vaporizes and the pottery shrinks slightly, emerging lighter, the gray clay turned a flesh-pink.

Until just a generation ago, Miyama potters skipped this bisque firing, piling the glazed raw pieces directly into the wood-fired kiln. The process, called *namakake*, is still carried on by Sataro-san in the yearly noborigama firings. In that technique the glaze must be applied in a thin layer or its weight during firing will cause the pot to warp and twist, splitting it like a ripe watermelon. As a result, old kuromon pottery is rarely the dark, rich black of the tourist pottery made in Miyama today. More commonly, the work comes out a dull greenish-brown. Losses in namakake firings run as high as 20 percent.

With the introduction of oil, propane gas and electric kilns in the late fifties and sixties, Miyama potters were given a choice of methods. Potters of shiromon quickly switched to electric kilns. The oxidation atmosphere of these new kilns gave the clean, unblemished surface necessary for the later stages of painted decoration. Although pottery fired this way emerges a yellowish color, the almost risk-free firing process means less breakage and thus higher profits. Satsuma pottery connoisseurs and collectors, however, consider the stark ivory color of old wood-fired shiromon to be superior.

Of the eight kuromon potteries in the village, only old Kodama, who works alone, and Sataro continue to fire the large wood-burning noborigama kilns. "This is the way pottery should be made. It's the way they made pots when they first came from Korea. Tradition is tradition!" Sataro-san will grumble. "Potters today have it too easy." But even at the Sataro workshop, the five-chambered climbing kiln is fired only once a year to supplement the monthly firing of a large gas kiln.

I study the half-full kiln. Three boards of small-necked vases will fill the bottom shelf. Survivors of the batch that froze, they must be fired by Sunday. Rice bowls stacked five deep will fill in empty spaces and cover the tops of vases like a row of clay hats. As long as water vapor can escape through a crack or opening, stacking pots is both safe and necessary. Nagayoshi-san wants all eighty of the rice bowls I made before New Year's to be fired in this kiln. If they come out well, they join a set of two hundred and complete my graduation to small plates.

When an intricate layer of rice bowls and teacups, slanted

saucers and inverted coffee cups fills the bottom of the kiln, I am done. The entire mass looks like a pile of jackstraws, but it is actually a careful balancing act; if one piece on the bottom cracks or slips, the entire honeycomb of stacked clay can come crashing down.

As I step out of the kiln room, cold strikes my face in a refreshing rush. Next door in the workshop the popular radio music called *enka* fills the room. The country-and-western music of Japan, enka is a post-Meiji stepchild of traditional Japanese music, complete with Western rhythm and operatic solos to a background swell of electric organ. Today a nasal female voice narrates her misfortune: "*Anatawaaahhhhh.*"

I wait until Nagayoshi-san's wheel comes to a stop. "Excuse me, I'm finished," I say loudly, over the radio. Gripping the finished plate deftly in a two-pinkie hold, he lifts it off the wheel and onto a waiting board. "That was quick," he says as he jumps down from the bench. I lift his finished board of plates up into the holding racks and follow him into the kiln room.

"*Yōka, yōka.*" Nagayoshi-san adjusts his glasses to inspect the loaded kiln. He lifts the large bowl balanced above and, sucking in air through his teeth, sets it on the top shelf of the kiln as gently as if it were Steuben glass. The wide rim of the bowl is gray, with clay grog added for strength. After the bisque firing, Nagayoshi-san will design and glaze the piece, using layers of wax resist and colored oxides until a repeating geometric design emerges, reminiscent of ancient Southwest American Indian pottery. A second bowl taken down with equal care fills the entire top shelf.

Despite the cold, sweat beads on his face. The pieces are heavy, and a corner or edge nicked in loading will crack when fired. I crank down the steel-and-brick top of the kiln, leaving a two-inch space for water vapor to escape. Today's firing will take eleven hours. Pottery that is not bone-dry before firing cracks and warps. But in the damp winter months drying may take weeks, and to meet the coming deadline, Nagayoshi-san has gambled that a slow buildup of heat will dry the pots during the firing.

"*Hirugohan desu yo!* Lunchtime!" Reiko calls from the kitchen.

"O-kay, o-kay—" answers Nagayoshi-san, using one of his two English expressions. While he damps the flame in the kerosene stove I cover the board of plates by his wheel with moist cloths.

In the small dining room Reiko sets out bowls of steaming *udon.* Like spaghetti, only twice as thick, the noodles swirl in a sweet soy-sauce broth. Shaved brown curls of dried fish, a square of fish cake dyed hot pink, and finely chopped green onions decorate the top. Nagayoshi-san stops in the kitchen and grabs a bag of leftover New Year's mochi, a tin of seaweed strips and a bottle of soy sauce.

"Hurry up, it's getting cold!" Reiko calls, already seated seiza at the low table, but not until he has pulled out the toaster oven and placed inside three square mochi cakes to grill does Nagayoshi-san sit down with a hearty "*Itadaki-masu*—Let's begin." Reiko and Nagayoshi-san eat with hollow sucking noises, slurping their noodles gustily, as if trying to inhale rather than swallow. Within minutes the noodles are gone. Nagayoshi-san holds out a bowl for the second course, white rice. Bowl in my left hand, chopsticks in my right, I take a breath and begin. *Slurp . . . slurp . . . slurp.* My table instincts are definitely Western—hands in your lap, back straight, no noises. Slurpers and fast eaters soon found themselves in the kitchen in my house, pushing two drooling dogs away from their plate.

Reiko gave me my first lessons in Japanese etiquette. Why do you pick up your bowl with the left hand when eating? "Because if you don't you put your head down and look like a dog."

Why do people always slurp over noodles? "Because if you don't it means you don't like the food."

Why doesn't anyone ever talk over meals? "Because asking too many questions gives everyone indigestion."

Brought up in Kobe, Reiko comes from a samurai family. It took her a long time to get used to Kagoshima, where sugar is liberally poured into all foods and the polite way to accept pickles at tea is with an outstretched palm.

Bing. From the toaster oven pop three steaming mochi. Extricating the melted cakes from the oven grill requires two pairs of chopsticks and the patience of kiln loading. Nagayoshi-san gingerly guides the gooey white mass onto a waiting plate of soy sauce. Sandwiching the melted rice cake between sheets of seaweed, he quickly begins to eat. With a consistency between rubber cement and chewing gum when heated, mochi reverts to the hardness of a rock when cold and will not spoil, which is why samurai carried them. A square of mochi the size of a small apple has the calorie content of five or six heaping bowls of rice.

By the time I finish my bowl of noodles, Reiko and Nagayoshi-san are already sipping tea and quietly peeling tangerines. As usual, TV replaces mealtime conversation. Noon programs range from quiz shows, hosted by samurai-costumed announcers, to nutrition experts in white coats who explain how to boil white rice most efficiently. On the news, Coast Guard boats valiantly race the waves to rescue a half-submerged fishing ship near Kushikino. To the north a major earthquake has left an entire town homeless; three large Kyoto companies are sponsoring programs for food relief. In Hokkaido thatched houses drift in a blizzard of white, while a team of determined scientists scrambles after rare snow monkeys in the mountains.

Reiko switches the channel to a popular game show. In a model classroom setting, six gaijin, three women and three men, sit in oversized blue school smocks. Most of the foreigners are wide-eyed blondes, while the "teacher" is a trim Japanese. Pacing at the head of the class, long ruler in hand, he questions the students on Japanese trivia. Subjects range from medieval Japanese poetry to details of the latest in Japanese household conveniences, heated toilet seats. Correct answers earn five points. The winner receives a cash equivalent of one thousand U.S. dollars as well as a trip to Hokkaido, and all contestants win complimentary bath towels. Making a fool of oneself can be lucrative.

"Hey, you should try that. You'd be the only foreigner who could speak Kagoshima ben. You might win, you know," jokes Reiko. The hot tea burns as I swallow. Just watching makes me feel like a snow monkey on roller skates. But to my hosts the show is hilarious, and they break into laughter when a blond woman is dunked in a tub of water for giving the wrong answer.

Quiz and game shows featuring Westerners are not the only uses for local gaijin. A popular chocolate commercial depicts a woman with silky blond hair stretched out on a couch, languidly nibbling chocolates. A typical motorbike ad shows a group of golden-haired American students riding off into the sunset. Yet even TV advertisements reflect dual attitudes toward foreigners. In one commercial exhausted

American workers perk up and become productive only after consuming a popular Japanese health drink. When I ask Reiko why foreigners are so popular on TV, she only tells me that most Japanese people have never had the opportunity to meet a Westerner in person but wanted to. "Japanese people are *hazukashii*," she explains.

I often heard Japanese describe themselves this way, and it always left me dissatisfied. According to the dictionary, *hazukashii* can be literally translated as shy or bashful, but it also means embarrassing, or disgraceful. Children who ran behind their mother's skirts were affectionately called *hazukashii*, but so were rude adults. When a high school friend of Eri's came back overweight from a year away in Great Britain, her family told her not to leave the house until she was thinner—her condition was *hazukashii*. Japanese in general are ill at ease with strangers, and may in fact find it easier to encounter foreigners on TV, where they often come off as caricatures. While Americans tend to assume—language apart—that all the world thinks like them, Japanese believe that their world view is unique, and they are comfortable when cultural distinctions are reinforced. It did strike me as a pretty complicated expression of "shyness."

Back in the workshop, I start the afternoon's first chore, sanding pots. Sanding the once-fired pottery is not done in all workshops, but Nagayoshi-san feels that this extra step provides a better surface for the glazes. It is tedious work. I begin with a line of rice bowls.

When he speaks of fine ceramics, Nagayoshi-san alludes to Kyoto pottery. Eggshell-thin and clean-lined, it is the pièce de résistance of Japanese ceramics, although it was the warm, rustic quality of Korean-style kuromon that first attracted

Nagayoshi-san to Miyama. While still in Tokyo, he had read an article about the village. The pictures of Miyama, then a maze of narrow streets and thatched-roof houses, caught his eye. He wrote to the author, an anthropologist who had been studying and recording an oral history of the Korean shrine festivals from Miyama's native Shintō priest, and later met him in Tokyo. A year later Nagayoshi-san and Reiko made arrangements to move to Miyama and open a pottery workshop.

A sample of Nagayoshi-san's first pottery sits on a bookshelf in the center room. The small, heavy form is a copy of a seventeenth-century Satsuma tea caddy. The work is poorly thrown but shows a strong form under a dark kuromon glaze. After six months of struggling to master traditional shapes Nagayoshi-san made a fateful decision: he dropped all Naeshirogawa pottery forms completely and instead began designing and producing pottery of his own style. "I just couldn't make Naeshirogawa pottery. Maybe if I was a Miyama-born potter I could, but it just wasn't in me," he explained to me one day. His models were angular Kyoto-style rice bowls and the ceramic works of one of Japan's great twentieth-century artist-potters, Tomimoto Kenkichi. Eleven years and numerous prizes and successful exhibitions later, Nagayoshi-san's order book is filled with requests he can barely meet.

In the past he had not considered taking on an apprentice, on the grounds that one would take up valuable time. Last year, when I asked Nagayoshi-san and Reiko if I could study at their workshop as an official apprentice, a long silence had followed. "I don't have anything to teach," Nagayoshi-san finally said quietly, folding his hands. I had been prepared for a direct refusal; all I had to do, I thought, was to convince him and Reiko that I could work hard. For weeks I had practiced the necessary phrases. Already I had found a place to live outside of Kagoshima City, just a twenty-five-minute ride away in a dance studio that needed a nighttime caretaker. But this flat denial left me stumbling.

"I'll learn anyway. I want to study in the Nagayoshi workshop. I'll work hard," I had insisted. Nagayoshi-san looked at me closely, unfolding and folding his hands on the table. "You know that this is not a traditional Satsuma pottery workshop, don't you?" Again we sat, bound in a long silence.

The fact was that I wanted to study pottery under Nagayoshi-san precisely because he wasn't "traditional." After several months of observing the Miyama workshops I was frankly sick of "Satsuma pottery," almost all of which, both the black pottery and the white, was merely a repetition of the same styles and forms. For a month I had even practiced kick wheel in the traditional Sataro workshop. While I loved the slow rhythm of the kick wheel, I realized that I would soon grow bored practicing the same heavy folk pottery shapes. And I doubted that as an American female I would ever be taken seriously as a student there.

"I have studied enough about Miyama's traditional pottery," I continued. "Now I wish to study Nagayoshi pottery." I held out both hands, adding "*Onegai shimasu*—I entreat you," the polite expression accompanying a request.

"But I'm not a good potter," Nagayoshi responded quietly.

"Yes, there are better potters in the village," Reiko chimed in.

The room began to swim. Panicking, I slowly repeated myself. "I wish to study ceramics under Nagayoshi-san. . . ."

Pushing back his hair with a quick gesture, Nagayoshi-san

turned to his wife. "Well, I suppose she can do the same work as I do," he said quickly, and left the room. I was horrified: was his answer yes or no? But soon Reiko was discussing with me how I would live and when I wanted to begin. As an apprentice I would receive meals and a place to sleep. Until the winter exhibition, while the extra room was in use, I would stay in the Kagoshima dance studio, but afterward I could stay in the house. No wages, but I would receive a percentage of the money made from my own pottery. In a sense, the apprenticeship was a natural progression. I had already been in Miyama for several months; since my arrival I had helped with cleaning and small tasks in the workshop. Already I had learned how to wedge and often prepared Nagayoshi-san's clay.

Only the next morning did I get a chance to speak to Nagayoshi-san directly. I asked him if he thought my apprenticing in his workshop was a good idea and how I would study. He smiled broadly, as if he had never had a doubt. Concerning my study, he said simply, "I'm your teacher. Let me think of that." And so I had become Nagayoshi-san's first apprentice. That week we went to dinner at one of the most expensive restaurants in Kagoshima, where we ate Chinese food and drank beer before a panoramic view of Sakurajima.

Dust flies everywhere as I sand, and I glance at my wheel, wishing that I could begin on the last twenty rice bowls. Back at his wheel, Nagayoshi-san continues trimming plates, a jar of cinnamon candies cradled among his pile of tools. The afternoon radio program of *sumō* (wrestling) begins, with shrill whistling calls and the clacking of wooden sticks.

Bang! A sharp crack sounds from the area of the electric

kiln. Nagayoshi-san jumps up from his wheel. He holds his head close to the top of the kiln, listening like a bird after worms. From within comes another small *pop* and a faint cracking sound. The sound comes from the upper layer. It must be one of the large bowls cracking in the heat. "*Wareta!* Cracked!" Nagayoshi-san heaves a long sigh. What will he say to the Sendai people this Sunday? I slip back to the workshop and continue sanding pots.

Nagayoshi-san comes in. Looking at me, he laughs. "Maybe I'll send your rice bowls to Sendai instead." Everything seems to be going wrong in the workshop today except Nagayoshi-san's mood, which remains bright and fresh as snow.

"*Samu gowandonahhh!* Cold, isn't it!" The lilting Miyama greeting announces next-door obāsan's slow progress down the lane. "*Samui desu ne!*" answers a soft voice in standard Japanese. A pottery guest? A fashionably dressed young woman steps into the yard. By her side bob the yellow hats of two small children. In one hand she carries an enormous gift box of Japanese sweets. "Welcome, welcome," says Nagayoshi-san, jumping up, and leads them into the house through the front entrance. I glance at the clock: 2:30, and only a few more pots to sand.

Suddenly a horn beeps and the round face of Someura Okusan peers around the hedge. A heavyset, ruddy-faced woman in her late forties, she has a youthful and generous smile. Her bobbed hair, slightly curled and dyed a rich raven-black, peeks out from under a print scarf.

She calls hello as I step out to meet her. "I brought you some mochi, as I promised. It's not good at all—in fact, I'm embarrassed it's so bad, but please take it. I put in extra so you can send some home. I bet your parents have never had Japanese New Year's food."

"Thank you, thank you," I say, inwardly amused to think of the reception my family would give a bag of rock-hard mochi.

On the sixth a great bonfire in the community field had signaled the end of New Year's festivities. All day the children, usually unseen, ran everywhere to collect the straw rope, pine bough and fern New Year's decorations from doors and entryways around the village. That night they threw them into the blaze. Pine boughs crackled in the flames, chasing away *oni* (devils), and everyone ate a square of mochi toasted like a marshmallow on a long stick in the flames to ensure a year of good health. When I met Someura-san's wife there, she had generously offered me some of her own home-made rice cakes, but since I couldn't pick up the gift without stopping for tea, I doubted that I would ever be able to take her up on the offer. I am Nagayoshi-san's apprentice, and visiting another workshop complicates this allegiance. He would never forbid me to go, but I know not to ask.

At first this unspoken code of not visiting other potteries had seemed unfair, if not wasteful: I had come a long way, after all, and wanted to see as much as I could. Sometimes in the early fall I had visited other potters. But returning to the Nagayoshi compound I felt twinges of guilt; simply doing what others did not do somehow felt like betrayal. Slowly, I was becoming Japanese.

Even if one is not an apprentice, casual visiting is not common in Miyama, and the New Year's bonfire was the first time I had seen so many villagers together in one spot. As with other village festivals, like the October shrine gathering in Ijuin and the Tanabata *matsuri* in July, New Year's provided a rare excuse to celebrate and socialize.

During the rest of the year not even neighbors casually dropped in on one another the way they might in small American towns. Only obāsan, who met one another walking to and from the fields and at the local stores, stopped to chat over impromptu cups of tea. The young men in the village commuted early to jobs in surrounding towns or Kagoshima City, children were at school or at home studying, and housewives kept busy in their homes. Only in the potteries did visitors drop by unannounced and linger over cups of tea; for a retail business, providing "service" to customers was expected.

If I didn't wake up in time to get in a walk or run before breakfast I felt confined and irritable, but whole days would pass without the Nagayoshis' ever leaving their home. Once I showed Nagayoshi-san my favorite walks in the village— the old Buddhist graves in the woods below the shrine, the far ridge from which one could see the East China Sea, the tea fields that overlooked Sakurajima—and he said he was surprised to learn of such beautiful places in Miyama. He and Reiko never went anywhere in the village except to the Kirin store to buy beer and Coke from the vending machines, or to catch the bus to Kagoshima City. From banking to cough syrup to life insurance, so many goods and services came to the door that it was almost possible not to leave home at all.

Reiko had understandable reasons for avoiding local obāsan, who criticized her for pursuing her own work instead of devoting all her time to her home and husband. "Miyama has big ears," she once said with a frown. Walking was considered an old person's pastime, and she worried that if people spied her taking a stroll, they would say she was lazy. Even

Nagayoshi-san, who loved socializing with pottery guests, never walked around Miyama. Several times in my presence he told guests that I was an *erai hito*, a "great person," because I would say hello, stop to talk to anyone, even farmers. But when I asked him why that was so unusual he just shook his head. "You can talk to anyone because you are a foreigner. We Japanese just can't." In such a crowded country, privacy had to be protected. And in the strict hierarchy of Japanese society, spontaneous socializing, what Americans call "being friendly," only created chaos and confusion; people lost the sense of order and place that was felt to be the backbone of social "harmony."

Today, although Okusan has cleverly solved the problem of getting me the mochi by bringing it herself, I notice that she does not step into the yard but stands in the lane, one hand on her motorbike, carefully positioned so that she can peek into the workshop while we talk.

"How's business?" I say, taking the white plastic bag bulging with rice cakes. "There are lots of buses in town these days."

"Just terrible!" answers Someura Okusan. "Those bus tourists, they only come and look. They don't buy anything unless it's from a famous kiln. They don't know handmade pottery when they see it. I told my son, 'You'd better not become a potter like your father. You'll never get a bride!' "

I shake my head in sympathy. According to Someura-san's wife, business is never good, but ranges from "*zenzen dame*"—absolutely terrible—to "*dame*"—bad—to "*muzuka-shii*"—difficult. But the Someura workshop, famous for her husband's wheel-thrown white vases, cups, incense burners and teabowls, attracts Satsuma pottery painters from around the prefecture, who paint the clear-glazed pottery with bright-colored floral designs, firing several times in small electric enamel-overglaze kilns. Someura-san, whose father was a kuromon potter of the Korean family name Chin, is said to be the last potter in the village who can throw the tall, fluted white vases, crafting the base and top section separately and then attaching them in the middle. All but one other one-man workshop now produce shiromon vases by mold.

"Anyway, I'm holding you up, and so much to do myself," says Someura Okusan suddenly and jumps on her motorbike. Before I have time to say good-bye, she zooms down the lane. From the kitchen door Reiko calls us to tea.

In the center room the table has been set. Seated before bowls of steaming *azuki* (red beans) and plates of heated mochi, the two visiting children in immaculate matching blue jumpsuits sit quietly, chopsticks busy with the New Year's treat. Although allowed to run loose as small terrors at home, even two- and three-year-old Japanese children sit quietly when they are guests. Seated between two kerosene stoves, their mother gracefully bends over tea. Although normally etiquette requires that teatime gifts not be opened upon receipt, today's present, a large box of Japanese rice-and-bean sweets, lies open. The colorful handmade paper wrappings encasing each cake are the handiwork of a noted Japanese bakery. The guest, the wife of a Tokyo banker, has been in Kagoshima visiting her husband's family for New Year's. Having seen Nagayoshi-san's work in a national ceramics exhibition in Kyoto, she has come to place an order for a large decorated bowl as a housewarming gift for her friends. But she needs the piece in several weeks. "I'll fire twice in February. We can do it," Nagayoshi-san answers promptly, nodding in my direction. Reiko looks at him dubiously and pours tea.

"*Konnichiwa*." The front door rattles open to reveal an elderly obāsan in a dark purple skirt and jacket. The Nagayoshis bow in formal greeting. Reiko quickly pours another cup of tea. I have the feeling that she is someone I have met before, but can't remember where.

Suddenly I remember. She was one of a group of housewives from a Kushikino calligraphy class who came last month to the workshop to decorate plates. With them was their *sensei*, an older man with a swelling potbelly and a black briefcase full of brushes, inks and samples of calligraphic style sheets. It was my job to watch over the process, supplying brushes, pans, water, and grinding more color when needed. I was to call if there was a problem; otherwise, Reiko and Nagayoshi-san would be working out back.

It had been a long, noisy morning. I was kept busy supplying brushes, cobalt and iron oxide mixed with water, and wide bisque-fired plates that had been dipped in a white bath of clay slip before pre-firing. The group decorated Nagayoshi workshop plates with names, individual characters, poems and pictures in flourishes of cobalt blue.

Everyone thought I was *kawaii*, "cute." Hands touched my yellow hair. One woman thought I should wear a pink ribbon, while another wanted to practice her English. Everyone was talking at once. Someone suggested that I needed a Japanese name and the characters *ri*, pear, and *ra*, net, were chosen. "I already have a name," I protested, and wrote down the characters my teacher had chosen for me from the name of an ancient Korean village. But it was to no avail, and for the rest of the day I was "Pear Net."

Caught up in the festivity, the teacher suddenly turned to me, reciting slowly:

> I gaze across the
> endless plains of the sky can
> that moon be the one
> that comes from the rim of Mt.
> Mikasa in Kasuga?

It was a famous poem, he explained, by Abe no Nakamaro, called "Gazing at the Moon in China," from the *Manyoshu*, an eighth-century book of Japanese poetry. Sent by the Emperor to China to study and unable to return home for many years, Nakamaro laments his fate. His recital finished, the sensei wrote the verse for me on a plate in sprawling blue characters. Thanking him eagerly, I carried it over to show my teacher.

"Can you read it?" he asked, putting on his glasses and examining the plate, decorated with stylized characters of ancient Japanese.

"No . . . but . . ."

"Neither can I." He laughed, handing back the plate and picking up his brush to resume signing boxes.

Today the obāsan has returned to request that their plates be fired in the hatsugama. After drinking a cup of tea and wolfing down several tangerines, I quickly excuse myself and head for the door. "Please mix the glazes," Nagayoshi-san says quietly, barely looking up, and continues with the on-going negotiations.

Outside, tatters of afternoon sun filter through the clouds, warming my spot for the remaining two hours of daylight.

All the bisqued pottery has been sanded and washed. Nagayoshi-san probably won't glaze until tomorrow anyway, I decide, readying my wheel. I will throw the rice bowls first and then mix the glazes.

In the quiet workshop my wheel hums. Despite red freezing knuckles and a stiff back I feel pleased; steady lines of rice bowls fill the board on my left. The clock reads 4:00, but Nagayoshi-san has not yet appeared from the house. I warm my hands for a minute by dunking them in a bowl of hot water. They emerge lobster-red. Only five more bowls to finish. I grit my teeth and press into the ice-cold mound of spinning clay.

The clay rises beneath my hands, smooth and straight, then down into a flat plateau. I form a small ball of clay at the top and press down in the center. The clay opens, spreads, then rises into a shallow bowl, responding to every touch of tool and hand. It is a godlike feeling. Within minutes a smooth-walled rice bowl spins atop the mound, gleaming like a jewel with a wet, silky sheen. I reach for the cutting wire and slice through, releasing the new bowl from its spinning base, then lift it with two fingers to the waiting board. It is the same process, again and again, day after day, rice bowl after rice bowl, and yet different each time. Tomorrow after glazing I can trim these last twenty bowls. Then finally I may graduate to plates, considered the most difficult stage in throwing practice. No longer conscious of the cold, I reach down and start again.

"Sayonara . . . Sayonara . . . Sayonara . . ." Tea is breaking up. Nagayoshi-san enters the workshop, looks around for a minute, and then departs. I wonder why he doesn't return to his work at the wheel. Several more plates wait to be trimmed. The sooner they are finished, the sooner they will begin drying and be ensured a safe firing. Suddenly a familiar hollow thumping noise comes from outside, the sound of a wooden pole hitting the sides of a plastic bucket. Nagayoshi-san is mixing glazes—*my* work! A hot flash runs the length of my spine, the board of rice bowls disappears like smoke. All that matters is getting outside as quickly as possible to take over my job.

My teacher's gaze is Sakurajima laced with ice and snow. Looking down, I pry the lid from the bucket of red iron glaze and begin stirring. The glue-like mass of precipitated glaze grabs at my pole. To free it I reach a bare arm into the freezing milky-red water. Nagayoshi-san works silently, as if his apprentice no longer existed. His message is ice clear. When he asks me to do a chore, he wants it done—immediately. If I work at being a student, then Nagayoshi-san is my sensei: "Your teacher is a door upon which you must beat and beat to be let in." The workshop comes first; he accepts no compromise. Without a word, the learning contract has snapped. Only the cold and the remaining work keep my mind off my mistake. Without speaking, Nagayoshi-san and I continue stirring and sieving glazes.

The winter sky gradually sinks in purple and touches of red. The cycle of a day closes. Darkness falls across the glaze kiln, shadowing the New Year's decoration now wilted and still. The first evening stars rise above the hedge as I finish stirring the last glaze. My arms begin to ache, I begin to wonder why I am here, why in Japan obedience means so much.

Nagayoshi-san breaks the silence: "It's gotten cold, time to quit now. Before you begin the glazing tomorrow, please finish your last rice bowls—they look good. How about starting plates?" He hands me a towel and pulls the last lid over the vats of glaze.

I nod and wipe my arms. Nagayoshi-san plucks the New Year's decoration from the kiln, pocketing the mochi and dropping the ferns into a small pile of leaves by the kiln. He reaches down with a lighter. A small fire crackles in the dark, leaping up past the kiln and workshop into the dark night, now shimmering with stars, as bright and clear as fine ice crystal.

Plum blossoms in the early spring
black pots catching silver rain
the old Miyama

Aɴ ᴏʟᴅ ᴊᴀᴘᴀɴᴇsᴇ sᴀʏɪɴɢ ᴇɴᴜ-merates the four most feared phenom-ena: fire, thunder, earthquake—and father. Low and flat, Miyama houses hug the ground below keening blasts of wind and typhoon rains that batter this tip of Kyushu. This morning after we ate bowls of golden miso soup and rice, green tea and then coffee, the smiling TV weatherman announced rain today, tomorrow and the next day too. It seemed as if the four weeks of rainy season that usually began in June had already arrived.

When it rains, Nagayoshi-san gets depressed. Recently a Tokyo restaurant ordered five hundred teacups as gifts to longtime patrons. Each cup will be presented in a wooden box tied with a blue cord and carefully signed by my teacher with a brush dipped in stone-ground ink. After break-fast, Nagayoshi-san quietly announced that he would go to town to pick up a load of boxes for finished pots that was waiting at the carpenter's workshop. Reiko jotted down a shopping list—rice, miso, seaweed—then added apples, butter, eggs, white flour and yeast; this week she wants me to teach her how to make bread and apple pie. The next bisque firing, for which Nagayoshi-san and I are throwing the ordered teacups, is a week away. After a winter of long days in the workshop, I have a day off.

A warm March wind rustles through the tall, rain-soaked bamboo. The road is an odyssey of rain pools. Bits of red and pink—camellia petals torn and scattered in a haste of wind—break the general haze of green and gray. Rain slides down roof lines, soaks the crouching stands of fern and ends up sloshing against my toes in flip-flop sandals. I walk down the main street, enjoying the absence of cars and people, once again in T-shirt and cotton mompei as winter's cold gives way to spring.

The rain makes Kirin Obāsan at the Kirin store shut the glass doors and run to pull in deliveries, one arm holding a frayed black umbrella. The children rushing down the road to school look like a band of bright fish, their uniforms a wave of blue under identical yellow umbrellas. The village cats, scruffy to begin with, look drenched and mean. The well-swept dirt of front yards becomes pools of mud.

Just ahead gleams the large sign for the Kirin store which is the bright canary-yellow of Manhattan taxicabs. I leave my brown umbrella by the door and step in, meeting Kirin Obāsan and her friend Shigenobu-san, who lives alone in a drafty old-style wooden house across the lane. Next to their hunched frames, I feel awkwardly tall. They move slowly, like rusted gates, although Kirin Obāsan is as talkative as usual. "Good morning. The day off, Ri-ra? My, what a rain. TV said all day, and Sakurajima just blew up. Ash all over. It's like rainy season. Do you have rainy season in America? No tōfu today, you know. Where are *you* going?" Shigenobu-san sits quiet, her back against a case of shōchū. She wears a tan wool vest that comes down past her knees, covering a dark blue kimono. On her feet are *zōri*, traditional sandals that have been adapted for the rain with clear plastic tips that cover the maroon thongs. I wear *zōri* too, but when she sees them she breaks into laughter. "Hey, what have you got on your feet? You're wearing old men's shoes!" One hand half covering her mouth, she points down at my feet with the other. Next to her small blue-socked feet, neatly tucked into maroon sandals, my own bare toes look enormous. "My new sandals. Got 'em in Kagoshima yesterday," I answer, lifting my foot. "They're comfortable, and they were cheap." Now both women stare down at my feet, giggling wildly. I begin to feel slightly miffed. What's so funny about wearing sandals with black thongs? They were the only pair in the shop large enough for me to walk in with ease.

I start picking through the cellophane-wrapped packages of rice cakes, Western-style jelly rolls, English butter cookies and chocolate-covered doughnuts. Junk food abounds in Miyama. A bag of the popular Satsuma brown sugar chunks seems the most portable. Today I plan to walk around Miyama. I haven't been down the streets in months. Who knows whom I'll meet, or whether it will be teatime?

Outside, the rain has stopped. The air is fresh, laced with the scent of damp earth and wet leaves. A new house rises from the corner along the main road. Like all the other post-war Miyama houses, it is one-story, with a sloping gray roof and white stucco siding; wood is far too precious for Miyama incomes.

In front of an L-shaped old-style house with a well-kept garden a bonsai tree, leafless and skeletal, shimmers with immaculate paper-thin pink blooms that seem squeezed from every tuck and bud in the scratching limbs. I slip into the yard to look. Most plums bloomed in February; this one is a month late. To me the tiny gnarled tree with its hundreds of blossoms looks absurdly like an old woman who has tied on too many pink hair ribbons, but hundreds of poems have been dedicated to the flowering plum.

"You can have a branch if you like. Here, I'll cut you one. Put them in water when you get home." A quiet, friendly voice startles me from behind, then a trim figure materializes, in a green polo shirt and khaki pants tucked into black rubber boots. Although he looks about sixty, he wears no eyeglasses, unlike most village men of that age. His eyes, bright and watchful, inspect me from under a wide-brimmed straw hat. Behind him I see glimpses of yard and garden, a tiny grove of plum trees and outdoor houseplants in old-style kuromon pots. Stepping back, I apologize for my intrusion. But the old man waves his arm, as if brushing away a swarm of troublesome gnats, and grins a wide toothless smile. There is something light and open, almost humorous, about his manner, and I feel suddenly at ease. "*Yōka*, please come in. I'm Mizoguchi Hideo. Anyhow, I know about you," he says quickly as he walks toward the house.

I follow him into the yard, where a cluster of strong thick-walled kuromon pots hold the late-flowering plum, various plants, water, tools, old seed bags, brooms or nothing at all. Years ago they would have held a winter's supply of foods: barley, millet, buckwheat, Satsuma potatoes, octopus, dried plums, oil and soy sauce. Now they merely decorate Mizoguchi-san's garden. In the corner, a rain pipe from the roof spills water into a squat, half-submerged vat. At the house entrance a narrow storage urn, its smooth sides twisting with *haritsuke*, applied clay patterns of vine, serves as an umbrella stand. All the pots are old, well-crafted examples of the tataki techniques that have all but disappeared from the village. Folkcraft collectors would vie for so valuable a collection, each piece exemplifying the mingei aesthetic of the beauty to be found in utilitarian objects produced by the "unknown craftsman."

Mizoguchi-san points toward a barn out back. "Over there my wife grew silkworms. It was a good business once. But I live alone now. Come in, won't you have tea?" Marching ahead, he disappears into the house. Until thirty years ago sericulture was a profitable Miyama industry, and traditionally women's work. Now, with the decline of small farms and businesses in Japan, only four or five women farmers in Miyama still grow silkworms to supplement their income from the fields; Mizoguchi-san remembers when there were over thirty. A few scattered patches of mulberry bush still overlap with rapeseed and tobacco, daikon, sweet potatoes, and small vegetable gardens. Once the silkworm larvae have hatched and begun their forty-five-day growing cycle, tender mulberry shoots chopped fine is what they like best. A good grower with a supply of mulberry leaves can harvest several crops of silkworms a year, buying eggs and feeding the newly hatched worms until they spin their peanut-shaped white cocoons. Once the worms have begun to feed, the long, shallow wooden troughs where they live writhe with green and the dark shed echoes with their steady nibbling. When their skins are a translucent white, the fattened worms crawl onto the waiting wooden racks, where at a rate of six inches per minute, they spin themselves into a series of tiny white mummies, each one wrapped in one thousand yards of silk.

I follow Mizoguchi-san through the sliding wooden doors. He puts a kettle for hot water on a portable burner that, along with a sink and some shelves, constitutes his kitchen. The sliding inner doors are half open, revealing a wide, dark central room divided down the middle by blue and white sliding screens, now faded and water-stained. No furniture breaks the symmetry of dark wooden beams and light tatami. Against the far wall to the right is the *tokonoma*, the traditional viewing place for pottery, scrolls and flowers. An aged and faded ink painting on silk hangs in the alcove above a white wide-lipped Satsuma vase, a plastic arrow from the Kagoshima shrine, several boxes still in department-store gift wrap, and a decorative clock that is stopped at nine. Next to the tokonoma hang pictures of two old people, a woman in a kimono and a man in a Meiji-era dark suit. Next to these are photographs of the present Emperor of Japan as well as the famous Kagoshima samurai Saigō Takamori. Enraged at the dismantling of the old feudal order, particularly the Meiji edict forbidding samurai to wear the two swords that distinguished warriors from common people, Takamori stormed the capital in 1877 to champion the cause of the samurai elite. The "Satsuma rebellion" was quickly put down and Saigō returned home, where he performed ritual suicide, becoming a Kagoshima folk hero. Over a far doorway hangs the wooden *kamidana*, the household Shintō shrine, decorated like a bird feeder. On a small ledge, next to cups of water and rice, are perched a few shriveled tangerines, a small unopened bottle of shōchū, a pack of cigarettes and stale rice cake from New Year's.

Mizoguchi-san talks as he bustles in the neat kitchen alcove. From the tidy kitchen have come a half-eaten bag of rice crackers, jars of pickled radish, a bag of hard candies, packets of Nestlé's hot cocoa mix, thick slices of sweet rice cake and crimson *umeboshi*, salted plums. Mizoguchi-san carefully hands me a plum, and I am reminded of a popular TV show in which foreigners are stopped on the street and asked to try such Japanese delicacies as raw fish, fermented soybeans and salted plum. One steel worker in Illinois spat the plum out so fast the announcer picked up his portable booth and ran up the street.

I pull out my bag of unrefined sugar. "*Nanimo nai desu kedo* . . . It's nothing, but . . ." I say, placing the bag on the table. "Oh, no . . . I couldn't accept," he answers promptly, carefully stowing the gift under the table. I begin to explain how I came to Miyama, but the old man cuts me off in midsentence, slapping me on the back. "You don't have to tell *me*! I see you in the morning. You walk a lot. Where do you walk to all the time? I'm old, but my eyes are good. I know all about you." Mizoguchi-san fumbles through a pile of papers on the low table and pulls out a series of newspaper clippings with my picture over a headline that reads "The Gaijin Apprentice," and a crumpled village bulletin featuring a haiku poem by an eight-year-old Miyama boy.

> Cutting rice.
> Gaijin in a rice field;
> How strange.

Now I am the one surprised, and I laugh. Each minute I am becoming even more curious about this old man, so friendly and eager I begin to get the strange feeling that he has almost been waiting for me to appear.

We drink tea under the dark eaves. Mizoguchi-san's story unfolds between bites of cracker and sips of tea. Born in Miyama in 1911, he remembers sledding on pieces of potsherd down the hill behind the community pottery dump and sneaking out to stay up with the men at the communal kiln firings. But his youth was spent in Taiwan. Although his grandfather had been a kuromon potter, his father had been encouraged to choose another vocation. In the 1920's, hard times for Miyama potters, Mizoguchi-san's father, along with many other villagers, went to Taiwan to seek government work on the railroad. Mizoguchi-san remembers Taiwan fondly. But after Japan's defeat in 1945 he was repatriated along with all native Japanese. He was then a bachelor of thirty-four.

During the war all the potters, with the exception of those who couldn't join for health reasons, were drafted into the military or ordered to pursue work of more direct benefit to the war effort. The manufacture of "luxurious goods" was illegal. Pottery production was limited to filling military orders for bowls, plates, cups, tiles, drainpipes and bombshell holders. But by 1947 whole pottery families had returned— from Taiwan and Manchuria, from the army or civilian jobs. Potters Yamamoto and Kodama returned from Taiwan, Araki from Manchuria. Like Mizoguchi-san's, their grandfathers had been potters, but their fathers had worked as civil servants in the railroad and foreign service. Returning to Miyama was not a sentimental act; they came to reopen the family business.

But the sudden appearance of so many would-be potters brought confusion and chaos. The sons of potters hadn't

worked in clay in decades, and the grandsons, like Mizoguchi-san, had only childhood memories of the workshops.
According to Mizoguchi-san, who ran the village agricultural
cooperative until he retired in 1982, of the many who returned
only ten or so had pottery skills. A temporary factory was
set up to train new potters, and attempts were made to fire
all six of the remaining communal kilns, but only two were
in good enough shape to fire successfully. Arima, Hayashi,
Hamazaki and Yamamoto all fired together at a kiln near the
present post office. The kuromon potter Sameshima Sataro,
who had kept his workshop open during the war, fired with
a separate group of potters in the kiln below the shrine.

All were kuromon potters except Arima Takao, who ran
a small operation for white pottery. "*Taihen deshita yo*. It was
terrible. We ate sweet potatoes every day—for breakfast, for
lunch, for dinner. I hate sweet potatoes. But we made out
somehow—everybody needed pottery, you see," Mizoguchi-san explains. For a while the potters had ample business;
Kagoshima people, their homes destroyed by the bombings,
needed bowls and cups and pottery for cooking, as well as
vessels to store foodstuffs and water. A nationwide metal
shortage made pottery essential.

As Mizoguchi-san describes the war years I think of
Okuhara-san, the thin-faced old man whose rice fields adjoin
Nagata-san's paddy. Repatriated from Manchuria in 1945,
Okuhara-san worked as a potter for a while, but quit to farm
full time. When we meet on the street or in the rice fields,
he always talks to me about the "terrible times" during the
war. "Your father and I fought on opposite sides of the war,"
he once exclaimed, then broke into a short laugh, "And now,
here you are!"

My father was grazed in the head by a bullet on Iwo Jima

and, although he says it was just a "Hollywood wound," received a Purple Heart. Later, in 1945, his marine division readied for a second invasion. But in August the atomic bomb fell and they went instead to Sasebo as occupation forces.

From the start of the war, Kagoshima was a major Kyushu bomb target for U.S. planes because of its active harbor. In the prefectural museum, pictures from the war years depict flattened, smoking rubble in the area of modern-day Kagoshima City. With no tall city buildings in the way, Sakurajima towered over the waves, a brooding column of smoke in the bay. Today in the hillsides surrounding Miyama, one can still see the shadows of shallow caves built as temporary bomb shelters along roads and railroad tracks leading to Kagoshima.

Soon after arriving in Miyama I had traveled to Nagasaki, just a few hours northwest by train. At the epicenter, which was once a gaping black hole, there is now a museum, and a peace park full of flowers, sculptures of women holding children, and a monument to victims of the bomb. Ironically, of all Japanese cities, Nagasaki has the longest history of contact with the West; after 1637 it was the only port open to Western traders throughout the time of official isolation during the Tokugawa era.

The day I visited the memorial was sunny and bright, but the small, dimly lit museum seemed deserted. Halfway through, however, I came upon a sea of blue uniforms. Schoolchildren dutifully followed their teachers in straight lines, or clustered in tight groups around the exhibits, some solemnly listening to their teachers, others scuffing their feet along the floor. I hurried through, feeling their eyes on me even after I had passed.

Case after case contained black-and-white photographs and relics of the blast—scraps of charred clothing, bits of furniture, bottles misshapen from the heat. By the time I reached the last room I was so depressed I decided to skip the rest of my planned sightseeing and walk back through the city to my room. On the way I stopped to rest in the courtyard of a small but prosperous-looking Buddhist temple, where I was greeted by the resident priest. He invited me in and we had tea in his office. He asked me the usual questions of how and why I had come to Japan, and then I told him where I had just been and asked what he thought about the bombing of Nagasaki.

"Oh, the bombing," he said quietly, gathering the edge of his brown robe. "Yes, the atomic bomb was a terrible thing. But now, you can see, the city has been rebuilt. It is modern now and new—better than before."

Even Miyama villagers, who often mentioned the war years, would never tell me their feelings about the bombing. I only heard, again and again, the same stories of hard times and food shortages, and how much better things were now.

After the war, debts ran high to cover taxes and rising fuel costs. Wood, much needed for reconstruction, heating and cooking, became scarce. The potters worked in continual debt, borrowing money from the bank to pay for firewood, materials and living expenses for the months before the firing. In 1948, along with two other village members, Mizoguchi-san tried to reorganize the village pottery cooperative (*ku-miai*), which had fallen apart during the war. Sataro-san's father had been its president for several years. At that time the cooperative set pottery prices and kept a warehouse for pottery on the way to market. Photographs of prewar Mi-yama show mounds of black pottery from workshops across the village heaped in the cooperative yard, waiting for transport to buyers in Kagoshima.

But, according to Mizoguchi-san, one well-established workshop owner, fearing loss of profit, vehemently opposed re-forming the kumiai, and the effort failed. Ever since that time, Mizoguchi-san explains tersely, his brow knit in a sudden frown, "*Naka ga waruku natta.* Relationships between people have soured." I question him further, but he only shakes his head and leans forward, half whispering, "Miyama has secrets, you know. There was one very bad potter," and says no more. Who? I want to ask. When? Why? But I remain silent.

There are many such Miyama *naishō*—"secrets." Not long after arriving I had discovered that the wealthiest and most prestigious workshop owner, Chin Jukan, who advertises himself as a "master," can barely throw. When guests arrive by busload or limousine he dresses in the clay-spattered garb of a traditional potter and sits before a potter's wheel. In similar garb (without the mud spots), he regularly appears on TV talk shows to speak about his Korean heritage, and at least once a year he travels to Korea to publicize his "roots." But most of the pieces in his showroom are mold-cast in a small factory on the hill, then carved and painted by his workers. Meanwhile, Chin Jukan drives a white Mercedes-Benz.

One day when I was visiting the Someura pottery across the street a Jukan worker came rushing in. "One incense burner, quick!" she said. Someura-san, who had once been an apprentice at the Chin Jukan pottery, calmly took the order and threw the piece. The waiting kiln worker then rushed it back to the Jukan workshop—just in time for the arrival of British embassy dignitaries who had come to tour the pottery.

The incident was not all that unusual. Workshop owners in Japan are often not potters themselves, but serve as business managers for what is essentially a pottery factory. In such cases, however, the ware is not sold as the work of an individual master but is stamped with the generic workshop mark.

Once I had visited a well-known workshop in Bizen in Okayama Prefecture. The potter's apprentice picked me up in a black Mercedes-Benz, announcing my arrival to the main house by car telephone. The workshop itself was a potter's Sturbridge Village; not even a plastic bucket broke the symmetry of clay and weathered wood.

At first I was indignant at Chin Jukan's hoax. This was corruption of tradition, wholesale duping of the Japanese consumer—and what was worse, nobody seemed to care. Even people in Kagoshima City knew the truth, but no one said a word. When I approached my Japanese friends on the subject, they responded with a shrug. Some pointed out that in the long run Jukan's publicity benefited everyone by making Miyama's "Korean" background known. For generations Miyama potters had hidden their Korean roots for fear of discrimination, but now it was a major selling point. Others said that if Jukan was exposed, the whole village would lose face. Most villagers simply felt that while the present Jukan might not be a master potter and his sales practices were dubious, he was still fulfilling his family duty as *chōnan*, eldest son, by preserving the name for future generations—perhaps his own son, the fifteenth Jukan, would become a true potter. It was common knowledge that Chin Jukan himself had hoped to become a doctor.

In the end my own views reluctantly began to change. I had only to look around to see that much of the world of Japanese traditional arts was concerned with name, status and lineage. "Form first, content after" is a well-known Japanese saying. It was clear that when Japanese customers spent exorbitant sums on a Jukan pot, they were investing not in the individual piece but in the tradition it represented and its connection with their own past as well. When Jukan walked around in old-fashioned handmade indigo-cloth work clothes that other potters couldn't afford, he was simply catering to the romantic notions of folk art and tea ceremony ware aficionados, who demanded that the "traditional" potter exemplify a way of life long gone. While Americans are drawn to images of youth, innovation and the endless frontier, in Japan a cachet of history and tradition is what matters and what sells. Chin Jukan brought in what some felt was much needed tourism. A large yellow billboard along the road now welcomed visitors to *Miyama no Furusato*—"Miyama my hometown." Middle-aged Japanese tourists came to Miyama on a sentimental journey to their own mythic roots. If the true Chin Jukan was revealed, the chain of tradition would be broken, and what would Miyama have left?

The irony, of course, was that the village, being of Korean ancestry, had a background with which no Japanese would wish to be affiliated. Throughout the Edo period (1600–1868), the potters had benefited from Shimazu's protection. Most years they were exempt from the heavy rice tax levied on the surrounding peasants. Certain potters were even commemorated with *gōshi*, rural samurai status. The appointed head of the potters, Boku Heii (Pak Py'ong-ui was his Korean name) was allotted four *koku* (twenty bushels) of rice per year and living quarters. Several kilometers away in Kushikino, a Korean potter named Kinkai (Kimhae) was given a pair of swords and the Japanese surname Hoshiyama, completing his naturalization as a rural Japanese samurai.

But in 1868 the Meiji Restoration transformed all of Japan. *Sonnō jōi*—"Honor the Emperor, expel the Barbarian"—had been the rallying cry of the restoration movement, and the new imperial government abolished the old system of fiefs and class distinctions in the name of national security and the Meiji Emperor. In 1875 the last Shimazu-operated kiln was shut down, ending almost three hundred years of Shimazu protection and patronage. For the first time Miyama potters had to market and sell their ware independently.

As of 1852, five Naeshirogawa families had obtained gōshi and *mongamae* (the right to erect gates in front of their houses), but in Meiji 5, 1873, when the family registers were compiled, following the abolition of the Edo social system, all villagers were automatically listed as commoners. In the postfeudal order, they would face a whole new era of racial discrimination as Koreans in the rigidly structured society of modern Japan.

But Japanese tourists to Miyama tended to lose sight of such facts in the pleasure of buying pottery straight from a workshop, and of taking a drive in the country. Housewives came in groups with their children, businessmen arrived on bus tours, families brought picnics, and groups of young working women drove out from Kagoshima City in immaculate white cars.

"Mizoguchi-san, after all these years, do you think there are still things about Miyama that make it different, that maybe still speak of its Korean heritage?" I ask. This is a sensitive topic and, as always, I am uncertain of the response. Even old Sataro-san, who tended to be nostalgic about his past, will mumble, "That was a long time ago. . . ." and say little more. Once when I asked Nagata-san if Miyama people still kept any Korean customs or traditions, she looked at me as if I were crazy and stalked off in a huff.

Mizoguchi-san rubs his chin and looks out into the rain. He pours another round of tea before answering. "Well, you know, the place marked Motoyashiki—everyone knows it as the place where the first Naeshirogawa kiln was built, but it also marks the area where the first Koreans were forced to live. They were called *Tsuboya no hito*, the 'pottery people.' The surrounding people didn't like them because they were Korean. The old people, they didn't want their children to have the same problems they did. So after the Meiji Restoration they had them all adopted into Japanese families and given Japanese names. Sometimes brothers would go to two different families and end up with different family names. That's just the way it was."

On the surface Miyama looks like any other rural Kyushu town. But I occasionally heard similar comments from others.

"Sure, there was discrimination; there still is. Our ancestors came from Korea. But they were kept apart, they couldn't leave the village."

"As children we were teased and harassed by other kids."

"It's because of discrimination that Miyama people have insisted that their children get an education and study hard at school. Only the ones who weren't smart in school continued in the potteries, everyone who could went on to other jobs. That's why there are so many retired schoolteachers in the village."

"Miyama girls have a hard time finding husbands; they don't get marriage offers sometimes because their ancestors were Korean."

Mizoguchi-san's fingers gently strum the tabletop. I cannot read his silence. I quickly veer the conversation back to kuromon. Mizoguchi-san breaks into a smile. "The last tataki? Well, I'll tell you, the last good potter of kuromon was old Tanaka, you know. His pots had strength! But he's dead now, died maybe fifteen years ago. He had no son to continue," he says, pouring a third round of tea and piling more candies, pickles and rice cakes on my already crowded plate.

When Mizoguchi-san was a boy, Miyama was a bigger, livelier village. "There were houses and workshops all up and down the street. There was always a kiln being fired someplace. And then there were the shrine festivals. It was busy, all right." Kagoshima prefectural records correspond to his memory. In 1920, when he was nine, sixty-four pottery households and twenty-five kilns made up the village. Miyama potters produced over seventy-five thousand ceramic utensils in that year alone. This marked a steady growth from 1890, when the first prefectural records list forty-four workshops. By 1925, however, Miyama was beginning to shrink; only forty-seven workshops and twenty kilns remained, and since the 1960's its population has remained at roughly six hundred. During the "pottery boom" of the early seventies, the number of workshops increased, then fell to the current number of fourteen. No communal kilns have survived.

Mizoguchi-san remembers that in his childhood six community kilns were fired by kuromon potters and five more individually owned kilns fired shiromon. Communal firings occurred once every two or three months. Potters drew lots for rights to kiln space and their order in the firing in the large seven-chamber kilns. When shiromon potters fired with kuromon potters, they used the second and third chambers. If fired in the first chamber, shiromon would darken and crack from the blasting heat of the firebox. Cooler temperatures in the top chambers turned the black pots a brownish yellow and the white pots a bluish gray. Even in good times a badly fired kiln was a financial disaster.

Yet nostalgia for *mukashi*, "old times," when potters worked together firing the huge communal kilns, abounds in Miyama. "Back in the old days," Sataro-san says sternly, "everyone fired together, and everyone was the same." From scattered comments I have pieced together that the advent of gas and electric kilns, the trend to produce smaller ware and the general decline in the number of potters contributed to the demise of the communal firings: the large wood-fired kilns were economically unfeasible. In other traditional pottery villages, though, such as Onta in northern Kyushu, potters still made their own clay, used wood-fired kilns and maintained a strong pottery cooperative. But while Miyama farmers mingled freely, the potters remained aloof, each workshop an island unto itself.

"See this?" Mizoguchi-san says, pointing to his teacup. "My niece painted it, so I use it, but the thing cracked immediately. It isn't really made to be used. All you can do with shiromon is look at it. And after you have one or two pieces in your house, that's enough." I nod. Frankly, I agreed. With its gaudy designs, much of white Satsuma was among the ugliest pottery I had ever seen. Turning the straight-sided cup so that I can see its light enameling of yellow flowers, Mizoguchi-san suddenly brightens. "Have you found all the old community kilns yet?" When I confess I have not, he picks up a pencil and begins to draw a detailed map on the back of an ad for Shironami (White Wave) shōchū.

When Mizoguchi-san is finished, a rough maze of lines maps out the location of the six major community kilns, in some cases fired as late as the 1950's. I am suddenly eager to get going. Although I have been in Miyama over a year, this is the first time anyone has explained in such detail the recent history of the village. But every time I rise to leave he tells me to wait and disappears into the back, reappearing with another present. By the time I am on my feet, my pack holds a tin of seaweed, three sweet potatoes from his garden, a half bag of candies, a small kuromon cup and a gift pack of instant coffee left over from New Year's. "Thank you, thank you. I'll visit again soon," I say once more and slip out the door, almost forgetting my umbrella in my haste to be gone.

The Kannongama kiln site is in the forest, now a soaking green sponge thickly covered with ferns. Mizoguchi-san's map shows a site on the left side of the road to the shrine. The ground is caved in, full of boggy holes. Stumps of cedar, bamboo poles and heaps of potsherds lie everywhere in tangled heaps. All that remains of what was once a long seven-chamber noborigama heaving with flame and billows of smoke is a sloping rise in the hill, a giant mound of turf spreading into the woods. Rain falls in a gentle mist; from the piles of broken red brick an eerie steam rises. Here and there, angular pieces of tile and drainpipe—relics of the war years—jut up from the ferns, like the ruins of an ancient fort. Digging down with a piece of shard, I find an underground colony of greenish-black pottery.

Nearby is a flat area curiously devoid of bamboo and level as though someone had planted a small garden of cinnamon leaf and fern. A few stone grave markers rise there, with lotus-petal designs on the base. Later I learn that this style of grave was reserved for Buddhist priests. The clearing once contained a Tendai-sect Buddhist temple, built in 1714 and used by the Shimazu lords when they stopped over in the village on their way to Edo. But in an 1871 decree setting up the ranks of shrines, Shintō was proclaimed the national religion and Buddhist temples across Japan were torn down. Potters still call the site Kannon, however, after the Buddhist deity of compassion once worshiped there.

Across the village I discover the ruins of Nankingama. Built in 1846 by Murata Hoami, this large kiln was meant to initiate the production of white porcelain in Miyama and help the struggling Miyama potters. But sources of kaolin-rich porcelain clay were scarce in Kagoshima and the effort failed; in 1880 the huge kiln was shut down. On the far side of the kiln site, three or four brick arches poke through the underbrush along the hill slope. Abandoned for a century, the kiln has a Shintō marker that is kept clear of fallen leaves and brush, and the small white cups with the Shimazu sign that rest on the ledge are filled with water.

I scramble up the hill through ferns and broken pottery, my feet sliding on broken bits of porcelain. At the top, where the kiln's chimney once funneled out continuous black smoke, a stand of young bamboo reigns over the valley. This back side of the kiln, overlooking the East China Sea, was once the village pottery dump. Under cover of vines and brush lies an avalanche of cracked white porcelain bowls, black grinding bowls called *suribachi*, as well as roof tiles and water pipes from the days of wartime production. It was here that Mizoguchi-san remembers sledding down the slope on potsherds.

Next I discover the Nyomongama site, under the foundation of Yamanouchi-san's new house. For twenty-five years Yamanouchi Obāsan worked at the Sataro workshop as a general helper. She is the same age as Sataro-san and remembers him as a boy. Five years ago, when she retired and built her present house, she hired a bulldozer to smooth over the ruins of the old kiln. The house is modern style, with white concrete siding and a well-swept dirt yard. A thick wall of concrete holds back the hillside where the kiln once stood.

Sataro-san remembers when Nyomongama was built. He was twenty and had not yet gone off to study pottery at the National Ceramics Laboratory in Kyoto. The Sataro workshop fired with four or five other potters at Kannongama on the hill, but when it collapsed in 1945, they built a new climbing kiln that looked like a series of enormous connected beehives stacked up against a hill. Sataro-san contends that mud-clay kilns built over a thin framework of bamboo are better than those made of brick. If one brick falls a whole kiln can be lost, while in a mud-clay kiln you simply patch any holes: the firing seals and vitrifies the patch.

Nyomongama, however, was made from bricks. The mortar of clay and soil was carried down from the shrine area on horseback. Four bricks of clay were packed onto a horse in one load. Sataro-san figures that the horse climbed the hill over three hundred times. Five years later, only Sataro-san and one other potter were left firing the enormous, crumbling kiln, the last communal kiln in the village. They gave up in 1950. For the next ten years Sataro-san used a smaller, independent kiln nearby until he asked experts from the pottery center of Arita to build the present noborigama on his workshop grounds.

When I first came to Miyama, I couldn't wait to see the famed wood-fired kilns described in books on Japanese ceramics. I had seen a documentary film about the venerable folkcraft potter Hamada Shoji, and read the travel accounts of the British potter Bernard Leach, as well as essays on traditional crafts by Yanagi Sōetsu. In an issue of the Japanese folkcraft magazine *Mingei*, Yanagi had lauded Miyama as a rural village that still maintained the traditional pottery-making methods of its ancestors. One of the photographs in Yanagi's book *The Unknown Craftsman* was of a Miyama choka.

It had not occurred to me that in computer-age Japan, potteries would modernize as well. Everything that I had read and heard about Japanese pottery suggested a tradition fixed in time. Discovering gas and electric kilns in all the potteries had been a disappointment equal to my surprise at meeting my first Miyama potter—a middle-aged man in a white T-shirt, blue jeans and a blue baseball cap who glanced at a small black-and-white TV to the right of his wheel as he worked. Later I learned that only two workshops used the remaining noborigama, once a year at most; the firings would begin in late spring. Indigo-cloth work clothes and wood-fired kilns were too expensive for most workshops to consider.

Yet all that is forgotten about Miyama lies in the woods: every inch of wooded area is a graveyard of ancient black pottery. Pots dropped in haste or pots thrown in anger, discarded for the need of something new. Made by whom, and in what year and workshop? Nestled in the bases of cedars are broken plates imprinted on the bottom by seashells placed between layers of pots during firing—a practice discontinued over a hundred years ago. One finds wide-rimmed bowls to hold water, crafted thick and sturdy to stand the rigors of country living, or rough-scored bowls to grind miso and make balls of buckwheat flour. Small cracked teapots for tea and hot potato liquor wait in the fern bracken, amid broken cedar and dirt.

Even the bamboo holds secrets. Once I found a discarded

black pot that the bamboo had pushed up from its hiding place. In less than a week it hung four feet off the ground, dangling like an old feed bucket. When someone finally took it away, I felt robbed.

Following Mizoguchi-san's directions I find seven more kiln sites teeming with potsherds. By day's end I feel rich, triumphant, and thoroughly soaked. Back at the workshop, a tall stack of sweet-scented cedar boxes fills the table just under the sloping tin roof. I open the wooden doors and look into the damp, dripping work area. Several boards of freshly thrown flower vases sit by Nagayoshi-san's wheel, two abreast in the shadows. From the house come voices of guests and laughter. Inside, amid tea and conversation, pots are slowly being sold.

The boards of vases and a waiting mound of clay mean that even though it is Sunday Nagayoshi-san will work this evening. I put down my umbrella and backpack heavy with gifts and potsherds, carefully setting aside the branch of delicate flowering plum from Mizoguchi-san's garden. I lift up three twenty-pound bags of plastic-wrapped clay and set to work. Steam rises from my wet hair. I catch my breath, rock back on my heels and then lean forward again, moving slightly with each turn of rolling clay. In generations of change, wedging remains a simple if essential task. Revolving on an unseen core, well-turned clay spreads out and lifts, turning and opening like the petals of a large, sun-warmed flower.

March; spreading green, breezes
dawn in the workshop
rising steam

A͟T 5:30 A.M. THE EMPTY WORKSHOP
waits like a gear stopped in mid-
motion. Outside, the yard is empty,
shadowed with predawn moonlight,
save for a tailless orange-and-white cat
that slinks toward the compost pile and
some scattered fish bones. Not even
the paper boy has made his rounds.
Beyond the hedge the lane gleams, a
long stretch of silver veiled with mist.

Cats make Nagayoshi-san's skin
crawl. Even when he is working, if a
cat strolls into the yard he rushes at it
with stones in hand, or sticks, potsherds, anything he can find. The cats
flee before his onslaught, then slink
back again the next morning. During
the winter they continually find their
way into the kiln room, leaving behind
piles of scat and the lion-cage stench of

S
P
R
I
N
G

urine. The other day an orange-and-white cat came skidding into the yard with a large brown tom in tow. Both cats leaped into the window of the showroom. Howls and the crash of falling pottery made Nagayoshi-san and me jump up; we found two vases smashed on the floor. Dogs are no help in keeping Miyama's wild cats in check. The population of small canines in Miyama spend their lives chained down; they bite if approached.

Sometimes I think Nagayoshi-san imagines the wild cats to be certain Miyama residents. *Zing*. One small pebble for the slant-eyed obāsan who to this day never says hello. *Zing*. A rock for the clay salesman who sold him bags of unusable sandy clay. *Thump*. A sharp stone for the local contractor who used only cheap materials on the workshop and house, pocketing the extra money.

My first week in Miyama big cats haunted my dreams: night after night I imagined myself running from shadow-fast tigers, their yellow eyes everywhere at once. Those days I walked around the quiet streets so many times I seemed to have the bamboo memorized. Gradually my circles grew smaller and smaller, and then led directly into the workshops. For months I gazed enviously at the potters and their place of daily work in clay. Villagers looked at me with surprise, even suspicion. Only the Nagayoshis would speak to me. At first I thought it was a language barrier, or shyness, the Japanese reserve one reads about in books. But as soon as I became affiliated with the Nagayoshi workshop, and thus attained a recognizable niche in village life, the problem vanished; soon I was unable to go anywhere without someone wanting to stop and talk. Now I rarely have time to walk the village; the hedge is a wall of green blocking out all but the workshop. With a last glance toward the long silver street I head inside.

I take a deep breath of the musty pond smells, my sandaled feet suddenly cold on the dirt floor. A lump of clay rises from Nagayoshi-san's wheel and tools lie scattered across the cushions. A glass jar of cinnamon candies is wedged into the windowsill, while the mud-spattered cassette player lies on its side. To the right a full board of smooth-walled vases rises like a stand of cedar. For the next kiln firing, in two weeks, Nagayoshi-san must produce a piece for display in the annual Kagoshima ceramics exhibition at the prefecture art museum. Acceptance into the exhibition is determined by a panel of judges from Tokyo and Kyoto. Technically, anyone can submit a piece, although in a province like Kagoshima, with a large population of potters and only one main ceramics show a year, competition is stiff.

When the green entry forms arrived last month, Reiko handed me one at breakfast.

"Leila, why don't you submit some of your pottery," she said, "some of your cups perhaps?"

"But I don't have anything to enter," I answered quickly. "Besides, I'm only an apprentice."

"Well, why not make something! There's time, if you work at it." I watched a splash of white cream swirl and melt into rich black coffee.

"You could try," said Nagayoshi-san quietly, his fingers resting lightly on his chin. "How else will you know where you stand?" He didn't smile.

"Work hard!" said Reiko, handing me the entry form.

That was three weeks ago. Now, at 5:45 A.M., with a cup of green tea in hand, I look over my last board of unfinished cups. As I watch the stump-tailed cat scratch through the garbage, my stomach rumbles. Two silent, undistracted hours stretch before me. I can finish trimming these last five cups for submission to the ceramics show. Over the past month I have made some fifty different shapes and styles of teacup. Which one to use? Which one least resembles Nagayoshi-san's work and is something closer to my own? One short, rounded form felt particularly good in my hand after trimming. I chose it for a model to make sets of five.

Repeating the form was an entirely new problem. Although I made measuring sticks and pulled up what felt like equal amounts of clay on the spinning wheel, I couldn't quite catch the swell at the bottom, or the cup's slight bend inward at the lip. In the end I settled for mere quantity, hoping that in trimming, a matched set of five would emerge. On the back shelves a finished line of cups waits under shrouds of dampened cloth. They must be kept wet enough to absorb a thin coat of white clay slip without cracking. I set a board with the five remaining cups beside my wheel. Covered with plastic to keep moist, a trimming chock is still fastened on the wheelhead. Sitting down cross-legged, I finish the cup of strong tea, turn on the motor and reach for tools.

Centering an upside-down piece of "green"—raw, or unfired—pottery as it spins on a cone-shaped chock takes concentration, attention to detail, trial and error, a certain hair-splitting patience. When I first began small plates this past month, my teacher weighed each one. If they were more than 187 grams they had to be redone. Last week, fed up with plates, I slipped the last three into the drying room without retrimming, although each one felt a touch overweight. The next morning I found all three carefully wrapped in a damp towel next to my wheel. Even though he regularly lost pieces from working too fast, he wanted Nagayoshi pottery to be light, paper-thin.

I carefully tap the revolving cup on the side each time it passes, gradually persuading it to spin on center. With an index finger pressing down on the top, I cut into the side with a trim tool. Peels of clay twist off in long curls. Soon the bottom and sides are smooth and light. The next step is carving the foot. I dig in with the edge of the steel tool and watch a clean groove widen, spreading into the pot's concave base. I tap the pot as I work, listening to its hollow echo. A dull thud means that a thick layer of clay still needs to be trimmed. What I want to hear is a light, hollow ring.

Tap, trim, tap, trim. The wheel and I negotiate. More curls of brown clay fill my lap, a muscle nags in my lower back. Finally the pot spins evenly, transformed into a smooth round-walled cup with a shallow indented foot. I pull the pot off gently, only to find that it has a leaden heft—too heavy. Time to re-center and trim again. The vision of my cups trimmed and set out to dry before breakfast slips away.

I find it hard to imagine this row of small teacups behind a glass case in the art museum. I wonder which potters in Miyama will submit work to the show. Nagayoshi-san plans to enter a large round-walled piece painted with his new motif, a repeating design inspired by the double-arrow recycling graphic used in advertising. Kubo Masayuki, another first-generation potter in Miyama, also relies on exhibitions for exposure. His pottery is a white slip ware, modeled on the Yi Dynasty Korean ceramics admired by the mingei leader Yanagi Sōetsu. Like all pottery couples in Miyama, he and his wife, Miwako, who have lived in Miyama for ten years, work with the endurance of farmers, firing a gas kiln twice a month to keep up with orders. "When we moved here from

Shigaraki there were a lot of young people and apprentices. It looked like a nice place," Kubo-san explained. "But everybody left." No one would sell the couple land, but they rented a half-fallen building and a small shed on the hill by the old community kiln. They plan to build a new house and workshop soon, but not in Miyama.

Finally my cup is light to the touch and rings like a muffled bell when tapped. Then I catch sight of my teacher's clay-spattered wheel and concentration splinters. Usually Nagayoshi-san cleans the wheel carefully before leaving the workshop, but yesterday we had worked up until dinner, and then we had stayed up late talking. Now the mound of clay has hardened. Should I be doing my own work when his lies unattended? Yanking my wheel to a stop with a sigh, I throw a damp towel over my cups and start cleaning.

Last night after dinner, I showed my teacher and his wife the copy of *Ceramics Monthly* that had just arrived from home. When he saw the magazine, Nagayoshi-san jumped up from where he had been watching a samurai movie on TV with Reiko and rushed into the kitchen. By the time he emerged, balancing a tray of teacups in one hand and the green-and-white thermos in the other, Reiko was already looking through the magazine.

"Hey, Otōsan," she called, "come here and look at this. How interesting!" The magazine was opened to a color plate of porcelain cowboy boots painted with pop-art designs in red, yellow, blue and gold. Across the boot tops waved miniature American flags. Nagayoshi-san poured tea so quickly that the hot liquid sloshed over the sides. Reiko leafed through the glossy pages: a hot-pink teapot, high-fired plates in bright red and gold, enormous vessels with snakes twisting around the sides, pastel vases in pink, green and yellow, punk-style coffee mugs in bright green and black, and sturdy sets of oatmeal-colored dishware.

When she turned to a large wood-fired piece, split down the center as if someone had attempted to rip the piece in two, Reiko suddenly sighed and handed the magazine to her husband.

"What are you doing, studying pottery in Japan." she asked me, her brown eyes serious. "It's so much more interesting in America. Strong. Free."

"Perhaps it's too free," I offered.

"Well, I don't know anything about ceramics anyhow. I never did like mud," she joked. "Anyhow, don't stay up too late." Taking up her small blue teacup, she went back to finish her crocheting in front of the TV. Even in her leatherwork, Reiko likes *kawatta mono*, things that are new and strange. In the Yamakataya department store exhibition last December, she displayed free-form masks and a framed piece of tan leather molded into a curvaceous behind that she titled "My Mountain." Yet her question lingered.

Studying ceramics in Japan might be compared to pursuing English literature in Great Britain, sculpture in Italy, winemaking in France: the centuries of tradition were a powerful lure. I had seen Japanese, Korean and Chinese pottery in museums before I began to work in clay, and even the beginner's instruction books I had read at age twelve all made references to Japanese ceramics. It was inevitable that as a student of the craft I would eventually look to Asia for inspiration and technique. Like generations of artists, potters and scholars before me, I had come to Japan because of all the contemporary Asian traditions Japanese pottery is the most thriving and celebrated.

In the States, while a vibrant crafts movement grows, "potters" still evoke images of the sixties: a lone craftsman throwing coffee mugs in the Vermont woods. To be successful an American potter must carve out a name as an artist, not just as a potter. But in Japan the pottery trade, far from representing an alternative life-style, constitutes a respected industry. At one end of the spectrum, production potters are essentially no different from factory workers across Japan, throwing the same shapes day after day in a production line where the emphasis is on speed and precision, not originality. At the same time, tōgeika, such as Nagayoshi-san, who specialize in fine art pottery, rely on galleries and exhibitions to sell their work. Meanwhile, a boom in ceramics hobby-classes has resulted in a population of amateur potters. Master potters and workshop owners regularly appear on TV to discuss their work and the status of ceramics as a traditional art. The average Japanese household, which generally uses factory-made Seto ware for everyday use, will own a set of handmade ceramic dishes or a flower vase from a major pottery center. In the best Japanese restaurants, patrons dine on a carefully selected display of handmade pottery ware.

Whether pottery is a craft or an art form is not the important debate in Japan that it is in America. Since the height of the tea ceremony in the sixteenth and seventeenth centuries, pottery has remained one of Japan's most treasured arts. What matters in the strict, status-oriented and fiercely competitive world of Japanese ceramics, however, is a potter's name within the group and division in which he or she works. A gift from an established traditional kiln such as the Jukan workshop is as prestigious as Tiffany silver.

While Nagayoshi-san eagerly studied the magazine, I leafed through a book on old Miyama. "What do you think?" I finally asked.

He looked again at the page he was studying. "They're good. Nice forms. Strength. Look at these," he said, pointing to a set of half-twisted black teacups. "Japanese potters would never think of making that. They already have the shape of how a teacup *should* look too much in mind—they can't think of new ideas like these."

Opportunities to talk to Nagayoshi-san about ceramics were rare. Once work began he was moody and rarely spoke. "Just wait, I'll show you," he would say in answer to my questions, his voice tight with exaggerated patience, or, saying "Never mind," he would jump up to do the task himself. At first I thought it was a language problem. But although I have been fluent for months now, in the workshop I speak less and less. Sometimes whole days pass with my having said barely more than *"Ohayō gozaimasu"* in the morning, *"Ocha?"* at 3:00, and *"Sayonara"* when I leave at night. "Through association one naturally comes to understand," Nagayoshi-san would say. In the workshop, silence unfurled.

I poured another round of tea. Still squinting at the pages through his brown plastic and wire-rimmed glasses, Nagayoshi-san continued, "Well, they're good. But, well . . . it's just not my style. Besides, you can't drink tea from them." He turned the page and, staring again at the multicolored boots, laughed abruptly. "You think too much," he said, tossing me a tangerine. "I make rice bowls and teacups, tableware, to make a living. But in my free time I make the large exhibition bowls. That's enough."

I turned the tangerine in my hand like a globe. "What about Miyama," I asked suddenly, changing the subject. "What will happen here?"

"Such questions!" he said, scratching his head, then pointed to a photograph of old kuromon in the book I was reading.

"Tradition is difficult, you know," he answered slowly. "How much *good* pottery do you see being made in the village anymore?"

I looked down at the photograph. As always, the old black pots, swelled out at the base, seemed as timeless and complete as river-worn stones. There was nothing like them produced in the village anymore. Plastics, prepackaged foods and running water have all diminished the need for storage bowls and jars. In tiny Japanese apartments, where would one keep a barrel-sized kuromon vat?

"It's a different time," said Nagayoshi-san. "Pottery too must change."

My teacher's response was no surprise. My first month in Miyama I would often come back depressed from visiting workshops. Of the twelve remaining Miyama potteries, most produced quantities of mass-produced souvenir ware, often by mold. At first I assumed that the situation was unique to Miyama; never a famous pottery center to begin with, it had quietly slipped into decline. But that winter I had traveled to more famous Japanese pottery centers like Shigaraki, Tamba and Bizen, only to find workshops piled high with their own versions of tourist schlock. What had happened to traditional Japanese pottery? Pottery centers across Japan were mired in a sense of their own past, mass-producing a few chosen "traditional" forms from their area, which they sold as authentic mingei.

"What about folkcraft pottery?" I continued.

"Perhaps it's fine for certain traditional kilns. But you see, I am not that kind of potter."

Although he never talks about mingei ideas, there was a time when Nagayoshi-san read everything about the movement. Thick volumes by Yanagi Sōetsu, as well as writings by Tomimoto Kenkichi and Bernard Leach, fill the living room shelves. The term *mingei*, literally "popular art," was coined by Yanagi Sōetsu in 1926. Although mingei has come to represent the dominant Western view of what is "Japanese" about Japanese crafts, Yanagi's original concept of a mingei movement was inspired by the British arts and crafts movement of the nineteenth century. An ardent admirer of William Blake, Yanagi was also influenced by the writings of Thomas Carlyle, John Ruskin and William Morris.

"Nature, cooperation, tradition—these are the three ingredients of folkcraft beauty," wrote Yanagi. Mingei reflected Yanagi's interest in religion as well as antimodern philosophies, the Buddhist concepts of *mushin*—"selflessness"—and *tariki*—"absolute faith in another." Folkcraft workshops must produce simple, functional ware and emphasize the preservation of traditional skills, forms and glazes of its area.

Mingei ideas became popular in the rapid modernization of Japan after the war. By the 1960's a new Japanese prosperity combined with a fervent nostalgia for things "Japanese" culminated in the "mingei boom," which lasted through the mid-seventies. Although Miyama was too far from the major cities to receive the full impact of the folkcraft movement, Naeshirogawa pottery had been admired by Yanagi, and as a result of this publicity, kuromon from the traditional Sataro workshop sells well in folkcraft stores as far north as Kyoto, Tokyo and even Hokkaido.

While I had long ceased to be a mingei admirer, I had to admit that it had served an important role in keeping intact small villages like Miyama, where pottery had always been a corporate rather than an artistic venture. If it had not been for the consumer demand for folkcraft pottery created by the mingei movement, much of what survives of Japan's traditional potteries today would have vanished completely after the war. It was true that the strict canons of the mingei gospel prevented potters from experimenting or trying new forms, and that as a consequence most of the pottery one now found in pottery centers was junk. But there were signs that with more money to spend, the Japanese consumer was beginning to look beyond generic mingei ware to better-crafted, more expensive objects. While sales in all but the three main Miyama workshops had fallen off, first-generation potters like Nagayoshi-san could hardly keep up with orders. Even so, the mingei market had kept the potteries in business throughout the critical postwar years. And mingei ideas continue to provide an intellectual background and context for the modern Japanese potter.

For folkcraft and other potters, the highest honor is designation by the Agency for Cultural Affairs as a Living National Treasure. An individual designated a Living National Treasure receives a modest annual stipend toward continuing traditional methods and training apprentices. Most important, his name becomes a household word and he can charge outrageous prices for his work. When I went to Okinawa to see the folk potteries there, I brought back teacups from the Kinjo Jirō workshop as mandatory omiyage, travel souvenirs for my friends. Nagayoshi-san, who disliked mingei pottery, looked at the cup I gave him for a moment and then gave it back, saying that I should take it home to the States: he could always go and get another one. My other friends were similarly unimpressed. But several months later Kinjo Jirō became a Living National Treasure, and the next time I visited one of the friends to whom I had given a teacup, it held the place of honor in his tokonoma.

In 1955 thirty-three people in twenty-eight categories of traditional crafts and performing arts were announced as the first Living National Treasures. By 1979, seventy-nine individuals in performing arts and sixty-nine in traditional crafts had received this distinction. Some say that money and connections have become as important as lineage or skill. Village rumor has it that Chin Jukan is working to become the first Living Treasure of Miyama.

As a self-taught artisan, Nagayoshi-san falls outside the categories of *sensei* (master or teacher) and *deshi* (pupil) of the traditional craft system. Therefore, he is technically not eligible for consideration as a Living National Treasure. Instead, he relies on department store and gallery exhibitions to establish his name as a potter and thus his price, competing with other contemporary potters by submitting to large Tokyo-based national exhibitions, such as the Dentō Kōgeiten and the more avant-garde Nitten, "Japan Art Exhibition," founded in 1946 as a continuation of the prewar Imperial Art Exhibition. Nagayoshi-san submits to the Dentō Kōgeiten because his work is functional. "You have to decide which competition you want to be in, and then stick with it. Japanese people are like that, they want to be in one group or another," he explained.

Last night before the conversation faded, I asked Nagayoshi-san about his own pottery study. He sat quiet for a minute, then pulled two faded photograph albums from the shelf. The potter's photographic history begins with a black-and-white snapshot of him on the way to school, barefoot and half frowning in a kimono. He remembers himself as a mischievous student, having his knuckles rapped by teachers for drawing in his books. "The only thing worse than school was working in the rice paddies," he explained. "And I didn't want to work in those fields."

In the next photograph he poses in a brown uniform, on his way to serve on a Japanese battleship. Then it is 1950 and he stands bright-eyed in khaki pants and a visored cap, just twenty-three and on his way to Kyoto. The next five years he studied painting on the top floor of a department store building with Kuwada Michio, a painter now teaching at Kyoto University. Most of the pictures from this time show the young art student beside his paintings, two fingers hooked around a burning cigarette.

After five years he left Kyoto and moved to Tokyo. "It was time to move on. You can't stay with your teacher forever, you know." On the next page he stands before the wall of Osaka Castle, one arm around his smiling new wife. Reiko was just nineteen and a student in art school when they met. It was not an arranged marriage and Reiko told me that before they could marry they had to wait two years until her older sister found a husband.

One year later Nagayoshi-san holds the white bundle of his month-old daughter, Eri; two years later, Keisuke. The following pages are filled with pictures of him in khaki work clothes and a white painter's cap, doing odd jobs as a sign painter, or with his young family in Tokyo. Several are of the government vocational school where he taught painting techniques and lacquerwork.

Nagayoshi-san paused, peering closely over the next section of photographs and exhibition announcements of his paintings. Dark, moody studies of working people and abstract geometric forms make up his early work. Despite the Japanese craze for French Impressionists, Nagayoshi-san preferred Van Gogh and Picasso, the Dutch masters and the riddles of Escher prints. His work became increasingly abstract, filled with dark studies of distraught, angular faces, tall buildings and complex machines. Postwar Japan was not a place to sell artwork, much less the paintings of an unknown. To support himself Nagayoshi-san did manual labor, from cleaning gutters and city toilets to splitting firewood. He also worked as a firewood carrier at a kiln headed by the famed ceramic artist Tomimoto Kenkichi. Later Tomimoto, the artist-potter who broke from the strict principles of mingei, became his idol, but at the time Nagayoshi-san saw pottery only as tableware or as teabowls for the rich. He talked to Tomimoto with only vague interest, for Nagayoshi-san was determined to become a painter.

Nagayoshi-san often reminisces about the hard times after the war. "It wasn't like now, with good food every night. I had to walk home from work because I didn't have money to take the trolley car." But he talks about those "terrible times" so much I finally asked him if it hadn't also been fun. "Oh yes," he said. "It was fine. All I worried about was my painting, I was free."

After his children were born Nagayoshi-san took a job at a government school. Painting at night and on weekends, he exhibited often. But after he moved to Miyama, he ceased painting altogether. When I asked him why, he said firmly, "Now I make pottery." The other day when Reiko was in town, he built a small fire in the yard and threw in reams of black sketchbooks and two of his large oil paintings that had been stored behind the kiln. "It's getting cluttered around here. These have no use," he said, pitching in a large flowing sketch of a bodhisattva.

Although in his clothing Nagayoshi-san prefers khaki, gray, or olive-green, he decorates his pots with rich browns and brilliant shades of cobalt and turquoise. Around the swelling sides of a bottle, bands of woven geometric pattern accentuate the form, making the whole piece seem taller, more strongly defined, and complete. His plates become canvases for Escher-like designs of repeating rectangular bands, and his small bowls reel with repeating designs not unlike those of Southwest American Indian pottery.

"My pottery started there," he says, pointing to one of his early works, an abstract painting of a waterwheel. "Back in Kyoto." In the geometric design of repeating rectangles and lines I saw the abstract painting of a bird that he often uses as a surface design on pottery. It was this motif on a large brown-and-white bowl that earned him national recognition in the Dentō Kōgeiten, only two years after he moved to Miyama.

In comparison with folkcraft potters, Nagayoshi-san emphasizes innovation rather than skilled reproduction of standard forms. "Sense study and technique study—both are important. A balance of both is most important. But too much technical skill and you'll get lazy," he has said repeatedly during my study, encouraging me to travel, visit museums and draw. Since September, Fridays have been marked off on the calendar for wheel practice on my own forms.

"Do anything you want," he once said with a grin, pantomiming the throwing of an enormous pot. Then he added seriously, "Anybody can get good on the wheel if they practice. Monday through Thursday, learn the Nagayoshi workshop forms, but Friday, make your *own* pots—cups, bowls, whatever." I was also not to address him by his official title of sensei, because in the workshop, he explained, he too was always learning. In an American art school these policies of independent study versus rote learning would be standard, but in Japan they turned the traditional concept of learning by repetition on its head. After the discipline of repeating the same forms all week, throwing without a model and a definite plan was unsettling. I was as lost as in the very first days of my apprenticeship, floundering to discover where to begin.

In the workshop I pry the mound of unused clay from Nagayoshi-san's wheel and gather the encrusted tools, then sponge down the wheel. Outside by the hedge I pour out the bucket of clay slip and rinse tools and sponges. By the compost heap two more wild cats are digging for bones. Beyond their excavation, the yard is cleared and empty. Holes in the dirt show where Nagayoshi-san and I pulled up the half-entrenched glaze vats to prepare for the carpenters who will arrive today to begin remodeling the hot tub and its tiled room. The paper boy enters, bobbing his shaved head and dropping a newspaper wrapped in blue plastic. A large dark cross within a circle is printed on the paper's plastic wrap— the Shimazu crest is now a logo for Kagoshima liquor companies. Across the valley a pair of crows caw and dive. Somewhere a rooster begins calling. The morning sky widens and spreads out in deeper shades of blue.

Suddenly the recorded Westminster chimes spread across the village, followed by the distinct crackle of a radio at full volume. "*Ichi, ni, san, shi*. One, two, three, four." Music begins and a woman's voice calls out calisthenic exercises to a fast beat. The 7:00 A.M. exercise program broadcast from speakers above the community exercise field has begun. I hear cloth flapping and peer through the hedge. In front of his lichen-covered stone walls and ceremonial garden, Suzuki-san does calisthenics in the lane, the wide sleeves of his blue kimono rising and falling to the music.

Suzuki-san comes from a family of potters. The large-roofed wooden gate over the entrance to his yard denotes the samurai status given to favored potters by the Shimazu clan. But Suzuki-san's father had urged him to get an education and choose another trade, so he was a schoolteacher until he retired several years ago. Cycling to the post office, he inevitably wears a brown suit. His wife wears a traditional dark brown or blue kimono or a long skirt and vest. Like the other older women in the village, she feels that white hair, once a token commanding respect in Japan, is unattractive and has it dyed jet-black in a beauty parlor in Unamoto. As a school-teacher's wife, she never wears mompei.

"*Ohayō gozaimasu,*" I call through the hedge.

"*Ohayō gozaimasu,*" Suzuki-san answers stiffly, his white mustache twitching, and, turning abruptly, heads into his garden to resume his exercises.

The small electric wheel beams on its red-painted stand as if new. I carry the board of finished vases outside and lift them up on the roof to dry. But what good is a clean wheel with no clay? I wedge quickly. Only when three conical mounds of clay rise next to the wet shaping tools and a bucket of fresh water sits by the wheel do I turn back to my own work with a sigh of relief.

"*Ohayō,*" calls Nagayoshi-san stepping into the doorway, carrying boxes of discarded paper. "What, no walk this morning?" He looks quickly around the workshop, and without waiting for an answer, slips outside. From the window I watch him tend a small fire of paper and leaves with an iron poker. He picks up a fish bone and places it strategically on a flat rock. Whiskers twitching, the wild cats watch from under the hedge. Nagayoshi-san waits, poker in hand and a pocket full of stones.

With a squeak the kitchen door opens and Reiko bends down to put on her high-heeled black shoes. She comes out dressed for town, in a brown linen skirt and jacket and bright red lipstick, her face powdered white. She carries her hand-made leather purse and two dark-blue *furoshiki*, cloths, for carrying home purchases. Today she will shop, and then go to an acupuncture appointment in the nearby spa town of Unamoto. "Don't forget to serve the carpenters tea at ten and three. Lunch is instant ramen." She rushes down the lane in a clatter of high heels to board the 7:05 bus.

Far from being a typical okusan, Reiko leaves the house more often than Nagayoshi-san, commuting to Kagoshima City and Kumamoto City to teach her leatherwork classes and show her work in exhibitions. Sometimes we eat dinner amid sheets of drying leather, or breakfast is delayed while she finishes tooling a particular piece. The strain of managing the pottery, the house and her own work, however, has taken its toll, and she is a regular patient of the Unamoto acupuncturist. When my knees began to hurt from the long hours sitting cross-legged before the wheel (a common potter's complaint), Reiko insisted that I go to the acupuncturist myself. The first needles in my knees and legs had only hurt a little, but when the doctor began on my lower back, each twist and tap as he worked the needle deeper sent a jet of pain racing along my spine. "That's good," said the acupuncturist calmly each time I shouted. "We must release the pain and then you'll get better." I begged for him to stop— my knees didn't hurt anymore. They were cured, I was sure. Around the room half-dressed obāsan, waiting on chairs or stretched out on tables with needles protruding from sore joints and muscles, turned to stare. Reiko quietly suggested that perhaps since it was my first visit, the doctor might cut the treatment short. I limped toward my clothes. On the way out Reiko handed the doctor six thousand-yen notes. I stared in disbelief as his hand missed the money and Reiko had to place it in his palm—the doctor was blind.

Today a team of carpenters from Nagayoshi's hometown of Sendai is coming to rebuild the ofuro. Since there will be no hot bath tonight, Nagayoshi-san and I will meet Reiko at the public bath in Unamoto. Once again my teacups disappear under a damp cloth. I go inside for breakfast.

In a ringing of hammers the morning speeds by. The carpenters work with speed and precision; by 10:00 the iron tub has been removed, and half the outside wall knocked away. Tea break is quiet and polite, an informal ceremony in the yard. Wiping layers of dust and plaster from their faces, the workers take seats in double lines before the head carpenter. Dressed in white pullover shirts and baggy maroon pants that tuck into black cloven-toe boots at the calf, they sit like a team of jockeys.

As I pour the tea they watch, too dumbfounded not to stare. When the cups have passed from hand to hand down the line, the head carpenter speaks. "Weren't you on the TV? Yes, I saw you. Why did you come to Miyama? Do you like pottery that much? Do you really eat tōfu?" The group of workmen leans forward, suddenly curious and alert. Their headman's inquiries gather momentum; I sense a coming avalanche of questions.

In the winter I had appeared on a local television station's special news program about foreigners in Kagoshima. The day of the interview at 8:00 A.M. sharp the news announcer had arrived, stylishly dressed in a red suit. She stayed all day, asking me questions as I worked: How did I find my teacher? Why did I pick Miyama? What do I like about Japan? The finished tape reminded me of a Walt Disney special, complete with music and long takes of my blue eyes and beat-up Nikes.

Nagayoshi-san had encouraged me to do the interview. "It will be good for Miyama, and for Kagoshima to know that you are here," he said. "Most people have never met a foreigner, you know."

But after the show I became even more of a curiosity and an outsider. Just a few weeks ago an old couple wandered into the yard. I jumped up to greet them.

"Where is she?" asked the old man.

"Yes, we came all the way from Sendai," added his wife. "We want to see the gaijin who makes pots."

"Is it true she can eat tōfu?"

I was about to introduce myself when the old woman asked again, peering about the yard. I realized that she could barely see. Since I was speaking Japanese, she assumed that I couldn't possibly be the gaijin.

"Come right this way," I said, and took them to the front of the house, then slipped back into the workshop. When Nagayoshi-san led them back, I smiled as if I had never moved from my work. They looked over to where I sat with great interest, nodded a few times in approval, then ambled back out into the lane.

That night I complained to the Nagayoshis about all the visitors that were coming to see me; I couldn't get any work done, and I felt constantly on display. Reiko scolded me soundly. "Think of all the nice things people have done for you just because you are a foreigner!" She was right. People flooded me with gifts. At the camera store I received film at half the price, and when I bought mompei shopkeepers gave me a discount. I determined to be more patient.

But now before the carpenters I suddenly feel foolish, serving tea and smiling quietly like a Japanese wife. "Yes. Me a foreigner. I come from America. Japan is nice," I answer slowly, in polite, deliberately broken Japanese. Nagayoshi-san looks at me in surprise. Immediately the questions stop. The headman looks down into his teacup, and the sunny yard is peaceful and quiet again; three pots of tea and both loaves of brown cake disappear. Promptly at 10:15 the ringing of hammers and crowbars resumes.

At noon Nagayoshi-san and I eat a lunch of hot noodles in silence. When we are done he suddenly leans over and turns off the TV.

"Have you decided on your entry?" he asks, rubbing his mud-spattered glasses vigorously with a small towel.

"Not quite," I explain. "I've got a few designs, but . . ."

"Good, shall I look at them?"

"Yes, I'll get them ready," I answer quickly. Only three weeks remain before the exhibition entries are due.

In the warm afternoon sun the four slip-glazed cups glisten like fresh snow. Looking over the group, each cup carved with bands of geometric design, Nagayoshi-san nods and comments briefly.

"Simple is good. Too much design gets noisy. But don't be indecisive. Carve in deep, big. Anyhow, do your own work this afternoon." Today his informal joking manner has vanished. Carefully brushing off crumbs of clay left over from trimming, I sort the cups by size and weight. Wherever possible I divide them into groups of seven. I want a set of five and have to allow for accidents and discoloration from atmospheric changes in the kiln. Soon five sets of seven line the boards. I stir the bucket of freshly sieved white slip, finally ready to begin.

"*Konnichiwa*," an abrupt voice calls from over my shoulder in gruff local dialect. "Hey, where's your teacher?"

Turning around, I almost bump into the thin, blue-clad figure of Sataro-san. Usually smiling and cracking jokes, today he too seems serious. He stands tall, with the full seniority of his status as the oldest master potter in Miyama. "*Hai.*" I bow quickly, and run to call my teacher from inside, where he is talking to the carpenters. With a look of concern, Nagayoshi-san rushes outside. Relations between the two workshops and potters are friendly, but the visit of one master potter to another is not a casual event. I put on hot water and grab Reiko's best can of new tea. Under Sataro-san's cup I place the wooden saucer reserved for guests. I rummage through the glass-paned cupboards for crackers, sweet seaweed and salted plums. I lay out everything in separate dishes and make my way slowly back into the workshop.

Arms folded, face tight, Sataro explains his visit. Pouring tea, I catch fragments of the conversation.

"What's this I hear about a newspaper calling your work Naeshirogawa pottery?" Sataro-san says quickly. Apparently a Fukuoka newspaper has printed the news that Nagayoshi-san's donation of a large bowl to a charity organization last month was "Naeshirogawa kuromon," the traditional black pottery of the village. As a native and resident of Kagoshima, Nagayoshi-san produces "Satsuma" pottery, made in the former province of Satsuma, the pre-Meiji name for Kagoshima. Whether he is a "Naeshirogawa" potter, however, is a matter of perspective. He produces pottery in that village, the old name for Miyama, and he works in the dark, iron-rich clays of kuromon potters. But Nagayoshi-san does not use local clay, he is not Korean in heritage, and his work is modern. Thus, according to strict folkcraft standards, he is neither a "traditional" nor a "Naeshirogawa kuromon" potter. With newspaper reporters and at ceramics competitions, Nagayoshi-san is careful to state that he is a first-generation "Satsuma" potter only. He was unaware of this particular mistake, but it seems that Araki-san and Chin Jukan have complained to Sataro-san about the article. As a village elder, Sataro-san must talk to Nagayoshi-san, and he is clearly displeased with his mission.

I watch Nagayoshi-san carefully. Though underneath he must be steaming like Sakurajima, no anger shows. In a village as small as Miyama, all must get along. And Sataro-san is Nagayoshi-san's *sempai*, senior; when Sataro-san speaks Nagayoshi-san responds with rapid bows of his head and a prompt *hai*. Apologizing, he fiddles nervously with his wool hat, occasionally sweeping one hand through his thick gray hair. He insists on calling the newspaper company at once. While Nagayoshi-san makes the phone call, Sataro-san looks suddenly relaxed, even slightly bored. He chews his gums as if rolling a wad of chewing tobacco and glances at my line of cups. His eyes begin to droop. After pouring another round of tea, I slip back outside.

When four cups are dipped and gleaming white on the board, I cover the bucket of white clay slip and set them out to dry. If the thin-walled cups, already weakened by trimming, are not dried enough, they will collapse under the weight of the slip. But if the cups are too hard, the slip will not bond, and will peel off like old paint. The sun feels suddenly hot through my light sweater. I cover the remaining cups with a damp cloth and set the four glazed pieces in partial sun to dry.

"*Konnichiwa.*" The traveling bank man in his gray suit

makes his way to the front door. I run after him, explaining that the lady of the house is away. As quietly as he has come, he glides serenely away, his money bag, bulging with collected bank deposits, carried loosely in hand. By the front entrance I notice that the large bound cardboard boxes of a pottery shipment still wait to be picked up. Usually the delivery men in brown uniforms roar up in their narrow white truck before noon. The boxes of pottery are due in Tokyo in forty-eight hours. Before I get a chance to look at my cups another "*Konnichiwa*" sounds: the stout, smiling traveling salesman has arrived. The Japanese version of AMCO, his company sells everything from dried seaweed to mammoth bottles of drain cleaner door to door. Today he carries a bottle of rice vinegar, packets of seaweed and a package of paper towels. Do I want any soap this month? He has a good deal on dried fish.

"Sorry, but Okusan isn't home today. Please come tomorrow. Thank you. *Sayonara*," I say and throw the packages in the kitchen.

Just as I am heading back outside, the door opens and a cheerful round face peeks into the kitchen.

"Hey, what are you doing? You look like an okusan in there! Those carpenters got the whole wall quick, didn't they? Have you been working on your exhibition entry?"

It is Miwako, the potter Kubo-san's wife, dressed in a red running suit and pink Nikes. Laying down a plastic sack of fern heads and the edible stems of *tsuwa*, a wild broad-leafed plant, she laughs and takes a seat on the entryway step. She is on her way to Ijuin, where there is a sale on work pants and sports shoes. Do I want anything?

"No, thanks," I say, squatting down on my heels to talk. The last time I went to a sale with Miwako she had insisted that I buy a pair of hot-pink sweat pants. According to Miwako my dark clothes were too solemn, I dressed like an obāsan; a young girl like me should wear bright pink and red. I haven't worn the sweat pants once.

"What about a run?" she continues.

"Sorry. I wish I could, but Reiko is away, it's really busy around here." Miwako laughs. Her eyes are shadowed green, her lips bright pink; she will not even go to the supermarket without makeup. We arrange to meet on Sunday afternoon to run to a nearby hot spring on the coast. In between helping in the pottery, running the house, carting her daughter Ayumi to daily *kendō* (fencing) practice, weekly Japanese dance lessons or English class, Miwako trains for marathons.

At the hedge, I see Miwako off and notice a stooped figure down the lane bending under the weight of a thin yoke with two wooden buckets suspended at either end. Nagata-san moves slowly down the road toward her rice paddies. Though most rice growers have switched to chemical fertilizer, she continues to recycle her outhouse deposits. Sour sulfurous fumes rise from the wooden buckets.

Back home in upstate New York, spring has begun as well. The orchard rows should be thick with prunings and brush, the small pond ringing with tiny peepers calling for mates, and deep in the woods the swamp is carpeted with the red-purple shoots of skunk cabbage. How did winter pass so quickly? I practice small plates now. Hundreds of my teacups and rice bowls have been fired and sold.

Suddenly the telephone rings. I run to answer and take a long order for bowls. It rings again. This time it is Nagayoshi-san's friend Muraoka-san, a potter from Ijuin. The spring rice-planting festivals have begun to the south; do I want to go next weekend? I eagerly accept, mentally counting the days until my cups are due. The kitchen clock reads 2:45. Almost time for tea. No time to bicycle to the Kirin store for more cakes. I put the kettle on, hoping that today no guests appear.

"*Yōka, yōka, sayonara.*" Sataro-san nods and grins as he steps out from the workshop. He strides lightly into the sunlight, eyes squinting in the glare, then stops at the table to look over my cups. "*Hayasugita yo!* Too fast!" He points to where four cups have crumbled under the weight of the slip, their too-wet sides collapsing them like toppled snowmen. Luckily I have many more.

"The noborigama firing will be soon," Sataro-san continues. "The paddle builder has already begun work. Watching him would be good study, even if you do make these kinds of pots. If your teacher doesn't need you, ask if you can come over." Surprised at his generosity, I nod eagerly. Nagayoshi-san comes out from the workshop with a board of finished cups balanced lightly on one palm at his shoulder. After several stiff bows, Sataro-san quickly leaves. From across the village the 3:00 chimes sound.

No cups today, there won't be time to let them dry enough to slip-glaze before catching the bus to Unamoto. Once again the reality of "every day"—not the mingei ideal—has gotten in the way. "Nature, cooperation, tradition," indeed. With a sigh, I carry the whole board back into the holding room. I look toward my teacher. Despite the interrupted workday and his own imminent deadline for the exhibition, his movements in the warm sun are light and quick, cheerful. He hums a bar from his favorite koto song and pulls up stools for tea. I linger a minute, watching in the strong sun, then go to get tea and call the carpenters. By the time tea is over it is almost time to clean up and get ready to go. Promptly at 6:05,

Nagayoshi-san and I grab towels and rush down the lane to catch the green-and-yellow bus for Unamoto at the corner.

Steam rises from the murky green bath in gentle clouds. I test the water up to my ankle and then jerk it out. My foot is a bright, glistening red. All around the blue-tiled room dark eyes are watching. One old woman goes to get her glasses, peering out through the steamy frames. Reiko laughs and eases into the scorching sulfurous hot spring. I try again, this time with my toe, but still the water feels hot enough to brew tea. I retreat to the faucets lining the room and douse my whole body once more with tepid water.

Public bath etiquette dictates that one rinses first, dips into the hot water for a minute and then gets out for a thorough scrub. Once completely soaped down and rinsed, you slip into the large hot tub, wide enough for thirty to sit in without crowding. I was introduced to the Unamoto hot spring a year ago, when I accompanied my teacher's mother into the public bath on New Year's Day. I had no idea of bathing etiquette but followed the old woman, first washing and then sinking slowly into the bath. Around the edge of the pool, two obāsan took turns scrubbing and massaging each other's back. Although the tub was almost empty when we arrived, by the time we had both slipped into the green mineral water, so many women had gathered to sit and stare that we were wedged in like fresh sardines. The bath manager, a stooped old man in his seventies, suddenly walked in; curiously, all the faucets needed immediate attention. I sank further down into the hot green water, letting only my red face and blue gaijin eyes show.

Today the bath is again packed with women and children. By the time I have succeeded in dipping into the tub, a group of six children have lined up against the edge to watch the gaijin bathe. Though adults are separated into men's and women's sections by a low wall, kids wander freely from one side to the other. They stare like a line of solemn wide-eyed dolls.

"*Konnichiwa,*" I say. They run laughing and screaming to the far end of the room, only to creep back slowly, like the Miyama cats. I smile and sink down into the water. The muscles in my back, sore from the afternoon's rush, relax in the steaming bath. My hands bob along the surface like reeds. I think back to Miyama's silver predawn streets. My own unfinished work today no longer matters. A puff of cool air brushes my cheek, petals of steam curl up from the water. I close my eyes and watch small white cups and random geometric designs swirl in clouds of heat and rising steam.

Fire in the kiln, stacked kuromon
in orange flames ash falls, softly
over green bamboo

THIS MONDAY SATARO SAMEJIMA,
master potter of traditional kuromon,
called at breakfast to say that his workshop will unload the long noborigama,
which finished firing two days ago.
For the past two weeks I have been
helping at the Sataro workshop, bundling firewood, carrying pottery to the
kiln and assisting in the loading of the
long five-chamber kiln. Sataro-san had
invited me to participate and my
teacher had thought it an opportunity I
shouldn't miss.

Sataro-san's five-chamber brick kiln
is the last climbing kiln used regularly
in the village. Noborigama technology,
brought to Japan by Korean potters in
the sixteenth century, had marked an
important advance for Japanese pottery. Before, potters in Japan had fired

one-chamber tunnel kilns, much less efficient for high-temperature firing. Compared with modern gas and electric kilns, however, the wood-fired noborigama are expensive. Roughly three hundred bundles of wood are needed for one firing—two hundred to feed the fire from the kiln's mouth and twenty to twenty-five for firing each successive chamber. Bundling the wood had taken two full mornings with everybody working together.

Gimp-legged Kodama-san, who works alone to produce large kuromon vats and planters, used to fire his long kiln yearly. Although he took up pottery only in 1945, when he was repatriated from Taiwan, Kodama's heritage is Korean. His grandfather had been a kuromon potter, and Kodama is skilled in *tataki*—paddle-building. Last fall I often saw his small white truck parked above the ridge where he cut firewood for the kiln. But his work schedule has become erratic. "*Kotoshiwa dame.* This year is bad," he had said with a twisted smile when I asked him about his kiln. As in many of the potteries, business in the small back-alley Kodama workshop has tailed off. This year he will not fire his kiln at all.

I had a vested interest in participating in the noborigama. Before apprenticing to Nagayoshi-san, I had practiced kick wheel at the Sataro workshop. It had been Sataro-san's idea—since I was so interested in "the old Miyama," why didn't I learn the old pottery-making techniques? He would teach me the way it was really done. For four weeks I threw sturdy Sataro workshop teacups on a wheel powered by kicking with my right foot and pulling with my left. At the end of the month my calf muscles ached, but dozens of mingei-style teacups filled the storage rack; Sataro-san had decided they would be fired in the next noborigama.

The way to the Sataro workshop takes me down a narrow

lane, past the bamboo grove and Shigenobu Obāsan's house.
Today the entrance to her kitchen is strung with necklaces
of drying tangerine peels and ivory lengths of twisted white
radish. Bent over in a loose brown kimono, she looks a part
of the landscape. While she leans over her garden, pulling up
shriveled fall vines of sweet potatoes and limp white radish,
cabbage and remnants of sweet peas, I slip by unnoticed.

When I arrive at the workshop Sataro-san himself is outside
in the entrance area making glaze. He pours buckets of rust-
colored water through a sieve into large wide-rimmed water
vats made by his grandfather. In the corner on a bag of clay
a fat yellow cat basks in the sunlight.

Sataro-san still makes the simple ash and clay glazes of his
Korean ancestors—*kuro* (black) and *soba* (greenish yellow)—
by traditional methods. To make kuro glaze, iron-rich sand
or crushed rock is soaked in water until the muddy red iron
and traces of feldspar are released. This iron-saturated water
is then carefully sieved and left to stand. The iron precipitate
that settles will be mixed with wood ash and water. Good
ban, iron-rich sand or rock for kuro, is always in demand.
For the greenish-yellow soba glaze, a yellow clay is mixed
with ash and water.

When Sataro-san was seven his mother died, and he remembers many boyhood days helping his father, who
worked alone. After high school he learned tataki from his
uncle, Samejima Tsukasa, then went to Kyoto to study glazes
at the National Ceramics Laboratory. On his return he joined
his father's workshop. Large pots were sent by horseback to
Sendai and Kushikino for a monthly fair. But smaller pottery,
such as choka, they carried house to house, in neighboring
towns and hamlets, bartering and selling. At that time a large
water vat sold for fifty or sixty *sen*—in those days roughly

the price of ten pounds of rice. Today a large hand-built water vat sells for several hundred U.S. dollars.

Sataro-san's jaw tightens when he mentions the 1930's. "We never had free time. Every day after school I helped my father in the pottery. Some days I never even went to school," he says, crossing his arms. "Young people today don't know what it means to really work." In 1950 Sataro-san saw his first television show. He remembers crowding into a room to watch the small black-and-white set. Eventually he got a projector and showed movies at the village orphanage.

"In the old days people didn't worry about how a pot looked," said Sataro-san. "They didn't worry if it was black or brown, as long as you could use it. In the old days kuromon was made for you or me, for everybody. It was all the same and was for everyone! Now people want to make fancy pots—modern pottery—I don't understand it!"

According to Sataro-san, the mingei founder Yanagi Sōetsu sometimes visited the Sataro workshop to buy pottery from his father. Sataro-san himself is a staunch believer in the movement. He subscribes to the monthly *Mingei* magazine and wears traditional indigo work clothes, but his observance of mingei ideals is not superficial. He makes his own glaze from scratch, and still uses local clay. Even today, bowls and plates from the Sataro workshop remain unglazed on the rim, a characteristic of Korean folk pottery. Kuromon from the Sataro workshop is famous in mingei stores across Japan, and the workshop is listed in international kiln guides. Sataro-san can afford to hire apprentice-workers, who are paid a weekly wage to throw a progression of teacups, bowls, plates, sake holders and choka, in precisely that order. He will not allow any "strange, new pottery things" in his workshop, and in keeping with the mingei ideal of the "unknown craftsman," the pottery is signed only with the "Naeshiro-gawa pottery" mark.

I visited the shrine with Sataro-san during the October festival, when he is honored as the oldest working pottery master and, on behalf of the other potters, offers the ritual branch of *sasaki*. The kami-sama of the village shrine is said to be a *yakimono no kami-sama*—"pottery god"—who looks after the well-being of the potters, kilns and workshops in Miyama. We knelt without speaking inside the weathered board structure. In the corner the Shintō priest sat swaddled in his white robes, beating a slow, steady rhythm on a small white drum as villagers, mostly older men, entered. We sat seiza, as the priest banged faster and faster, moaning with the crescendo. No one moved in the silence that followed. A prayer was read, and all heads before me touched the floor in a long bow; then one by one we rose to receive potato liquor from the priest. The small white shiromon cup was marked in gold with the Shimazu crest.

Sataro-san placed his ceremonial branch before the closed doors to the inner shrine and nodded to the priest's attendant, who pushed a similar branch in my direction. Taking up the offering, my hands crossed palm over palm, I went forward awkwardly. Sitting seiza had cut off the circulation to my feet and my ankles were numb. In front of the closed wooden doors I fumbled through what I could remember of the series of bows, nods, claps and pauses that accompanied the offering, then quickly returned to my place. As suddenly and abruptly as they had begun, the drumbeats ceased. The ceremony was over. Sataro-san and I walked slowly down the hill.

At the last stone gate he turned to me. "Now that you have given to the kami-sama it will be a good year for you.

You know, you might even find a husband." With a sly grin and a hasty "*Sayonara*," he strode off down the path and was gone, his thin figure lost in evening light and the green hedge.

Today Sataro-san works slowly, bending over the vats in the warm sun. "You'd better hurry in. Everyone's waiting for you," he says gruffly. I walk back toward the long shed where pottery is made and stored before firing. The glass-paned doors to the workshop slide open with a familiar screech. To the left in a separate room Arima-san sits cross-legged before a wheel, wearing tan sweat pants and a blue T-shirt. From a small radio by his wheel comes the twanging of samisen music as the long board steadily fills with cylindrical flower holders. Each cylinder is a perfect ten-inch column of clay.

Arima-san's mother is Sataro-san's only sister. She works in the Sataro workshop now, helping glaze and pack pottery, as well as finish choka, deftly twisting lengths of soaked vine into sturdy handles. As a child, however, she wasn't allowed to work in the pottery. When no one was around she would sneak in and play on the wheels. But when her father found out he was furious. Women pounded clay, mixed glazes, and carried the heavy baskets of pottery to and from the kiln. But pottery-making and firing were reserved for men.

Later she married Arima Takao, a Miyama native from the Korean family Ri, who works in shiromon. Of their eight children only this Arima-san has become a potter. And although he began studying at seventeen in his father's shiromon workshop, he prefers the kuromon tradition of his uncle. Since Sataro-san has no children of his own, Arima-san will take over the workshop. It is expected that his newborn son, Hiroaki, will continue after him. Now in his thirties, Arima-san is the main thrower in the workshop. Each movement of his hands is steady, precise and light. Yet as the slick red clay rises even and straight, he pauses for a moment and then pulls a slight twist or warp into the form. "It's too perfect otherwise," he says with a touch of a smile.

Against the window-lined wall of the inner room, two apprentices work at adjoining electric wheels. Graduates of the Kagoshima prefecture ceramics trade school, they sit upright, legs extended. Toriyama-san, who wears the top half of a blue cotton kendō uniform over his blue jeans, was once a hospital clinician in Kagoshima City. He began pottery in a hobby class in Kagoshima City and has been working at the Sataro workshop for the past two years. Next spring he plans to open his own workshop in a nearby town, where his parents run the local fish store. Working quickly, his small electric wheel grinding under the speed, Toriyama-san pulls up ball after ball of the red clay into choka. But the form isn't right and, dissatisfied, he crushes many. To his right works Okada-san, the younger of the two, who began in the Sataro workshop six months ago.

Fragments of angry bickering in Kagoshima ben drift in through the windows; Sataro-san and his wife are arguing over the unloading.

"Well, look who's here," a bright voice pipes up from the rear. Yamanaka-san grins as she settles down at her workplace next to the wheels. A slim, handsome woman in her late thirties, she has quick, capable hands and an even faster tongue. Divorced many years ago, she returned to her parents' house in Miyama to raise her son, who is now in high school. She began as a general helper in the workshop several years ago, and supplements her income by working nights in a *sunakku*, a hostess bar in Unamoto. Today she is busy finishing teapots. Each foot or spout is carefully shaped by pressing into a mold and then trimmed before attaching.

"I have the morning free," I tell her. "I've come to help."

"Good, then you can come over for lunch. I have fresh bamboo shoots—dug them yesterday."

"Hey, what about me?" says Toriyama-san, slowing his wheel.

"No men allowed," she answers, sticking out her tongue. We go out into the yard, arms linked like schoolgirls.

Loading five months' worth of pottery had been a long, tiring process that took three days. I worked with Arima-san on the third chamber. After hours of meticulous work, the narrow brick cavern of the third chamber was crammed with a honeycomb of pottery: thirty large flower pots, forty saya (cylindrical containers of fireclay in which pots are stacked to protect them from direct contact with the flames) filled with rice bowls, sake cups, teacups, plates and small choka, two large bowls, sixteen flower holders, sixty teapots, and countless sake cups and other small items. Our aim was to set the individual pots in level, or at a bit of a slant against the slope of the hill. This is particularly important for pots in the first chamber, which are exposed to direct flames from the firebox—an inferno of flame and heat that reaches up to 1,300 degrees centigrade. The side of the pot facing downward will become the shōmen, or front; this side will meet the fire as it rushes up the slope and through the kiln, becoming "flashed" with ash deposits, which fuse to the pot's surface as glaze.

After a morning of loading, we paused to examine our work. Out of the jumble and jagged mess of broken brick and shelf emerged a beautiful architecture of stacked pots.

Grouped inside the old kiln, now crusted with layers of melted ash and cinder, the smooth, clean-lined pottery coated with a layer of beige-green glaze sat like a clutch of giant eggs. Suddenly, a high-pitched voice broke our reverie. "They're all slanting to one side. They'll fall over in the fire! Do it again—and this time, take the long road and walk it slow," scolded Sataro-san, poking his head into the chamber. We had accounted for the slope of the hill, but the entire kiln shelf was slightly tilted to the right. For the first time, Arima-san looked annoyed. "*Hai*," he answered slowly, sucking air in through his teeth. Obeying Sataro-san's request meant handing out each pot one by one and shifting each of the bottom supports one quarter inch to the right; gaining this precision amid the chaos of broken brick would take the rest of the day.

Last to be loaded were the two large bowls made by Ike-noue-san, Miyama's last itinerant shokunin. For a month the old man had worked at the Sataro workshop, paddle-building large vats, bowls and flower pots for the noborigama. Gaunt-cheeked and thin in loose khaki work clothes and a blue baseball cap, an unlit cigarette half dangling from his lips, Ikenoue-san could have been an American farmer. He is one of the last craftsmen in the village skilled in the Korean techniques of paddle-building. When he is gone, only Arima-san will carry on the tataki skills, said to take ten years to master. Yet this "unknown craftsman" barely ekes out a living, farming and making pots on commission for Sataro-san. Prominent, well-worn hands mark him as a potter, and as he works he holds them like sturdy tools. When he cuts a small gash in his knuckle, no pain registers—damn blood in the way, he keeps working. Watching him, my own hands hurt. On his feet he wears the blue cloven-toed shoes worn by farmers in the rice paddies. He is so slight that seated before the wheel he has to hunch forward to reach the mound of dark red clay.

Although Ikenoue-san may not feel Korean, his hands make "Korean" pots. One morning I watched him make large bowls. He ripped off a chunk of clay, which he slapped down on the wheel. Taking up a long wooden mallet, he pounded the red clay with a rough, blunt confidence, his right foot slowly kicking the wheel. With each blow the clay sank into a low disk, until a thick pancake circled on the wheel. His practiced hands grasped another even handful from the waiting mound of dark red clay. He rolled a rough ball between his palms until a long, thick tail of clay hung downward. When the coil was about eighteen inches long, he applied it to the base with twisting motions of one hand, supporting it from the outside with the palm of the other. A rough cylinder rose. He paused, pursing his mouth as he smoothed out the seam in the inner wall with his knuckle.

When the thick walls were several hand-widths high, he was ready to begin the process of paddling and shaping. Taking up a short wooden paddle (*shure*) in his right hand and a mushroom-shaped wooden anvil (*toke*) in his left, he leaned back over the wheel. Inside the pot, he used the toke tool to support the sides against the blows of the shure on the exterior. The hollow sound of pounding filled the workshop. He talked to the growing pot, he sang a gruff, half-whistled tune. It seemed to me the very force of the blows ought to smash the entire mass into red mush. I watched for a mistake, a misplaced blow. But the mallet struck the clay wall just over the molding tool, and the walls of the pot grew higher and thinner until Ikenoue-san himself seemed dwarfed by them. Within fifteen minutes, a bowl the size of a birdbath turned slowly on the wheel. Smiling for the first time, Ikenoue-san looked less a craftsman than a gnome.

A hot kettle was brought up from its nest of red coals in the hibachi under the table, but Ikenoue-san ignored the tea and me, stopping only to light another cigarette. He took up two thin wooden ribs and began carefully scraping the walls of the bowl, the cigarette dangling from his pursed lips. Then he pried off the bowl and its supporting wooden bat with a bamboo knife. The entire process had taken thirty minutes. He slowly scraped red clay out from under his thumbnail and reached for another hunk of clay.

By day's end sixteen identical bowls stood in the drying room, and in two weeks Ikenoue-san produced ninety-three flower stands, ten large bowls, eight flower pots, and ten large water vats. As each piece came off the wheel Sataro-san himself gingerly carried it off to the holding room. Until the pots were safely glazed and stacked in the kiln, he was as protective as an old troll.

Across the East China Sea in Korea, the sound of tataki paddling fills the streets of entire pottery towns. Modern-day Korean potters use similar skills to paddle-build huge black vats called *onggi* for the storage of *kimchi*, spicy Korean pickles. Months before, I had traveled from village to village in Korea's South Cholla province, in search of clues as to the roots of Miyama potters. Armed with a Korean dictionary and an article that explained the transport of the first Korean potters in 1597 and the subsequent founding of Naeshiro-gawa, I went to many onggi workshops. The potters I met were large burly men with arms like construction workers' from building and carrying the large, heavy vats. My Korean dictionary was hardly needed, as everyone over forty had learned Japanese during the occupation. Potters and workshop owners were eager to talk about Miyama, and all were familiar with the sixteenth-century "pottery wars."

According to local histories, during the seventeenth-century religious persecution in Korea, many Christians and other state criminals were smuggled in and out of towns by onggi potters who hid them in their larger pots. More than one Korean Catholic moved throughout the countryside in the guise of an onggi peddler. Even today it is clear from the rough working and living conditions that onggi potters occupy a low social status in modern Korea, and none of the potters I met wanted their sons to continue in the trade. As in Japan, changing ways of life have made much functional pottery obsolete. And in Korea, there has been no mingei movement to stir up nostalgia and a market for vanishing crafts.

Still, the potters I met worked with pride. At one busy workshop near Kwangju, when they heard that I was studying ceramics in Japan, the young men immediately lined up to show off their skills. "You won't find skills like this in Japan!" a young man, who had just finished throwing a large jar on the kick wheel, exclaimed proudly. "You should study pottery here in Korea."

By the time I left, my pack held three black onggi, which I had been asked to carry back to the potters' "cousins across the sea." I gave the bowls to Sataro-san, and he stared at them keenly before speaking. "Did you say it was easy to find these workshops, and they spoke Japanese?" Then he leaned forward and asked in a low, excited whisper, "How much did you say it cost, your trip to Korea?" Later each bowl was labeled and carefully placed upstairs in the small

Naeshirogawa People's Museum above the showroom. There they sat among generations of kuromon vats and jars, and displays of old tools—samples from the homeland.

The firing of a kiln is fraught with superstitions. In Miyama, the kiln kami-sama, like the supreme Shintō deity and the progenitrix of the Japanese people, Amaterasu, is said to be female. But mortal women of menstrual age as well as people who have recently been to a funeral are believed to make the kiln kami-sama jealous. According to one village story a man who had been to a funeral came by a firing kiln. No matter how many hours the potters labored, they couldn't make the kiln reach temperature. Only when he was told to leave was the firing saved.

Sataro-san had begun the fire in the mouth of the kiln at 6:00 that morning. Alone, he offered salt, rice and sake in small black cups, then made a quick prayer to the kiln's kami-sama for a safe firing. When I arrived a few hours later, I noticed that a ring had been drawn in the dirt around the kiln. Sataro-san's okusan shrilly warned me not to step across. Confused, I turned to Arima-san. "Oh, it's an old custom, from now on you can't go near the kiln—only men. It can't be helped," he added apologetically. "It's tradition." I felt shocked and betrayed. All week I had helped to carry pottery, load the kiln and bundle firewood. But now, at the most critical stage of the process, I was excluded. It seemed a convenient belief, this jealous kiln-god story—and a low blow.

That night when I told Nagayoshi-san and Reiko they looked concerned. "Well, that's Miyama for you. Traditional!" said Reiko. I smiled weakly, accepting a cup of tea. "When you get back to America, you can build your own kiln—no men allowed!" Nagayoshi-san joked. But there was nothing to be done. I was a visitor, after all; none of my beliefs were going to change the sexism of centuries. I could either sulk and stay away, missing out on the firing, or abide by the restrictions. I decided to accept my role of observer.

When the last vats and bowls had been loaded, the doors to each chamber bricked shut, a small fire was lit in the mouth of the long kiln. Once lit, the fire takes twenty hours to attain a bed of coals that will maintain the fire at a constant 900–1,000 degrees centigrade. When a high enough temperature is reached, wood is thrown in to entice the flame upwards. Fire chases after the wood, hungering for new fuel and jumping over the fire wall to enter the next chamber. A strong draft, running from the kiln's mouth up through the chimney at the opposite end, furnishes oxygen for combustion and pulls the fire on. In addition, the bricks themselves radiate heat, further warming the air, which creates currents that help pull the fire onward. That heat also keeps the pottery in the lower chambers from sudden cooling as the fire moves up into the next chamber.

Moving the fire is a critical, delicate process. Potters must throw wood in evenly from both sides or the fire will wander inside the kiln, overfiring some pots, underfiring others. Once fire enters the first chamber, they must throw in enough wood or the fire retreats, sulking in the firebox while pots in the first chamber crack from sudden cooling. If they add too much wood, however, the fire consumes the pots, warping and twisting them in intense bursts of heat.

Over the ridge at the site of the oldest communal kiln lies an entire hillside of failures, the village pottery dump. Pots that never made it—bowls fused to plates, teacups slumping and warped from heat, enormous storage vats split down the center like ripe melons, homes now to sleeping snakes and hairy, yellow-bellied spiders.

The fire is about to take the critical jump into the first chamber. Yamanaka-san and Sataro-san's wife are standing fifteen feet from the mouth of the kiln, armed with a thermos of hot water for tea and plates of rice cakes and pickles, while Sataro-san crouches by the mouth of the firebox, his small silhouette lithe and spry in the orange glow behind him. "*Yōka! Yōka!*" he shouts. Two apprentices spring to the left side of the kiln, while Arima-san and Sataro-san move to the right. "*Iku yo!* It's going!" Arima calls across the kiln, adding five sticks of firewood to the first chamber. "Five sticks," comes the response from the other side of the kiln. From that point on, the firing is a continual dialogue between right side and left.

When Arima-san adds wood, the flames shoot out the top windows. A steady ring of fire surrounds the clay plugs on top. Tongues of flame spread over the kiln until it seems to want to crack apart. Fire bellows up from the firebox, moving through the center of the kiln in pursuit of the sticks of wood. Sweat beads on faces. With quick, stylized motions the men thrust wood into the kiln. Each throw stops just short of the bricked door so that the wood shoots in like an arrow. If the wood hits a saya, or a kiln shelf, the entire chamber of stacked pots can come tumbling down. When Arima-san feels that more fire is needed, he shouts again, "*Iku yo!* Going!" and adds another five or six sticks of wood. On the far side of the kiln the two apprentices respond to his call in kind. Soon they add wood every fifteen minutes. The fire moves up, fast and even. When the first flames subside, the kiln belches out black smoke, and they throw in wood faster, now at five- or ten-minute intervals.

By the following evening, fire rages in the third chamber. The area below the kiln is littered with teacups and candy wrappers. Half of the bundled wood has burned. Sataro-san watches like a director, arms akimbo, a bottle of shōchū at his side. Every so often he glances to where Arima-san crouches in the orange glow and nods approvingly. The first test ring of doughnut-shaped glazed clay is pulled out with an orange rod. No pyrometers or test cones register the kiln temperature. Firing a kiln, says Sataro-san, takes a certain *kan*—"sense"—plus *keiken*—"experience." One must watch the way the fuel is burning, the color of the flames. When they burn white and the pots glisten, reflecting shadows, the kiln is reaching temperature.

At 10:00 P.M. Arima-san pulls out another test ring from the last chamber. When it cools it gleams a dark brown, meaning that the glaze has melted and fused to the pot's surface, but is not yet mature; when the glaze is black, the kiln is ready. Inside, the flames are swirling, incoherent waves of light touched with smoke and heat. When short chunks of wood are added, the fire bursts forth, threatening to consume the clay plugs covering the stokeholes. Arima-san gives the fire a few minutes to quiet and looks inside. The inner chamber is clear and white; the pots gleam against the night.

"It's almost time, Uncle," says Arima-san quietly. But Sataro-san looks and shouts, "Slow it down, it's too fast!" Arima-san nods and slows his additions of wood, according his uncle infinite respect. In fifteen minutes Sataro-san is back by the kiln, impatient and eager. Arima-san hands him a stick of wood, which he hurls into the kiln, and then runs around to check the other side. The fire rages in the third chamber. By this time I have edged so close that I sit on a pile of firewood, still outside the line, but if I leaned forward I could touch the hot kiln.

Arima-san leans to one side so that I can peer inside the kiln. I squint in the blast of yellow-white heat, feeling beads of sweat line my forehead. The inside of the kiln is a volcanic fissure of energy, light, heat. "More wood! more wood!" shouts Sataro-san, jumping back to this side of the kiln. "Hey, *you*!" he yells in my direction. "Wood!" I quickly pull up five sticks of wood and hand them to him. He pushes them through the stokehole and then squats beside Arima-san, peering into the flames. Next to the great kiln heaving with smoke and flame, the two men seem more like boys catching pond frogs than a master potter teaching his nephew the tradition of centuries. Sataro-san starts to sing a little jingle of his own making—"Ri-ra . . . ri-ra . . . ri-ra-kun"—adding the male form, *kun*, after my name. He looks at me perched on top of the firewood and starts to chuckle. Arima-san turns his head, catching my eye, and we all laugh, then are suddenly quiet. The hollow rushing sound of fire bellowing up the long kiln fills the night.

Half past midnight, after almost forty-three hours of continual tending, the fire is steady and bright, extending the entire length of the kiln. The last test ring is taken out and the glaze cools a shiny black. Arima-san wipes the sweat from his brow, his flannel shirt damp with sweat and streaked with ash. Although the others have taken breaks for sleep, he has stayed with the kiln throughout. "*Yaketa, yaketa—owari!* It's fired, it's fired—done!" shouts Sataro-san suddenly, breaking the silence. Stokeholes are quickly plugged, and everyone helps to push the remaining firewood back from the kiln.

"*Gokurōsama*—good work," we say to one another as we file out into cooling, star-filled night.

Now, two days after the firing, daylight streams over the kiln's lower end. Outside, the road is a bright yellow glare. By the entrance Okusan tends a fire of bamboo husks gathered from the road to make ash for glaze. Wisps of smoke trail across the blue sky like white string. It is almost noon. Box after box of black pottery has been carried into the lower display room for sorting. A pile of broken and warped pots grows in the corner. I am reminded of apple harvest at home: steady work, endless boxes of fruit, the bushel of spoiled apples in the corner.

Inside the dark shed, Sataro-san crouches beside the unbricked first chamber. Gingerly he hands out pots to his wife. Their surfaces are dull in places, spotted greenish-brown where wood ash has collected during firing. Old kuromon rarely fired coal-black, ranging in color from reddish brown to honey; iron was scarce and thick glazes tended to crack during firing. Only thirty years ago customers would not have bought these pieces, preferring the shiny, enamel black of postwar pottery, made with glazes darkened with manganese and fired in a gas kiln. But today, thanks to the mingei boom, folk pottery collectors will pay as much as double the price for wood-fired kuromon. Wealthier Kagoshima citizens, who can afford to build wooden Japanese-style houses, place the pottery in their tokonoma or in their formal gardens. Tea ceremony teachers vie for wood-fired black Satsuma, not only out of nostalgia for the past but also because in the world of tea no price is too high for ceramic ware that embodies the tea aesthetic of *wabi*—"simplicity and poverty."

Squinting toward a sunbeam, Sataro-san holds a small

choka up toward the window. Brushing off some remaining ash, he purses his mouth in concentration and readjusts his glasses. The black beret tips back. Everyone, even steady Arima-san, stops working to watch. Sataro-san ignores us, silently studying the black surface of the pot. Then, as if surprised by the quiet around him, he abruptly looks up, puts the pot down, and steps inside the kiln. Arima-san has been standing so stiff it seems he has forgotten to breathe. From within the kiln comes a high-pitched voice.

"*Yōka! Yōka!*"

May; month of camellia and bloom
azure sky and bamboo breeze
rustle of fern, tea harvest

Sᴜᴢᴜᴋɪ-ꜱᴀɴ, ɪɴ ᴀ ᴡɪᴅᴇ ꜱᴛʀᴀᴡ ʜᴀᴛ,
bends down over the narrow black tar
road, cracked and twisted where thick
bamboo shoots push toward April
light. Beside him, on her knees, is his
wife in her faded blue bonnet. On
either side frail bamboo poles hold the
living grove back, away from the road.
New shoots will grow twelve inches a
day, ten, twenty feet in two weeks,
pushing through gardens, roads, walk-
ways, anything in their way.

   Armed with short-handled sickles
and blades, the old couple attacks the
irreverent plants in a silent fury.
Whack. Rip. Whack. Splinters of bamboo shoot fly from their tools. I stand
in the warm sun and watch.

   "Ohayō gozaimasu."
   "Ohayō gozaimasu."

GREEN TEA

"Need some help?" I ask casually, in Kagoshima ben. For the first time both heads rise. Okusan lifts the rim of her blue bonnet to get a better look. "Ah . . . *hora* . . . Ri-ra-san!" she exclaims, sitting back on her heels and smiling. "*Yōka, yōka.* It's okay." She wipes her brow with the back of a gloved hand before resuming her work. Her husband, who has looked up only once during our exchange, continues his furious reaping. I step forward to pass by, but Okusan looks back up, her eyes bright. "Where are you going?" she asks suddenly.

"Oh, just a little way, over there."

"Over there?"

"Yes, that way."

"Ahh, I see, a walk," she says slowly, nodding her head.

"Yes, a walk, I guess," I answer vaguely, pointing ahead to no place in particular. After months in Miyama I have come to realize that not all questions require answers. It is not that I mind telling her where I am going, but by tomorrow the news would be spread across the village. She laughs and waves me on, then bends back over the road, her small blade hooking neatly around a stiff brown shoot. *Whack. Rip. Whack.*

I walk on, scuffling through the bits and pieces of twig and scattered bamboo. On either side of the road amid the tall spires of adult growth a few new shoots poke through the bracken and broken fern. Some are already chest-high, others still barely visible spikes, their tips protected by thick layers of husk. They butt through the ground with the insistence of goats. Soon they will lose their rough brown coverings and shoot up higher, faster, green now and, tasting the light, unstoppable. It is a continuous spring battle: bamboo versus Miyama villagers.

Last week, one lone spindly shoot burst through the dirt floor in the workshop and Nagayoshi-san put a flower pot around the base and left it. When guests came he told them it was his new houseplant. He cut off the new shoots to keep it low and bushy, like a bonsai. It kept on growing. He cut some more; it grew some more. Finally he took a sharp blade to the shoot; cutting it down took an hour.

Yet because of this weedlike growth, *take* is a ceaseless resource. In January when everything was cleaned for the New Year, we placed fresh bamboo poles across the outside faucet area as racks for glazing. My new measuring tools, like all others in the workshop and many of Nagayoshi-san's brushes, are made from the green wood. Bamboo shoots, known as *takenoko*—"bamboo child"—are edible. Stewed with tōfu, white radish, thick *kombu* seaweed and carrots, they become the standard winter stew called *oden*. Sweetened bamboo shoots appear at breakfast alongside bowls of miso soup, at lunch with scoops of steaming white rice. For dinner we devour the thick yellow slices like steak with bamboo chopsticks.

The giving and receiving of takenoko is a spring ritual, predictable as the cherry-blossom viewing in late March, or the daily exchange of information about volcanic ash. With a gentle bow, Suzuki-san's wife comes over with three or four long shoots every morning. Nagayoshi-san brings them in when he picks up the morning paper. Reiko looks at them warily. Preparation is a long process of boiling in rice-rinsing water to extract the bitterness, then flavoring with soy sauce and sweet rice wine. On Saturdays when I go to Kagoshima City to teach my English classes, Reiko hands me a bagful for my students; the boiled yellow meat is a country delicacy for city people. When I gave some to my ink painting (*sumie*) teacher, a tall, elegant woman who always wears dark red lipstick and a formal silk kimono, her husband was so pleased that he gave me a gift in return—a plastic wall clock in the shape of Sakurajima. On the back I made out the words "Compliments of Kagoshima Chamber of Commerce." My sumie teacher and her husband, who are quite wealthy, often give me small presents: a pink change purse from Kyoto, a miniature copy of a Japanese doll, a sake cup from Okinawa, an old silver fan. Even though they are clearly unwanted omiyage that someone had once given them, etiquette requires that I reciprocate somehow. I would stop along the way to the next class and buy some overpriced but beautifully wrapped rice-and-bean sweets. Once started, this cycle of gift-giving has no end and my pile of omiyage has grown. When Reiko discovered that I was buying a gift each week, she was shocked and insisted that I stop spending my own money. From then on she prepared something for me to take, usually a small assortment of sweets—leftovers from the boxes of teatime cakes pottery guests had brought.

Yesterday on the way home from town I passed Yamanaka-san from the Sataro workshop, to whom I gave the volcano-shaped clock. She promptly ran into her house and emerged with a bag of freshly dug takenoko. I gave the shoots to Reiko. She glared. Reiko gave them to customers, who were delighted, "Natsukashii!" they cried—"How nostalgic!"—and told stories of their mothers in the country who used to boil them every spring. In the evening Suzuki-san's wife with a soft bow brought more.

"Itte irasshai—go and come back," she calls when I reach the end of the lane. "Itte kimasu—I go and come," I answer, as expected, and continue on. The sounds of their energetic reaping fade and the bamboo grove ends, intersecting with open light and, to the left, a wide, freshly tilled and planted tobacco field. To the right on the corner is the single-story weathered-board home of Shigenobu-san. Like many Miyama obāsan, she lives alone. Her husband, once a famed shiromon carver, died two years ago, and all eight of their children left Miyama for jobs in major cities. It is a point of pride to Shigenobu-san that her children were educated, and have not become potters or farmers. One son, a schoolteacher in nearby Ibusuki, visits sometimes, but the others live too far away to return more often than on an occasional New Year's or at obon, the August festival of the dead. Shigenobu-san has lived to see the Depression, the war, postwar inflation, Japan's economic success, and now, in her early eighties, she says she doesn't mind living alone. "*Jiyū ga dekiru,*" she will say. "I can do what I want." Her house is dark and dusty. Dirty dishes fill the sink, and piles of papers lie everywhere. Only the boxes of fruit and other foods that her children send each month are piled neatly in one corner.

The other day I passed her house and, noticing that the sliding front doors were open, stepped in to say hello. Shigenobu-san sat waiting quietly on the raised entrance. She wore a long skirt as if on her way to town, but no shirt at all.

"Hello?" I said tentatively. She looked up with a wan smile.

"Oh, hello, I'm waiting for the mailman. Shall I make some tea?"

"Oh, no, not at all, sorry to trouble you," I said quickly, edging back out the door. It was once a common sight to see rural women, particularly obāsan, working in the fields bare-chested. But, like mixed bathing at the public baths, it has since been deemed "improper." A loud voice suddenly

sounded from the entrance. In the doorway stood a neighboring obāsan, dressed for work in the fields.

"Well, well, what's this?" she said, stepping in. Walking
over to Shigenobu-san she reached out and gave her a poke,
then whispered something in Kagoshima ben that made them
both break out laughing. "Oh, I am forgetful," said Shigenobu-san with a giggle, and slowly reached behind for a shirt.

To pass the time Shigenobu-san watches TV, visits with
friends, reads the paper every day and putters in her garden.
For a while she played gateball with the group of old people
who meet every morning on the community exercise field,
but she says she found it boring and quit. When she first met
me on the road in front of her house she immediately invited
me in for tea, and I go to see her sometimes. Each of my
visits she faithfully records in the small green notebook that
is her diary.

She has other rituals of her own invention. Before we sit
down for tea, which is usually cups of instant hot chocolate
with three teaspoons of white sugar, she carefully pries open
the package of whatever teatime sweets I have brought, and
then carries one over to the *butsudan*—the Buddhist altar.
Kneeling down before the gilded altar, she pushes aside the
fruit, cakes and other offerings, and places the sweet down
in front of a framed photograph of her late husband. Almost
every Miyama home has similar dark-framed photographs
of the late family elders next to the butsudan; many have
pictures of the Emperor as well.

"*Otō-chan . . . Amerika no musume ga mata kiyashta yo.* Daddy
dear . . . that girl from America has come to visit again,"
she calls in a mix of local dialect and standard Japanese, then
goes on to describe the weather, the gift of cakes that I have
brought, and what she has done that day. At first I was

alarmed. Whom was she talking to? Was this some prayer I wasn't supposed to hear? Should I leave? Was she perhaps senile? But I got used to these one-way conversations. Her direct manner of prayer-talk mirrored the way I had seen many villagers address the kami-sama at the village shrine. While ancestor worship is a declining concern for the younger generation, in Kagoshima many beliefs persist. In the August festival of obon, when the spirits of the dead are said to return, the usually crowded local beaches are not full, as it is believed that the returning spirits travel inland from the sea.

One early morning on the way back down from the shrine I met Shigenobu-san slowly climbing up the hill to her husband's grave. Carrying a tin bucket, two long-stemmed yellow chrysanthemums and a single-serving bottle of shōchū, she made her way slowly up the maze of gray markers lining the hillside. When I waved hello, she shouted for me to come down. "Shall we go together?" she said, handing me the bucket and taking my arm. Months before, a Tokyo anthropologist who had done fieldwork on Miyama had given me some cryptic advice. "If you want to learn about the old Miyama," he had said, "go to the graves—and listen." I had made it a habit to pass through the crowded cemetery on my morning loop through the village.

Scattered amid waist-high grass and thickets of low bamboo, the gravestones keep company with a colony of black pots. Squat wide-mouthed jars hold flowers and water; small cups hold shōchū and sake. By the grave of the famed kuromon potter Tanaka-san, two leaning urns mark his skill. In a thicket just below, Korean-style grave markers lie buried in bamboo and lichen. In the 1870's, when discrimination against Koreans flared, villagers tried to hide their origins, discarding the roofed Korean-style tombstones for upright

Japanese markers. Often I saw Miyama obāsan tending the graves; when they left, flowers, cigarettes, cups of liquor and dishes of rice, salt and water filled the hillside. But no one had ever invited me to come along.

Following Shigenobu-san that day, I climbed back up the hillside. When we reached a rectangular gray marker on a stone base, she promptly knelt down, clapped her hands twice, and began to murmur. She told her husband about the yellow chrysanthemums and jar of shōchū she had brought, about my coming to help, the latest news in the village. Holding the tin bucket, I waited awkwardly at a distance, gazing down over the village.

When she was done, she clapped her hands twice and slowly rose. "Now, the cleaning," she said matter-of-factly, and motioned for me to draw water from a nearby tap. While I poured buckets of water on the stone marker, washing away a thin layer of volcanic ash, Shigenobu-san poured out the shōchū and placed the flowers in two waiting black jugs. Before leaving, we lit two sticks of incense and placed them in the small blue bowl full of sand in front of the grave.

"Do you always bring shōchū and flowers?" I asked on the way down.

"Why, of course," she answered in surprise. "Don't you tend your graves in America?"

"Well, yes . . . but not quite the same way. Flowers, of course, but people don't usually leave liquor."

"Well, if I didn't, he'd be lonely," she said matter-of-factly. "And Otō-chan . . ." Her voice trailed off and she smiled fondly—"he did like to drink."

April gives way to May, bamboo gives way to tea. May is the month of *shincha*, the first tea. Every spring Yamanaka-san, who works six days a week, from eight to five, at the Sataro workshop, takes two weeks off from her job to help with the tea harvest. For generations her family has run the only tea-drying business in Miyama. Yamanaka-san's house is in the old style, with a mongamae entrance and a once ornate formal garden denoting old village wealth, but she insists that her family is of Japanese, not Korean, descent. Three times a year the long shed behind her home transforms into a tea-processing factory, but the first crop, the shincha, is considered the most delicious.

Tea was first cultivated in Japan with seeds brought from China in the late eighth century. Prior to the Edo period (1600–1868) it was a beverage known only to the ruling classes. Today, teatime in country villages such as Miyama is ten o'clock sharp in the morning and three in the afternoon. Cups of caffeine-rich green tea also appear at breakfast, lunch and dinner. Squat green rows of tea bushes line yards and gardens, and on the hillcrest below the shrine, narrow hedges of pruned tea stretch as straight and long as racetracks.

Once harvesting begins, the tea leaves must be immediately dried and processed. The factory will run twenty-four hours a day as long as villagers continue to bring the freshly picked leaves to the entrance. First they are weighed, then carefully separated into net bags and labeled by grower. The grades range from the expensive powdered *matcha* for the tea ceremony down to the coarse *bancha* for daily use. All Miyama villagers grow bancha, but each swears by the taste of his or her particular leaves. The tea is sent through a series of churning gas-heated drums for drying, then through cutters and brushlike tea rollers, all connected by a network of belts and gears. It enters the conveyer belt looking like a giraffe's green picnic, and emerges at the other end cut, dried and rolled into tiny balls that resemble freeze-dried vegetables.

Last month after morning services at the shrine the Shintō priest climbed into the back of a waiting blue Toyota truck, one hand still holding his conical black plastic priest's hat. The truck roared off, the priest's white robes flowing jauntily behind him, and stopped at the other end of the fields. From his perch the priest scattered rice and blessings over a waiting tea combine. He waved his wand of white paper over the new machine, read a prayer, and clapped solemnly. The farmer was elated.

In Kagoshima City one can buy green tea ice cream, Sno-cones, jelly, rolls and bread. Green tea is listed along with coffee and Coke at the McDonald's—popularly known as "Makkudonarudo." The Dunkin' Donuts store, popular among high school girls for its stylish "hatto pinku" decor, serves green tea and green tea doughnuts.

Drinking tea has many meanings, according to context. Accepting the tea offered by clerks in kimono shops means that you have come to buy. Eating the accompanying sweet signals clerks to wrap up everything you have seen. At the workshop, serving tea in Nagayoshi ware is good advertising. Pottery guests who have just come to look usually don't stay for tea. Those that intend to buy often accept only after several refusals and then apologies for all the trouble they have caused. When he is not rushing to entertain customers, a "Let's have tea" from Nagayoshi-san means that he simply wants a break or has something to discuss.

Nowhere is the drinking of tea more ritualized or important, however, than in the tea ceremony. A year ago last February I was invited to Chin Jukan's annual *ochakai*, tea ceremony gathering. The event was a plum blossom viewing:

tickets, costing over fifty U.S. dollars, and including a set lunch by a caterer who specialized in tea ceremony cooking, were by invitation only. But the day of the event I put on my newest blue jeans, a clean shirt and a pair of white socks and asked at the gate if I could enter. I had meant just to take a look, but Chin Jukan's wife appeared and invited me to attend the ceremony and accompanying meal. I eagerly accepted.

In the sixteenth and seventeenth centuries, the principles of simplicity, poverty and humility came to characterize the Way of Tea. Governed by the aesthetic ideals of *wabi* and *sabi*, meaning a refined poverty, the teahouse is built of natural materials and left undecorated. Likewise, all jewelry and ornamentation must be left outside. The tea utensils, including the bowls, are of simple and quiet design. The tea host and guests wear white cloven-toed socks, *tabi*, to symbolize cleanliness and purity. In his essays on the tea ceremony, Okakuro Kakuzo writes: "Teaism is a cult founded on the adoration of the beautiful among the sordid facts of everyday existence."

But looking around at the invited guests that day, many of whom were tea ceremony teachers and their students, I saw little that was everyday or Zen. The workshop grounds swirled with women in silk kimonos of colors as vivid and surprising as the hues of tropical fish, accompanied by men in dark brown kimonos or dark business suits. In the quiet teahouse, with its stark white-paper-covered sliding doors, rush-covered mats and dark brown wooden beams, the colors seemed brighter still.

Most teahouses have low entrances through which one must, according to ritual, crawl to enter, and seat only three or four people. But Chin Jukan's spacious room seated ten guests that day. When everyone was assembled and silently sitting seiza around the perimeter, the ceremony began. With a soft thump, the white sliding door was pushed back to reveal the kneeling figure of Chin Jukan's wife in a brilliant burgundy silk kimono. Beside her, carefully placed on a black lacquer tray, were the utensils and the main teabowl, an antique shiromon piece whose white rounded sides were decorated with delicate motifs of gilded branches and flowering plum. She bowed low, and ten heads responded. Placing the tray inside, she propelled her still-kneeling figure into the room by pressing down and pulling with her knuckles. After closing the door behind her she stood up carefully, back straight, hands gently pressing into the red folds of cloth just above her knees.

I sat transfixed; in the small room, her tall, graceful figure seemed to float. The iron kettle, resting on its sunken bed of coals, softly hissed. The next hour passed in a series of stylized rites for receiving and drinking the bowls of frothy whipped green tea. After the hostess had prepared a bowl of whipped green tea for the guest of honor, individual bowls of tea, prepared behind the screens, were brought out and served to the rest of us. When everyone had finished his or her tea and the accompanying sweet, and each bowl had been carefully viewed, Chin Jukan's wife slowly cleaned the main teabowl by rinsing it with hot water from the kettle. Then came the closing ritual. The head guest, a frail older man in a brown kimono, asked a series of formalized questions about the ceremony and the tea utensils used.

"From where comes the tea container?" (From Satsuma. Twelfth-generation Chin Jukan.)

"Who made the tea scoop?" (The abbot of Daitokuji.)

Layers and layers of rules concerning etiquette and style

and speech shaped each movement of the ceremony. Halfway through, my ankles had begun to burn from sitting seiza, and by the end I could barely sit still. By the time we ducked our heads and crawled back out into the sun, I was exhausted.

Afterwards, I made my way through the crowds of guests to sit under a flowering plum tree beside the small pool of fat orange carp. The gliding fish, the shimmering reflections of "sleeping dragon" plum blossoms restored my sense of what a tea ceremony should be. After a few minutes I was joined by the elderly tea ceremony teacher from whom I had taken a few tea lessons. She was delighted to see that I was finally seeing a "real tea." But after having met a ballerina from Kagoshima City, a man who owned an island in Okinawa, dozens of housewives and their tea ceremony teachers, and so many local businessmen, I felt I had been to a cocktail party. Guests rushed in and out of the showroom with bags of pottery, proclaiming the prices of their purchases like bargain hunters. The tea ceremony itself had a Zen-like concentration and grace, but the rest of the event, I realized, was a Jukan promotion.

I began to understand Nagayoshi-san's ambivalence toward this traditional art. Like all potters, he made tea ceremony ware; customers expected him to, and tea ware, priced higher than the other pottery, brought in necessary income. But he viewed it differently from the large ornamental plates that he spent hours designing and glazing. The few teabowls that he did make were not even displayed in the showroom, but kept in a separate cabinet in the house.

One night he and Reiko had a disagreement about the price of Nagayoshi teabowls. Nagayoshi-san had a habit of undercharging customers, which confused the finances and infuriated Reiko, who kept the workshop books. *Chawan* in particular had to be marked high, Reiko insisted, otherwise no one would buy them. Nagayoshi-san sat silent. The next morning I found pieces of smashed pottery scattered by the kitchen entrance, where a teabowl had been flung out the back door.

Yet it is Chanoyu—the Way of Tea—that underlies Japan's historic passion for ceramics. Yanagi Sōetsu wrote: "Tea taught people to look at and handle utilitarian objects more carefully than they had before, and it inspired in them a deeper interest and a greater respect for those objects." It had been the dream of fine teabowls that first inspired the Shimazu lords to found and sponsor Satsuma pottery. Centuries later, the making of tea ceremony ware is still a Japanese potter's bread and butter.

Today I have special permission to watch Hirashima-san, master carver at the Jukan workshop, make tea ceremony ware. When I arrive, she is waiting for me, anxiously looking up the road. A handmade white summer sweater covers her thin shoulders, and she wears a matching light purple skirt, stockings and orange high-heeled sandals. Tall by Japanese standards, with dyed reddish-brown hair, Hirashima-san looks younger than her forty-eight years. But today she wears no makeup, and her eyes look tired. When she sees me, she waves a can of fish in miso sauce and her stern face brightens. I park my bicycle across the street and push it firmly out of sight behind the store. It is the only lime-green ten-speed in Miyama, a village where people notice details, and I am in a rush today, not in the mood to answer questions.

The noon siren blows. The mailman speeds by on his green scooter, his black mailbags flapping empty in the wind. In the center of town chattering workers from the Jukan workshop spill out through the tall roofed wooden gates. Sandals clack against the road. Across the street at the Kirin store a crowd gathers. *Konnichiwa, konnichiwa, konnichiwa.* A group of six women in loose polyester slacks and white smocks, mold pourers from the Katsuragi workshop, banter as they pick out soft drinks and hot canned coffee. From somewhere comes the smell of boiling rice. Fukushima-san, the head painter at the Jukan workshop, walks out slowly, squinting through his black plastic glasses.

We hurry through the wooden gates of the workshop, where a large Korean guardian figure of stone proclaims its heritage with a bug-eyed stare. On the left, a low bamboo fence surrounds a small, tidy garden containing ornamental stones and a kidney-shaped reflecting pool full of gliding orange carp. The stones of the garden path lead to the low-roofed teahouse where I witnessed the tea ceremony last February. Chin Jukan is the only potter in the village who owns a teahouse, which has historically signified wealth and leisure.

Hirashima-san studied the tea ceremony and *ikebana*, the art of flower arranging, for two years after she graduated from a Catholic junior college in Kagoshima. Knowledge of these traditional arts is considered an important qualification for marriage. In part this is because, like playing piano in the West, it is a cultural refinement, but even more because the virtues developed through these arts—patience, attention to detail and inner strength—are considered good training for the duties expected of a Japanese wife.

Today, however, Hirashima-san rushes off in search of a can opener, leaving me to explore the two-story showroom and ceramics museum. Rebuilt five years ago in the style of a traditional Japanese storehouse, the white stone building is windowless to prevent fire. Just under the roof line is a dark circle with a cross, the crest that once barred entrance to all but Lord Shimazu's personal retainers. Climbing up a short flight of stairs into the museum, I find myself in a well-lit room, surrounded by cases of antique white luxury pottery that show the progression of Satsuma ware and Miyama history over almost four hundred years. In the far corner sit the simple *hibakari*—"only fire"—bowls made by the first Korean potters with clay brought from their homeland, the quiet lines and rough workmanship that gave way to centuries of simple black kuromon. Continuing around the room, I leave that rural world for the separate realm of shiromon, intended for the daimyō's use only.

From the beginning, Shimazu gleaned the best of the newly arrived Korean potters and moved them to Kajiki, near his castle town of Kagoshima. There the pottery leader Kinkai (Kimhae), who later received samurai status and the Japanese surname Hoshiyama, began the Chosa or Tateno line of kilns in 1601. While the makers of black Satsuma (kuromon) who remained in Miyama were left to their own resources, the white Satsuma (shiromon) potters in this group received the full advantages of sponsorship by one of Japan's richest clans. As early as 1602 Kinkai was sent to Seto for further training in the Japanese taste in ceramics. As the "Korea craze" of the early seventeenth century began to waver, favored Kago-shima potters were sent north to see "how things were really done" in Japanese pottery centers. In the late seventeenth and eighteenth centuries, Miyama potters studied overglaze polychrome enamel techniques in Kyoto. The result was a pottery far from the original Korean aesthetics of simple, undecorated ware. Lord Shimazu wanted pottery that would dazzle the eye and compete with the highly esteemed Kyoto ceramics from the Kiyomizu kilns. Satsuma ware came to

mean lavish gilt vases and elaborate water holders and teabowls, many of which are now enshrined with Japan's most
valued ceramic treasures.

In the center of the room an enormous gilded urn towers
over the surrounding pottery. Its four side panels depict winter, summer, spring and fall, an ornate tapestry of gold chrysanthemums, autumn grass, branches of cherry and plum,
and small human figures pulling rickshas across the gilded
landscape. The vase was discovered in 1978 in northern Italy
and brought back to the village in 1980; it was a wedding
present from Lord Shimazu to the Tokugawa shōgun in 1856.
In the same year the twelfth-generation Chin Jukan and Boku
Shokan became the overseers of Shimazu pottery in Naeshirogawa and began the production of white Satsuma there,
although strict controls still forbade the ordinary marketing
of Shimazu's prized shiromon.

Under the sweeping modernization campaigns of Lord Shimazu Nariakira (1809–1858), who also founded glass-cutting
and munitions factories and experimented with photography
and telegraphy, Satsuma production increased. In 1854 he
began the Iso-oniwa kiln, which produced some of the most
famous daimyō luxury pottery in Japan. In 1867, work from
this kiln would appear in Paris at the Exposition Interna-
tionale. Later, in 1873, an ornate Chin Jukan urn was exhibited in the Vienna World Fair. In Europe Satsuma ware
became synonymous with "Japanese" pottery. Back in Naeshirogawa, however, potters in Korean dress still worked in
low-ceilinged workshops, turning their wheels Korean style.

By the late 1800's Satsuma pottery was custom-made for
European clients. In the ceramics museum in Arita a collection of Satsuma ware includes Cupid-bedecked gold mantel
clocks, monogrammed coffee and milk pitchers, and tall urns

swathed in floral designs and gold. More Western than Japanese, they went well with dark Victorian furniture, tall ceilings and heavy drapes. The demand for "Satsuma ware" grew so great that ceramics factories in Tokyo, Kyoto, Kobe and Osaka began to produce it as well. From 1872 to 1881 the quantity of Japanese pottery being exported had increased a hundredfold.

One Japanese art scholar was so taken by a small white Satsuma figure of Fukurokuju, one of the Seven Gods of Luck, that he composed the following poem:

> I've bent o'er many an ideographic page,
> But cannot find, to give the men their due,
> Who made my little Fukurokuju—
> The nameless potters of a feudal age.
> Forgotten now, their secrets: gone their art!
> But I say this, I've found in them the heart
> Heart of Old Satsuma!

Today Satsuma pottery scholars are challenged to distinguish native Satsuma pots from later imitations. Recently a woman wrote the Freer Gallery of Art in Washington, D.C., to say that she had just inherited a pair of vases with the label " 'Original Satsumai' made in the Fuji mountains by an elderly woman who died years back taking the secret of making them with her." She had heard that they had been made by "an obscure order of nuns," and hoped to determine their value.

Fukushima-san paints detailed designs on curved shiromon vases at the Jukan workshop. It had taken me weeks to get up the courage to ask Jukan's wife for permission to observe the head painter from inside the glassed-in room where six women, kneeling in seiza, worked with him. Tall and slim, with thick eyebrows and a head of ear-length charcoal hair, Fukushima-san sat cross-legged, a vase cradled in his lap. He wore red sweat pants, and across the front of his blue T-shirt bright yellow letters read, ENJOYINGLY.

I have similar shirts that say, "Today's girls are be here now," and "Happy day Happy life." In Kagoshima department stores, entire sections are devoted to T-shirts, notebooks, sneakers, sweats, bookbags and pencil cases decorated with English words and phrases. With a printed word or two of English, anything can sell for a higher price. Reiko once hinted that this would apply even to pottery, but I refused to understand, and continued to sign the teacups, rice bowls and plates that weren't good enough for the Naga kiln sign with a simple "Ri-ra" in Japanese on the bottom.

In contrast to the thick yellow letters on his shirt, Fukushima-san's brush traced delicate border designs of yellow chrysanthemums on the vase. Surrounded by small bowls of red, blue, yellow, black, silver and gold, he sat slightly apart from the women, who decorated row after row of teacups with the speed of a production line. He also worked quickly, his fine-tipped brush flicking like a cat's tail. Where it passed it left patterns of chrysanthemum, cherry blossom and plum. A box of white vases to be painted waited by his side. The cat's tail flicked steadily, as again and again the same design emerged.

While he worked Fukushima-san neither spoke nor looked up. I was content just to watch. But when he had put the finishing touches on an elaborate rooster whose plumes draped down amid a profusion of gold and yellow flowers, he rested his brush.

"Why did you come to Japan?" he asked, his eyes down.

"Well, I came to study pottery. Japanese pottery is famous," I answered slowly.

"But—why Miyama?" Fukushima-san's brush quivered, and he kept his eyes down. I realized that he was painfully shy.

"Well, I saw pictures of Miyama pottery in books, and I am interested in Miyama's Korean ancestry."

"Oh," he said, and then seemed suddenly flustered. Without looking he put the vase down in the box with the others so quickly that it clanked against the edge and a small chip fell from the lid. I was horrified. It was an expensive Jukan piece. How many hours had gone into the painting? In the silent room the crisp clink of pottery had rung like a bell, but no heads turned. Fukushima-san looked straight ahead. At teatime I slipped away. Next time I'd watch from the outside.

Hirashima-san calls from the bottom of the stairs, can opener in hand. We hurry across the gravel, past the small coop of long-plumed Satsuma roosters. Blue-eyed Kuma (Bear), Jukan's large Siamese cat, follows in her shadow, leaping into the window of her workroom as we approach. "Go on in, I'll make tea," she says quickly, opening the door. I leave my sandals by the door and step up into her workroom. Under ceiling-length fluorescent lamps, the room is modern and sparse, a striking contrast to the dark-beamed, dirt-floored kuromon workshops. Though windows on two sides afford some natural light, Hirashima-san works under the glare of a swing-arm desk lamp, squinting like a librarian. Carved pots, three or four to a board, dry on racks by the door. This month she works on pieces for a coming exhibition in a department store in Osaka. Large vases, incense burners and water-holders for the tea ceremony will sell for thousands of dollars. The gray walls are bare, save for a calendar and a small black-and-white photograph of the present Chin Jukan. Adjoining is Chin Jukan's private workshop and, farther down, the room where I had watched Fukushima-san at work.

I set down three large pink apples I bought in the food section of the department store for 1,500 yen—about six U.S. dollars. On my family's apple orchard, fresh fruit sells for five dollars a half-bushel. But these apples, enormous and unblemished, are my necessary present to Hirashima-san. Laying down my lunch box, which Reiko has wrapped in its proper red scarf, I suddenly wish that my mompei were cleaner.

Hirashima-san returns with two teacups and a shiny black teapot in hand. Though she carves shiromon at the most prestigious workshop in Miyama, for tea she prefers kuromon because "black Satsuma has the flavor of real pottery." At her home in Ijuin, large black vats guard the entryway. Though she says she had hoped to become a pottery painter, not a carver, she considers most shiromon to be *hade*—gaudy and loud. We eat in silence, Hirashima-san facing the wall. After feeding leftover bits of fish to the cat, she pours tea.

"Your teacher's wife," she says casually, peering up from her tea, "is she busy at her leatherwork?"

I remember the first time I met Hirashima-san. I had expected some grizzled, creaking sensei tucked away in a dark corner. But there sat Hirashima-san, in a blue plaid kilt and a pink sweater decorated with red lace. Looking up through her bifocals, she waved. On the way home I met her again, standing at the bus stop with a brown vinyl bag under her arm, looking more like a housewife than a master carver. As a woman she will never gain recognition as a "master" crafts-man. Beyond the workroom her skill is unknown; even the pots she carves are signed and sold with the mark of the fourteenth-generation Chin Jukan.

For weeks every time I met Hirashima-san on the street she asked about Reiko's leatherwork. Taking the hint, I acted as go-between, telling Reiko of her interest. But although Reiko has invited her to visit, Hirashima-san still has not appeared. She says that she must come to visit while I am still there, because that way "there is a relationship," but some obscure fear, or shyness, or modesty still keeps her away.

"We must be quick. There is a lot to learn," she says. Only forty-five minutes before lunch break ends, and today may be my only chance to observe her at work. Taking up a fine tool the size of a ballpoint pen, Hirashima-san's long fingers gently pull the lid of an incense burner from a plastic bag. At this point the lid is in two pieces, a dome shape not much bigger than half a tennis ball and a flat base with a grooved rim. After carving, the dome will fit into the base.

When Hirashima-san carves, she bends so close to the pot that her bifocals slip down, almost falling from her nose. She doesn't notice, the room fades away. In the white silence I imagine that we are inside time, the only sound her steady breathing. Her tools are made of watch springs and umbrella spokes filed down and attached to pencil-sized sticks of bam-boo. With quick, precise movements she cuts into the smooth walls of clay. A repeating pattern of hexagons and triangles emerges, as perfect and fragile as bird tracks in soft new snow. To the untaught eye her work seems mystery itself, this ceremony of the hands opening windows in a closed gray dome.

The carving of white Satsuma pottery, especially incense burners, is a nineteenth-century innovation. The story goes that the twelfth-generation Jukan invented the techniques of relief work and open carving after watching the basket makers and bamboo artisans who abound in Kagoshima. But throughout the Victorian era, artisans at the Royal Worcester ceramics factory in Great Britain practiced this art, called reticulation in the West. One can find silver and gilt vases, double-walled urns, even ladies' slippers carved in ornate honeycombs of paper-thin porcelain clay.

Imitating Hirashima-san's movements, I measure the perimeter of the dome with a short string. I divide this circle at six equidistant points and mark them on the lid. Hirashima-san works quickly but exaggerates each step for my benefit. Neither of us speaks. She hands me a thin half-inch strip of flexible bamboo. With quick, certain strokes, she connects the points across the dome in a series of parallel lines. Soon the entire surface is crisscrossed with pencil marks. When carefully carved out, this mosaic of intersecting lines gives way to a repeating pattern of immaculate precision, resembling finely worked lace rather than clay.

Hirashima-san came to work at the Jukan workshop twenty years ago, by chance. A native of Kagoshima, she remembers visiting Miyama once on a school trip when it was very poor. Lining the narrow main road were scattered workshops and thatched-roof houses, half of which were falling apart. The next time she came to Miyama she was just married and looking for a job. Her husband, whom she met while working in Osaka, is a native of Ijuin. He works as a driver for a delivery company. His brother and sister-in-law run a small tōfu factory adjoining Hirashima-san's house. Not surprisingly, Hirashima-san was known as a skilled knitter and needleworker, and one day a friend told her of work at the Jukan workshop. For the first three years, she helped with glazing, finishing pots, pouring clay molds in the factory on the hill, loading kilns and running compression mold jigger wheels in the mass-production line.

"Originally I wanted to train as a pottery decorator. I have always loved to paint," Hirashima-san had explained to me. "But they didn't need a painter, so I learned pottery carving instead." Her teacher was Nagata Umeo, master carver at the Jukan workshop and brother of Ikenoue Hideo, the tataki potter I watched last month at the Sataro workshop.

"Every day I arrived at eight sharp and brought Sensei his tea with a formal '*Ohayō gozaimasu.*' Even then some girls didn't know how to behave politely, but I did because my mother was strict." Hirashima-san sat seiza, watching the old man work. She did not ask questions, and he did not speak. At 10:00 and 3:00 she poured his tea wordlessly. When she left, she again bowed low and thanked him formally. At night she practiced what she had seen, showing him her work the next morning. "Oh, he was a strict teacher, very strict. I cried every day. But after about a year of watching and bringing him pieces he let me sit there and carve alongside him."

In a year she could make the first shape, an incense burner lid. Then Nagata-san suddenly quit after a dispute with Chin Jukan and never came back. In the next few years, Hirashima-san took several apprentices, but they all left. "Wages were low then, you know, the workshop was half the size it is now. You have to like this kind of work to stay with it."

After working for twenty years, Hirashima-san says that she wants to retire. Even though she tries to rest, has given up reading and doesn't watch TV, she takes eye medicine daily. At home she collects antiques and old pottery. Her small entrance garden is full of plants, which she tends and sketches when she has time. But she often complains that she is overworked and underpaid, and most of all that she wants to design her own pottery.

Once I asked her why she didn't get her own kiln and make some pottery at home. "Oh, I couldn't do that, not while I'm working," she said, her black eyes wide with alarm, then bent her head to whisper, "But, you know, I have a plan!" She would buy a small electric kiln, she said, and purchase pieces from the Someura workshop to design, paint and carve. But when I asked her when she would start, she only sighed, her eyes half closed. "*Itsuka*—someday." Chin Jukan is against her taking an apprentice, though no one could replace her skill if she left. Even if she set up her own workshop, who would buy her pots? As a woman and an independent artisan, Hirashima-san does not have the status necessary to sell her work. Quitting would not only tarnish her reputation but would leave her without a job. Even in corporate Japan, true lifetime employment exists for perhaps only a tenth of the population, but filial obedience and loyalty are pervasive in the workplace. And as a master craftsman, Hirashima-san believes in her work; even without recognition, she will continue as long as the workshop needs her.

I want to ask her what sorts of pots she would design, but I keep still—I am the apprentice now. She takes up a triangular-tipped tool made from an umbrella spoke, with which she begins slowly poking holes in the center of the penciled sequence of triangles. I mimic her movements. Next she hands me a small, sharp blade made from a watch-spring coil and a piece of bamboo. Moving quickly, she slices perfect, symmetrical six-sided plugs out of the surface. Across the dome emerges an intricate hexagonal pattern. Hirashima-san begins to smile.

It looks as simple as making lattice crust on an apple pie, but after fifteen minutes of concentrated effort, a row of five wavering hexagons lies across my dome. In my cramped and sweating hands, the entire lid feels about as strong as a bar of warm chocolate. I keep on carving, wondering if she has a spare and trying not to imagine the whole lid crumbling under my thumbs.

"*Kirei desu ne*—oh, how pretty," Hirashima-san offers, looking over the top of her bifocals. Her politeness makes it worse. Now the top of the dome looks as if it had been pecked by a ravenous crow. I begin to wonder about the price of the piece I have ruined.

"No one can do it at first. That's not bad for a start," she adds, turning it over in her hands. "It takes time, you know. I'll fix it. You can take it home as a souvenir."

A sudden crunching of gravel startles us both. Two businessmen in dark blue suits, white shirts and neckties, with identical black-rimmed glasses stand and gape at the window.

"Hey, look over here!" one of them calls over his shoulder. "It's a gaijin." Two more men arrive. Hirashima-san smiles and waves. I feel caught in a giant fishbowl. I rush to put away my carving things and gather my hastily sketched notes. More men in blue suits are appearing by the minute.

"Hello, what's your name?" one of them calls in awkward English. "Do you like Japan?"

"*Ich spreche kein Englisch*," I say politely. I am not in the mood for an English lesson. Hirashima-san looks confused.

"Don't worry, I'll clean up," she says quickly. "Go on. You'll be late if you don't hurry. Come and see the tōfu shop sometime. The children are waiting for you. And don't forget to thank your teacher. Hurry!"

Outside, the world is startlingly bright. The entire workshop is a sea of blue suits—a bus tour of businessmen from Kumamoto. Luckily the men at the window have left for the showroom. I slip out the wooden gates and dart across the sunny street. Pulling my bicycle out from behind the stove, I turn onto the road basking like a lazy snake of black tar in the midday May sun. In the distance Sakurajima spouts a lazy plume of gray above the waves. Several obāsan line the road, deftly plucking the new green leaves. They are swathed in bonnets, long-sleeved shirts, gloves and long pants to ward off the sun. Bamboo baskets or blue plastic buckets hang from their shoulders. When I pass they raise their crinkled brown faces and stare.

Sakana! Sakana! Sakanaaaaa-san! Fish! Fish! Mr. Fiiiiiish man! The unmistakable sound of the fish truck blasts down the road. From the loudspeaker of what looks like a Good Humor truck sounds a grating jingle. Four times a week the fish seller passes through Miyama. When the white-aproned fish man opens the back of his refrigerated truck, a crowd of women compete for space, unmindful of the din. On a bed of ice, bright red octopus' legs curl up against gray shrimp and rubbery white squid. Packed in the corner are salmon steaks, squares of fried tōfu, fish cakes and paper-thin strips of expensive beef. Fukushima-san's shiny-cheeked wife, looking Chinese in her blue polyester pants and a blue kimono jacket, rushes away with a bag of fish heads for soup.

At the crossroads of the Kirin store I see Yamanaka-san racing down the road on her red scooter, high-heeled silver sandals flashing in the sun. By the end of the week she will be busy at home with the tea harvest, but today she hurries back to the Sataro workshop from lunch. Inside the store, Kirin Obāsan lays out fresh cans of cold juice for the tourists. Music still blaring, the fish truck turns right at the store, heading for the coastal town of Kaminokawa.

Sakanaa! Sakanaa! Sakananaa-san! blares the truck's loud-speaker. Today I turn right as well and take the back road home.

Back at the workshop I park my bicycle behind the kiln and step inside. Through a thick layer of spattered clay the old electric clock above Nagayoshi-san's wheel reads one. Next to my wheel sit three trimming tools, a sponge and a small white kitchen scale. Today's work—small plates—waits in the damp holding room to be trimmed, each turned carefully upside down so that the base dries evenly. For trimming, the clay must be hard enough to sit on the wheel without deforming, but not so brittle as to crack under the force of the steel-bladed trimming tool.

Yesterday I left a line of plates out drying too long in the sun, and by the time I brought them in they were a row of plaster-hard disks. When Nagayoshi-san saw what had occurred, he laughed. "That happens to me sometimes too," he said, and carefully dipped each one in water to wet the stiff clay before I trimmed them. But instead of peeling off clean lines of clay like shaved chocolate, the trim tool bounced off the hard surface with a high-pitched screech. Around the base of my wheel a mound of cracked plates grew. Clay crumbs filled my cuffs; the trimming tool left a burning red streak in my forefinger. In the hot, empty workshop my mind wandered. I already had enough plates to fill the order; trimming the rest felt like a waste of time. Carrying the board of ten remaining plates at shoulder height, I stepped outside. The yard was empty. The ten plates slipped under the brown water of the recycling vat, gurgled and disappeared in slow, downward spirals.

When Nagayoshi-san discovered my empty board, he frowned and said nothing. But at dinner that night Reiko delivered a brief lecture: if I was going to be a craftsman, then all my pots, no matter how small, were *sakuhin*—"works of art."

This time I have carefully covered my plates with a damp cloth before leaving for lunch. Opening the door to the holding room, I pull the remaining board of plates. From inside come the sounds of intermittent laughter, the clanking of the kettle on the stove. Pottery guests: once again time for tea at the Nagayoshi workshop.

Earth, water, fire, and air
journeys held still in
dark kuromon

JUNE. THE SKY IS CLOUDLESS, WIDE OPEN and blue. I walk quickly, sandals flapping on the cracked gray road, while a warm breeze brings the smells of cut grass and tall bamboo, murky rice paddy water—good weather for the *kamataki*, kiln firing.

Along the road, bright summer flowers poke through the grass. Almost two years have passed since I first came to Miyama. The kiln bulges with bowls, small-mouthed bottles, plates and custom-ordered teacups and plates from my last month of throwing practice. This is the last Friday I will be able to watch Nagayoshi-san at this critical potter's art. Any walking today must be done before breakfast; kamataki begins today, as always, at 8:00. All day long and into the evening I will work by the kiln, watching, waiting, listening, hourly checking the temperature, gas pressure and color of the flames. My teacher's twelve-year-old gas kiln is falling apart. Holes in the roof let out tongues of flame; mortar from the ceiling occasionally falls, ruining pieces on the top shelves. Firing this temperamental kiln takes thirteen to fifteen hours, depending on the weather, the amount of stacked pottery, and the length of time for oxygen reduction during firing.

Each step takes me farther from Miyama. If I walked for an hour I would reach the western coastline, the weathered-board houses and wide fields of Kaminokawa and the long sand beach that has collected driftwood, occasional sandals and, three hundred eighty-seven years ago, a boatload of Korean potters.

White signposts go by, inscribed with proverbs for Miyama's young.

> Children of Miyama never tell a lie.
> Never give in.
> Never torment the weak.
> Follow your senior, Togo.

They are reminders of Tōgō Shigenori, a Miyama native descended from the Korean family of Boku, who was a Meiji foreign minister. Samurai bravery is a point of Kagoshima pride. Portraits of the famous samurai Saigō Takamori and copies of his calligraphy hang in the viewing alcoves of many Kagoshima homes. Even today the Kagoshima school system is renowned for its samurai-inspired conservative codes. During the hot summer months, high school students must wear heavy black or dark blue uniforms, and throughout the winter

Miyama's young schoolboys run to school in shorts. Every fall the entire grade school lines up along the road in red and white costumes blazing with the Shimazu cross and circle. In a ritual reenactment of Kagoshima vassals' rallying to their lord Shimazu's aid in 1600 when he fought in the battle of Sekigahara, they walk all morning to the Shintō shrine in Ijuin. There they join hundreds of other schoolchildren, some of whom have walked over twenty miles from Kagoshima City. In front of the shrine, fat boys grapple one another in a junior league sumō tournament, and slimmer children of both sexes compete in kendō fencing play.

The lines of houses give way to thickets of unruly bamboo and bramble. A small pond appears, surrounded by deciduous trees. On the lower side a long irrigation ditch funnels water to the rice paddies below. Before work today I want to look at Nagata-san's fields. Did she get her rice planted on time? Is her crop growing well? Weeks have passed since I've left the workshop long enough to find her. At the top of the rise I stop to look across the hills of swelling green to a blue line of distant sea, then pass along the ridge and down to the road below. Once again I pause to look over a small valley of rice paddies, each banked by a narrow pathway and intersected by long irrigation streams. Beams of sun wander through the rows of waving fragile rice shoots. The whole valley gleams with a soft, silky emerald-green. I look for Nagata-san's half-moon field. When we harvested rice last October, the thick green shoots bristled with heavy heads of grain. Now the field is six inches shorter than rice in adjoining paddies. Insects? A blight?

Last week Nagata-san walked down the lane past the workshop with a small metal spray pump strapped to her back.

She wore a bonnet to ward off sun, cotton work gloves, and a thin white surgical mask. With this meager protection, she set off to spray her rice. In rural Japan white clouds of spray periodically hover over the rice fields throughout the summer, blowing across the village or settling down over ripe grain and the mompei-clad figures who move slowly, knee-deep in mud. Mizoguchi-san is the only villager I ever heard express concern about pesticides, and he grew his own rice and tea unsprayed.

In the kitchen Reiko scrubs all vegetables with soap, fruits with salt water. She peels their skins without question. When my friends heard that I ate brown rice, they were disgusted. "Brown rice is for cows," they would say; to the elder Miyama villagers, brown rice and sweet potatoes are unpleasant reminders of postwar scarcity. They much prefer white sugar, flour and rice to unrefined foods. Only in Tokyo has the American health-food boom ironically (it was inspired by traditional Japanese foods) caught on.

In a journal entry written shortly after my arrival in Miyama I had copied a line from Thoreau: "Half the walk is but retracing our steps." Today my walk has led me back to the intersection by the Kirin store, the crossroads within the larger circle of the village. Over three hundred years ago Shimazu rested here on his way to Edo, while nearby his tall banners flew. Next month I will be home and my morning walks will lead through thick orchard grass and sprawling apple trees instead of ferns, potsherds and tall bamboo. I will be free to walk and not be back on time. Will I miss bamboo?

In April one of my older brothers came to visit. We went to Kagoshima City and stayed up so late together that the waitress at the bar assumed we were husband and wife. My brother said I had changed. After several days with him, I realized that I was apologizing constantly and couldn't seem to make simple decisions or be straightforward about what I really meant. "Just say what you mean," he said, and complained that I was addressing him in the simplified phrases I used on English students. When I spoke in English I felt one way, but when I spoke in Japanese I felt another. Words began to lose their meaning; I drifted between two poles. Looking at my brother with his light brown hair and gray eyes was like peering at myself through a small periscope. I suddenly missed hot showers, the Sunday paper, summer evenings on the lawn. By the time he left I knew it was time to head home.

Across the street from the Kirin store the tall wooden gates of the Chin Jukan workshop stand closed. At 7:50, a bus from Kagoshima will pass through Ijuin, picking up Hirashima-san and other Jukan workshop members, as well as the women who work in the Katsuragi and Araki potteries. Just before 8:00, blue-uniformed schoolchildren will rush down the road in groups of three or four, dressed in identical white caps and blue uniforms and carrying red knapsacks.

One of my first mornings in Miyama, I made the mistake of walking into a horde of small children on their way to school, walking in columns of three and four like a miniature army. Catching sight of me, they broke ranks, hooted and ran. I was instantly surrounded by a solid ring of identical black-haired children. "*Haro, haro, gaijin da!*" they shouted, following me en masse down the lane. There was nothing to do but walk slowly on.

Today only Kirin Obāsan is busy on the road, setting up square tins by the entrance for the morning tōfu delivery. Dusty and straight, lined with houses and low stone walls hairy with fern and crawling weeds, Miyama's main street seems neither historic nor distinctive. At first glance only a few old-style samurai gates and workshop signs betray its history. When I first arrived I expected the village and this road to be somehow caught in time, like a spreading New England town, complete with hundred-year-old houses and shading elms. But wooden houses in Japan are vulnerable to typhoon, earthquake and fire, and do not last hundreds of years. Thick-limbed elms don't grow in southern Kyushu. Only giant bamboo pushes up, destroying anything in its way.

I cross the road and turn onto a shaded lane. A few paces in, a small path juts off to one side, pushing through a tall stand of bamboo and into a clearing. I step in. Sun pours down through the spiked bamboo leaves and over the clearing. At the far end of the grove a knee-high black vat sits under a crooked tree. The pot is plain and undecorated, but before firing a large square was cut in the rim to form a small gateway. Inside this opening zigzag strips of white paper blaze like fire. On either side, small blue cups hold water.

Kirin Obāsan explained that this site is a *tochi no kami* (Gods of the Land) site. I never quite understood exactly what was being deified. Was it the single tree? The whole area? The black pot? Perhaps it was the very bamboo, rising tall and straight, a towering circle of green in the forest. Though I never see anyone tending the Shintō sites scattered throughout the village, they are always clean—the dead leaves swept, fresh water poured in the cups, sometimes cut flowers placed in a waiting vase.

The lane loops, running parallel to the main road. If I turned around and walked straight, I would pass the tōfu shop, the gateball field, the site of the New Year's bonfire and the corner workshop of Miyama's guitar-maker. But today I hurry. I want to return via the Chin Jukan workshop. A new split-rail bamboo fence lines the pathway. Behind the fence the new bamboo shoots are already twice my height. I pass the silent noborigama of the Jukan workshop. Chin Jukan's wife has said that the kiln will be fired once again when their son returns from art school in Tokyo, but now it lies unused, an empty tunnel of red brick against the hillside.

Up ahead, the lane spills out onto the sunny main street. Back by the Kirin store, Nagata-san walks Chin Jukan's brown dogs. In a white sunbonnet and blue mompei, she rushes to keep up, one hand on her hip to steady her limping gait. I duck onto a narrow path toward the workshop. Once again bamboo closes in, the world of cinnamon leaf and forest lichen opens. The back of the kiln shed looms just ahead.

As I near the kiln an ominous rushing sound fills the forest shadows. A light fan of smoke, steam and unburned gas swirls above the kiln. At the line of spare gas tanks behind the kiln shed, the sound increases to a soft, urgent roar; gas is rushing through pipelines, charging into the kiln in streaks of blue. My teacher has lit the kiln early, without waiting for me. In confusion, I glance at my watch and rush into the workshop area, almost knocking into Nagayoshi-san. Facing the hedge, he is busy rinsing boards at the outside faucet and neither looks in my direction nor says a word. Two of the four gas burners on either side of the square brick and steel kiln are lit.

He must have begun the kiln a full twenty minutes ago. Soon it will be time to light the remaining four burners. I stand by the raging oven, too shocked to say a word. Lighting the kiln has been my unmissed ritual since the first days of apprenticeship, completing a month of work and signaling the start of a new kiln cycle. I don't dare ask him when he started. As his apprentice I should have been here. What have I done to make him this angry?

Then I remember. Last night, at the end of kiln loading, guests had arrived. No matter how busy Nagayoshi-san is, one of his unspoken rules is to stop work and have tea with the visitors. Two or three pieces had remained for loading, but some were mine, small-necked bottles made as parting gifts for the Kagoshima friends I would soon be leaving. While Nagayoshi-san took care of his guests, I had cleaned the last of the kiln shelves, arranged by color of glaze the remaining pots to be fired, and swept up the yard. I had nothing left to do but wait for his return. Inside I heard Reiko filling the hot tub. From the kitchen came the crisp smell of frying fish. I had been invited to dinner by friends, but soon it would be too late to go. By the time Nagayoshi-san came back out I felt as tired and sour as the leftover pickles I had chewed to keep my empty stomach from grumbling.

"Go on. I don't need help finishing these," Nagayoshi-san said quickly. "You were invited to dinner, weren't you?" Suddenly I felt too tired to think of anything but a hot tub and dinner. I didn't feel stoic and Japanese. It had been a long day, and I had done all that I could. "*Hai*," I answered quickly, and headed in.

But I have been working with Nagayoshi-san long enough to know that his requests and commands never come directly. When he wants tea, he asks me if I would like some. More important, my first duty as his apprentice is to stick with the work until done. But I left before the kiln was loaded, putting my own affairs before those of my teacher and the workshop. Nagayoshi-san knew that I was out walking, but this morning his apprentice does not exist. The bonds of apprentice and teacher have dissolved like smoke and he lit the kiln without me.

The workshop slips away; I see only the burning kiln. Taking a brick from the peephole, I look in. Flames shoot up around lines of teacups. I recognize in the slightly swelled forms the cups I had struggled to throw last month for a special order. Suddenly I no longer care if Nagayoshi-san wants me to help or not. The kiln bulges with four weeks of my work, nine to ten hours a day in the workshop, mornings, afternoons and evenings cross-legged at the potter's wheel. Back home in America there will be no sensei to decipher, my apprenticeship over.

I grab a piece of graph paper from the drawer and mark out an x and y axis of temperature and time. On the back I make notes. Settling for a starting time of 7:00, I mark the 7:30 temperature at 400 degrees centigrade. I stare again into the blue flames, licking orange where they meet the layers of kiln shelf.

"*Konnichiwa*," says a deep voice from outside the hedge. A tall green-uniformed figure strides into the yard with a bag of clay over his shoulder. Putting down the graph, I take a wheelbarrow to the road. By the time I get to the long blue truck, Nagayoshi-san and the clay salesman are already unloading plastic bags of clay. We form a chain to load the wheelbarrow. Nagayoshi-san wheels it off, and I run ahead to open the workshop doors and clear out a space for the shipment. When a tall pyramid of clay rises against the back wall, Nagayoshi-san and the salesman settle the bill, while I go in to get tea.

In the kitchen Reiko stirs a pot of miso soup. "*Arigatō ne*," she says gently as I take up the tray of tea. The clay salesman leans back on his stool and crosses his legs.

"What are you going to do when her study here is over?" he says, taking up the teacup.

"I will be lonely, won't I," answers Nagayoshi-san, looking over to where I am checking the gauge.

After breakfast, Reiko offers to wash the dishes. Together, Nagayoshi-san and I head out to check the kiln.

"What's the temperature now?" he calls from outside the kiln.

"Four hundred degrees. The flames are blue-orange," I say, bending down to read the battered dial and check the burners.

"Good," says Nagayoshi-san and turns up the gas pressure on the outside tanks. Immediately, the burners shoot higher and louder in a low, steady roar.

"We'll run out of gas in the tank this afternoon. I'll order more. Anyway, light the outer burners."

I ignite the steel starting rod and wait by the burners. Nagayoshi-san steps in to open the inside valve to .5 pressure and nods for me to start. I open the burners and gas flows in with a rush as I push in the flaming rod. In a burst of orange flame the gas ignites, then steadies into a straight column of tapered blue. When the remaining four burners are lit, the kiln's roar doubles in volume. Within seconds the temperature gauge rises fifty degrees. Nagayoshi-san steps back, peering at the wisps of smoke and steam exhaust that rise from the chimney.

He wants to fire the kiln longer this time so that the *temmoku* glazed bowls will fire a dark black. Lately the kiln has not been reaching temperature on the lower shelves. Black glazes have been coming out a brownish-yellow, blue glazes emerge gray. In addition, the kiln's left corner won't reduce. This time Nagayoshi-san hopes that by firing longer and increasing reduction time he can compensate for the problem.

In reduction, oxygen is cut down so that metal oxides in the glaze "reduce" to their pure or approximate state and leave metallic elements in the pottery glaze. Struggling to grab oxygen from oxides in the glaze, the fire does not gain heat. In the opposite process, oxidation, an abundance of oxygen raises the kiln temperature. Glaze color varies with the length of reduction and oxidation phases during firing. Copper turns red in a reduction stage and green during oxidation. Nagayoshi-san's favorite glaze is a solid green with occasional flashes of rusty cinnabar called *akebono*—"sunrise"—produced by carefully alternating the reduction and oxidation states during firing. In the past two months we have fired four kilnloads, twice the normal cycle, to produce pieces for the April ceramics exhibition and fill remaining orders from last December's show in Kagoshima. Besides the temmoku order, the kiln's top bulges with Nagayoshi-san's two recent exhibition pieces. If they turn out well, he plans to enter them in a nationwide competition. He designs the large bowls for layered glazings that create his distinctive style of curving geometric patterns. Timing is crucial: if underfired, the design will be faint and undiscernible; if overfired, the design lies hidden below a surface of deep blue or black. Next to these large wide bowls, my own small-necked vases, thrown during the final month of practice, are a line of sturdy dwarves.

"Well, what do you think. A good kiln today?" says Nagayoshi-san with a short laugh. "Shall we give the kiln god some whisky?" As suddenly as they had closed, the gates between apprentice and teacher reopen; the morning episode is forgotten as we fire the kiln together. Whistling softly, Nagayoshi-san heads out to the clay vats with a long wooden scoop in hand. I follow with a pile of canvas cloths. As he ladles the liquid clay into pots lined with cloth, I carry them into the kiln room. We keep clay out of the wind and sun so that it dries evenly, without a hard surface crust.

Just before noon the septic cleaner's blue "honey wagon" squeezes down the lane and parks by the hedge. Two men in blue uniforms come running in, dragging a thick plastic pipe connected to the tank on the truck. Nagayoshi-san grabs buckets and begins filling them with water and handing them to the men, who are already opening windows to the latrine. Reiko has left the kitchen and closed the door to her back workshop. I stand by the back window in the workshop, holding my nose against the rank smell, worse than any rice paddy's. Quickly pushing a long vacuum hose through the window, the men turn the truck motor on. When they leave fifteen minutes later, the septic tank is empty.

At 2:00 the workshop steams with heat. The kiln roars softly and flies buzz above my head in droning circles as I clean under the wheels. I give up trying to swat them and go out to check the kiln. A faint sulfurous rice-paddy smell lingers across the yard as I remove a brick from the peephole to check the kiln. An orange column of flames flares up past the kiln shelves, swirling around rows of white-glazed pottery. The temperature reads 1,090 degrees. I turn the gas pressure up as Nagayoshi-san had instructed and graph the temperature, noting the flame color. With increased fuel, the kiln roars harder, its flames bright. When I am sure that the burners are all flaring steadily, I go back to finish cleaning. Nagayoshi-san is still packing pots in the showroom; guests must be coming today. I begin to wonder who will come.

Suddenly there is a noise from the kiln. *Pop, pop, pop.* Silence. I throw down the sponge and run outside. The kiln is hissing a slim column of steam, unnaturally still. The gas burners are a row of quiet black knobs. Without flame the kiln is dead, stranded like a car on the highway. If the kiln temperature drops at this stage of firing, the stress of too-rapid cooling will crack the pottery. I run to get Nagayoshi-san.

"I'm sorry. The kiln is out," I explain in a rush. He leaps up, pushing aside rolls of plastic packing, and sprints outside. Running to the kiln, he shuts off the burner valves and runs to the gas tanks. "O.K., light the burners," he shouts, opening the valves to the spare canisters of gas, and closing off the empty gas tank.

I light the starting rod and begin again. The bricks radiate enough heat to singe my ungloved hands. With face averted, I turn on the gas valves and touch each burner with flame. In a familiar roar they catch fire, shooting up in blue and then orange bursts of flame. Soon all eight burners are once again burning brightly. Only a slight drop in temperature shows on the gauge.

"That was close. I completely forgot about the gas!" Nagayoshi-san says, wiping his brow with a white handkerchief. Satisfied that the kiln is firing steadily, he walks back toward the showroom. "Let's have a good time working," I hear him mutter as he goes. "When it's eleven hundred degrees, start reduction," he calls from the hedge. "*Hai,*" I answer, rubbing sweaty palms across my black work pants.

3:00. From around the brick wedges in the peepholes, orange flames are shooting from the kiln. Inside, the pots have begun to glisten in the heat, as glazes fuse to the clay surface in vitrification, the point of melting and bonding. Time for reduction. Squatting down by the kiln, I feel strong blasts of heat against my reddened face. The gauge reads 1,100 degrees, and the interior glows with orange swirls of flame. Still at work in the showroom, Nagayoshi-san is out of sight. Usually my teacher works this critical stage of the firing himself. I rummage through the drawer for last month's firing notes to confirm the sequence of steps that will reduce the kiln's oxygen intake.

With my head turned away, I gently slide a thin knife into the oxygen valve below the front burner. Even through thick cotton gloves, the heat scorches as I close down the valve to match the thickness of the blade. Immediately the burner responds with a low rushing sound. I continue around the kiln, reducing the air intake on all eight burners. The kiln's roar drops to a muffled rush.

Inside, the fire seeks oxygen molecules, pulling them from metal oxides in the glaze and leaving a metallic residue in the molten silica. I look over my shoulder to catch a breath of cool air. By the hedge I spy Nagayoshi-san, watching with folded arms. He concentrates on the tall chimney spouting curls of smoke.

"What was the temperature at this point in the firing last month?" he asks, still staring at the white flag of smoke rising into the blue sky. I read out my notes.

"*Yōka.*" Glancing quickly through the hedge for stray cats, he goes back to his work.

"*Konnichiwa. Konnichiwa. Konnichiwa.*" Over the hedge, arrival greetings spill into the empty yard, followed by three men wearing eyeglasses and dark business suits despite the hot sun. Three women in brilliant silk kimonos follow. As the women step into the yard they giggle and delicately pat white handkerchiefs to their hot brows. I nod and bow greetings as the procession passes on to the front entrance of the house. Instinctively I brush dust and bits of shaved clay off my mompei and red T-shirt.

Inside the cool middle room a banquet of costly Japanese rice-and-bean cakes and green slices of melon lines the table amid teacups and a large brown teapot. Following etiquette, the guests have brought abundant presents for the tea. I kneel before my small ocean-blue teacup. On my right, Reiko commences to pour, her businesslike manner fading away. Carefully warming the cups and teapot with hot water, she becomes graceful, upright and at ease. Hypnotized by her steady motions, I catch the bittersweet scent of clear green tea rising with steam. Across the table the three women sit seiza. I sip slowly, vaguely aware that in this quiet gathering I stand out like a chimney sweep.

Today's guests are from Kagoshima City. In the fall a daughter of one of the couples will be married, and they want Nagayoshi-san to make bowls to give to the attending guests. Gift-giving in Japanese weddings follows a prescribed formula: parents must give to all guests a present equaling a certain percent of the total cash gift they have received. Today they discuss the price of fifty decorated *okashi bachi*, bowls to hold sweets for the tea ceremony.

I eat the green melon slowly, enjoying its cold sweetness. Around me the conversation becomes a sea of polite verb forms and honorific phrases, flattering comments and self-deprecatory remarks. The bargaining and negotiation has begun. I feel like the heaving reduction kiln, oxygen-starved. Taking deep breaths, I stare at my melon rind, trying to think of an excuse for leaving. The deep blue-green of my teacup enhances its contents—a thought that would not have occurred to me before coming to Japan. In America little of a mug's original color shows through the black coffee. Even posh New York City restaurants serve food on simple factory-produced china.

Suddenly the conversation lulls, changes pace, then veers in my direction.

"Congratulations on your acceptance to the Kagoshima museum ceramics show," says the man across from Reiko. "I hear that the teacups sold too. What do you know, a Japanese buying teacups from a foreigner!" He laughs loudly and slaps his knee. I look down, my face red. Across the table, the women politely cover their mouths, oohing and aahing between giggles. "How quaint," says the tallest of the three.

Under the table Reiko nudges my foot. I look up. "Oh, they weren't very good," I say. "Just a bunch of cups."

Having my teacups accepted for the Kagoshima prefecture museum show in April had been an unexpected honor. When the winners were announced in the Kagoshima newspaper, Nagayoshi-san and Reiko were delighted. Reiko served pancakes with imported maple syrup for breakfast, and we dawdled over the meal for longer than usual. But when I read the account in the paper, I began to feel depressed. *Foreigner Accepted to Museum Show!* ran the headline. Had my entry been accepted simply because I was a foreigner, a curiosity, a news item? This was Kagoshima, after all; with yellow hair and blue eyes one had only to speak English to be a star. But when I asked Nagayoshi-san he answered, "The cups won a prize because they were something new, the designs were different. They were *your* cups." It was a sort of graduation for me. When newspaper reporters came to cover the story and asked Nagayoshi-san why he and Reiko had invited me to stay with them in Miyama, he pulled out a crumpled white sheet sprawling with clumsily written Japanese characters. Pointing to the mistakes in the letter I had originally sent them, he grinned. "We thought it was worth giving her a chance."

In a society where social status is critical, my acceptance had reflected well on the workshop, my teacher and his wife. But the exhibition was long over; for fifty dollars my cups had been sold to a banker in Miyazaki. Once again the next stage of practice and workshop duties demanded my full attention.

Though he is silent, I can feel Nagayoshi-san watching me carefully. I force out more embarrassed smiles, my face flaming crimson. The conversation rattles on as guests remark how different it is for an American to be interested in ceramics—and a female, to boot.

"You're so quiet, and interested in pottery too," comments one of the women. "What a shame you weren't born Japanese!"

"Yes," the man breaks in authoritatively, "she's not a *typical* American."

"Yes, you pay attention well. You'll make a good wife," says the woman on my left.

I listen in silence, my mouth set in a smile. Underneath I feel a jolt of anger, blue flames rising to orange, yellow, white heat. I'm fair-skinned, willful, impatient and inattentive to details—American, not Japanese, and suddenly glad to be headed home. I bow my head, sipping my tea with both hands, quiet; emotional control has become as secondary as breath.

The man who won't stop talking knows nothing of the

beautiful pottery produced by the Pueblo Indians of the American Southwest. He seems to forget that "Japanese" pottery styles trace back to Chinese and Korean models, and that the earliest Japanese potters, from the neolithic Jomon culture, were probably women.

Looking at me carefully, Nagayoshi-san suddenly speaks. "Ri-ra-san, I wonder what temperature the kiln is now."

"*Hai*," I answer and, bowing to the party with a hasty thanks, slip out the door. Outside, the kiln roars to temperature, now a steady 1,100 degrees centigrade. While hot sun spills over the hedge in bars of gold, I drop my last sack of clay trimmings and bits of dried pot into the recycling vat. A splash of muddy water cools my right cheek. The teatime talk fades, and I again accept my status of female apprentice, shadow potter. I wonder whether the copper-glazed bottle I will give Reiko is picking up its desired flashes of red. If Nagayoshi-san does not come out soon, I will have to go and call him; almost a full hour has passed since the start of reduction. Inside the kiln, flames are swirling more yellow than orange in the increased heat.

The vegetable truck makes its way down the lane, its roof-top speaker announcing the latest sumō results. Behind me the kitchen door opens with a sharp squeak. Reiko bends down with a brown wallet and a shopping list in hand. "Please do me this favor," she says, and adds, "Thanks for being patient."

By the time I get to the truck, two obāsan are already standing at the back. No one minds the radio. Suzuki-san's wife picks over bunches of Chinese cabbage, her basket already full of green peppers and heads of green lettuce. I pick out tomatoes, broccoli, carrots, bananas and bags of red apples. Sunday will be a small party, celebrating the unloading of the kiln and my last firing. Last week Reiko asked me several times if I didn't want to make apple pie. She will prepare sweet sushi rice, festival red beans, tōfu and vegetable stew, plus white daikon and Chinese cabbage pickles. Taking the hint, I plan to make seven pies.

My upcoming departure has instigated a flurry of gift giving and receiving. At Reiko's suggestion, I have made farewell presents of teacups and plates to give to all my friends and to people who have helped me while I have been in Japan. The kimono jacket of kasuri cloth in a handsome black, red and white pattern, for which I was measured on arrival, has come. I have also been presented with a handmade cloth doll, its saucer-blue eyes, bright yellow mop of hair under a red bandanna, and miniature mompei a tiny caricature of myself.

When I reach for the broccoli, Suzuki-san's wife, who has an informal arrangement with Reiko to sell the Nagayoshis her extra garden vegetables and bamboo shoots in spring, puts a hand out to stop me and rushes back into her house across the street. She reappears with two dark green heads of broccoli and puts them in my box. I thank her repeatedly, shouting over the radio, although my taste for her vegetables has decreased since I saw her hauling heavy buckets from the outhouse to her garden.

I put the vegetables inside the kitchen door and go to check the kiln. The temperature has risen two degrees, not a good sign in reduction. As I am heading for the house a clatter of shoes sounds from the kitchen entrance. Nagayoshi-san walks directly to the kiln, glances at the gauge and takes out a brick to peer inside.

"Let's end reduction," he says, running a hand through his gray hair.

"But it's early."

"I have a feeling," he answers firmly. Again I bend down and open the oxygen valve two turns to the right. Instantly the burner shoots higher, bright with its new source of oxygen. When all eight burners are open, the kiln roars. Putting on cotton gloves, I pull out a brick. The inner surface glows red as a poker, burning through the glove so quickly that I nearly drop the brick on my foot. Inside, the orange heat swirls with flame and unburned gases. No sound of cracking or falling has come from the kiln. Without mishap, the critical stage of reduction is complete. Nagayoshi-san studies the kiln for a minute and then looks at the even upward curve of my graph. "Looks good, even for a crumbling old kiln like this," he says. Next to the hot kiln he looks older than his fifty-six years, his brow seamed with lines of worry and concentration.

"What about Satsuma potatoes?" he suddenly adds. Roasting sweet potatoes on bricks under the kiln burners has been our habit in the hours after reduction. In the kitchen I scramble through baskets of produce, but find no potatoes. Nagayoshi-san scratches his head for a minute.

"Take the motorbike and go see if thè obāsan in Izakuda still has any. It's been a long time since you visited her anyway."

"But—the kiln," I stammer, surprised at his offer.

"Go ahead, I'll watch while you're away," he says quickly. "Now hurry." I run to get my license and helmet and wheel the green motorbike out into the lane. He throws into the basket a package of candies a guest had brought earlier.

"Don't dawdle, and be careful," he says quietly, giving the bike a push.

The gray sliding doors are slightly open. Sunlight streams through the cracks, across the dirt floor and up into the kitchen. No sounds of motion within. "*Konnichiwa, Ri-ra desu,*" I call through the closed door. No answer. I look beyond the long green garden, down across the fields of waving green rice and up the rising hills. Just above, the hillside crumbles in an eroded heap of tumbled grass and exposed red clay. No sign of a hunched old woman in a brown kimono. Behind me in the long barn, chickens cluck softly and scratch through the darkness.

The last time I visited it was raining. Yonemaru-san sat seiza on her dirt floor, sorting bags of harvested sweet potatoes. Around her a flock of bright-eyed hens gathered, pecking at the hem of her brown kimono. After tea I helped her tie an old umbrella over the blooming peony by the front entrance. Rain came down in thick sheets of silver, but the bushy, soft-petaled red blooms rose straight and fresh, camped under the arching black tent. As we worked, the old woman spoke to her flowers as she does to chickens and cats, in a soft melodic drone of unintelligible Kagoshima ben.

Eighty-five and the mother of eight living children, Yonemaru-san is still lithe and alert. She lives the widow's life now, alone with animals and a large garden, receiving monthly payments from the government and gifts from her children. While her husband lived she helped to dig and transport red clay to Miyama. Her sister-in-law married a Miyama shop owner and now runs the Aiko store by the rice fields. Yonemaru-san knows the potters in Miyama and many stories about them all. Each time I visit her, sometimes to dig clay, the time goes too fast. But where is she today?

"You've come!" a bright voice calls from the still house. The glass-paned inner doors slide back to reveal a kneeling figure. "I fell asleep. Are you well? Have tea. Come in." As she talks, the wrinkles on her face spread and fade beneath a soft smile. I put down my bag of cellophane-wrapped candies and step into the cool tatami-lined room. Yonemaru-san shuffles into the kitchen alcove, lighting a portable gas range and, in anticipation of an hour of talk, setting out teacups and plates of salty pickles, and hot tea.

The small hamlet where we talk is only a ten-minute ride from Miyama by motorbike, a thirty-minute loop through cedar groves if one chooses to run. Yet somehow this place is a world apart. Where the flat rice fields end, a long highway winds along the coastline, dividing greenery from a narrow sand beach. Trucks and cars speed by, but otherwise the hamlet is so still that the gray board houses seem to sit like empty shells or beached lengths of driftwood.

I first heard about Yonemaru-san and her hillside of clay from friends who had met her by chance one day while driving by. When I went to ask her if I could dig some clay, she offered me bags, a shovel and tea. The shovel cut easily through the thin layer of surface grass and loose black soil, sliding into deep beds of hard red clay and iron-rich sand. But firing the rough clay meant repeated trial and error. Glazes picked up rich tones from the orange-red clay, but the porous clay body leaked through the unglazed base. When I asked Sataro-san about the problem, he said that kuromon had always leaked, and that for tataki it was the elasticity of the clay that was important. "In the old times, sure, the pots leaked, but it couldn't be helped," he had explained. "No one had time to sift the clay any finer. Customers just weren't so fussy back then." Leaves and silt collected in the large water vats, plugging the holes, and smaller pots like choka were dipped in an underslip before glazing. Sataro-san still has some of this clay slip, dug from a secret source in Hioki.

Originally the characteristics of the clay in each area of Japan defined the separate traditions of Japanese pottery. Arita, with its lode of kaolin clay, became known for eggshell-thin porcelain, while Shigaraki and Bizen, with underlying deposits of coarse, sandy clay, became known for the rough finish venerated by generations of tea ceremony masters. In Miyama, iron-rich clay had given rise to dark kuromon. But the sources of good clay, never abundant from the start, have become scarce, and today the process of digging, sorting, pounding, drying and soaking local clay is too expensive for most potters; they purchase ready-made clay from a company in Fukuoka. Even at Sataro-san's workshop local clay is mixed with purchased clay in a one-to-three ratio.

Until the war, clay diggers and pounders rotated around the village, pounding seven or eight days in one workshop before moving on, leaving a supply that would last about two months. Clay was brought to the village on horseback by Yonemaru-san's husband. Sataro-san knows all the local clay sites, but when I ask him where they are, his eyes narrow and he answers briefly, "In the mountain," his hands waving in a different direction every time.

We drink tea slowly. From somewhere in the back room a loud clock ticks away. A few red chickens step gingerly into the doorway, heads cocked to one side, searching for crumbs. "If you want more clay, go ahead, there's a shovel in the barn," Yonemaru-san says slowly as she unwraps another box of rice cakes, piling yet more food on the crowded table.

"Well, thanks, but actually today is kiln firing, and I was wondering if you might have any more sweet potatoes."

"Kiln firing! You should have said so! Here, finish your tea," she exclaims. Putting down her own cup, she gets up stiffly, lurching forward and then back like a rising camel. While I reach for my sneakers, she steps down into her sandals and, pushing away two curious chickens, heads out the door.

Out in the shed she finds a bag and gives it a vigorous shake. Sweet potatoes tumble about, rolling under boards and empty boxes, even out through the door into the yard. She ignores the mess and shakes harder. Three more heavy potatoes drop. The chickens huddle in one corner. I reach out to help, but she thrusts five of the largest potatoes upon me and shoos me out the door.

"Go on," she says, "your teacher is waiting. Don't be late and make him mad." She walks me to the motorbike. "Aren't you going back to America soon? Oh, I'll never see you again." She suddenly sighs.

"Of course you will," I say quickly. She looks at me without speaking.

"Bring me a teacup before you go. Don't forget!" I had forgotten, but quickly I tell her that a rice bowl and cup I've made of clay taken from her yard are in the kiln and promise to bring them over on Sunday after the kiln is unloaded. I swing my leg over the bike and start the motor. Squeezing the accelerator, I race over the hill, down through groves of winter orange and tangerine, and past the boarded shrine at the corner. The hills of cedar go by, then the winding streams, and finally the rice fields on the road through Miyama. When

I arrive at the workshop, it is just 5:00: time to check the kiln temperature and peek into its blazing center.

By 8:30, darkness falls over the yard. From the hot kiln, the sweet smell of roasting potatoes rises. Bolt upright and silent, Nagayoshi-san sits next to the kiln with a white towel draped over his shoulders. Reiko comes forward humming a tune, a pair of long scissors in her hand. Tomorrow Nagayoshi-san goes to Kagoshima to see a gallery dealer from Fukuoka about exhibiting his work. At dinner, visiting Eri said that he looked like Andy Warhol, and Reiko announced that she would cut hair tonight.

She works quickly, talking as the scissors follow her hands through the silver strands. "Your hair has gotten so gray, you look like an old man," she jokes, shaping his hair with precise, even cuts. His answer makes her roar with laughter and threaten to cut his ear. In the orange glow they both seem young. When the haircut is over, Reiko goes in to finish her leatherwork. Nagayoshi-san runs a hand through his shortened hair and stoops down to roll a hot potato out from under the burner with a long poker. Handing me half, he asks, "When you go back to America, where will you get sweet potatoes for your kiln?" I blow on the potato and smile back, thinking suddenly of his continual refrain throughout my apprenticeship: "Your mind may forget, but your hands, never." I wonder if for me it will be true.

I hold my right hand up to the light and look at it slowly. The skin is cracked in places, wrinkled and dry from daily contact with clay, the nails filed down past the fleshy tip. It looks more like a tool than a hand. I flex the fingers, watching the tendons pull over the knuckles in long lines. What did this hand look like a year ago? The fingers are thinner now;

the muscles at the base of the thumb are thick and flexible. A long band of muscle running from my wrist up my forearm bulges slightly. Fall spent on teacups, winter repeating rice bowls, then spring concentrating on plates, and finally summer months of small-necked bottles and flower holders—my hands have been molded too.

Several nights ago I asked my teacher again about his own beginnings.

"How did you decide to come to Miyama?" I asked. "Didn't you worry whether it was the right decision?"

"Water always finds its way around the rocks," he answered with a laugh. "You think too much and your smile goes away." Although he often made fun of Zen, and the idea of Westerners sitting *zazen* in remote Japanese temples put him in hysterics, at times he could be as cryptic as an old monk. Once again I turn my hands slowly in the light. Nagayoshi-san watches me. Neither of us speaks in the kiln's steady roar. Suddenly he looks down at the temperature gauge and grins.

"What was the name of that king in Shakespeare," he says suddenly, "that king who couldn't decide—Hamurreto?" He grins. Cocking his head to one side, he looks so like a songbird that I laugh.

8:45 P.M. Inside, the kiln glows with a clean white heat, the final stage of flame color. The temperature reads 1,265 degrees centigrade. Nagayoshi-san raises the gas pressure a notch and the kiln roars harder. I pull out a peephole brick, jumping out of the way as a blast of yellow-white flame shoots from the kiln. Craning my head back from the heat, I make out the shapes of pots within the flaming swirl. They glisten like molten bars of steel, shadowed in places where flames crowd for air.

"The temperature is twelve hundred sixty-five degrees. It's been fourteen hours," I call. We have already fired a good thirty minutes past the usual time. Nagayoshi-san nods and paces the kiln's perimeter. He peers into the kiln through a peephole, touches the gas lines, and glances at the clock. He stares at the black box that registers the temperature.

Above the kiln, a yellow glow rises and shoots toward the tin roof where the flames seek holes. Nagayoshi-san pushes in the damper and waits, once again staring at the kiln. I hold my breath, trying to grasp what he is looking at so fiercely. In a few minutes he checks the kiln again. Five minutes later, he folds his arms and stands before the kiln, staring at it.

"*Yaketa. Owari!* Fired. It's finished!" he suddenly cries. Running to the outside tanks, I turn off the main gas lines. He flicks off the switches for the back-up gas pump and pushes in the damper. We stand back from the kiln, waiting for the residual gas in the lines to run out. Slowly the roar softens, growing fainter as the burners dim. *Pop, pop, pop, pop.* One by one they sputter and fall silent. Then we turn off all the burner lines. By 9:30, all that remains of the charging fire is an orange glow. Silence falls like a great sigh.

"*Gokurōsama*—Good work," says Nagayoshi-san softly. "*Gokurōsama,*" I respond. Pulling down the lead light, he flicks off the single electric bulb. In the darkness the kiln glows brighter, its heat visible in the cool night. I look up and see for the first time the wide circling stars. A slice of moon hangs above the kiln, persistent, bright, a silver scythe reaping stars from the wide dark sky.

IN 1986, ONE YEAR AFTER I LEFT MI-
yama, I returned for a visit. I arrived in
Tokyo on a hot, humid day in July and
traveled down to Kagoshima by train.
Again, Reiko met me at the station in
Ijuin—only, this time it was night and
there were no pink flowers. "*Okaeri
nasai*—Welcome back," she said simply, and gave me a hug. A white taxi
sped us through the dark to the village.
I had told only the Nagayoshis of my
return so that it would be a surprise to
friends in the village. As it turned out,
not only did my visit coincide with the
obon festival of the dead in August, a
homeward migration as important as
New Year's, but I had arrived in time
for the summer Lantern festival at the
shrine, the yearly noborigama firing at

the Sataro workshop, and the last firing of my teacher's old gas kiln.

While I had been away Nagayoshi-san's work had been accepted again in the national Dentō Kōgeiten, and the Nagayoshis had decided to rebuild the workshop and kiln, and to add on a spacious new showroom/living room to their house.

By the time I arrived, the showroom, with its large windows and shelves of pottery, was already finished. But even with the added space, the Nagayoshis' compact home seemed unchanged. The far room where I had slept, which smelled faintly of cut leather and soap, was still lined with Reiko's leatherwork and stacked wooden boxes for pottery. My old futon, which had replaced Eri's wooden bed, was still folded in the corner of the room, a purple furoshiki covering the top. The same pink guest pajamas were laid out on the pillow. Even the old yellow scrub towel I used to take to the public bath hung in the ofuro.

"It's as if you were just away for the year traveling in America," joked Nagayoshi-san as we sat in our pajamas after the hot tub, sipping a beer in the new showroom. I felt the same way myself; when the train had pulled into Ijuin, the dark station was so familiar it seemed as if I had only been to Kagoshima City for the day.

The next evening, when I wandered up to the Lantern festival at the shrine, villagers greeted me with warm surprise. "*En ga aru*—it's fate!" whispered a toothless old man whom I recognized as the farmer who worked the tea fields below the shrine. The priest nodded gravely, and fished among his things for a travel-safety amulet wrapped in plastic. The postman shook my hand and told me to come visit. Several of the obāsan with whom I had sometimes attended the monthly shrine service and cleaning gathered around to fill me in on the local news. There had been several deaths in the village. The old obāsan across the lane had passed away that winter and, in the spring, Ikenoue-san's wife, who had always jokingly complained that her husband liked the singing finches he kept in tiny bamboo cages by the front door better than her. The house of the cranky obāsan next door to Nagata-san was empty as well.

In the days before Nagayoshi-san's kiln firing, I helped in the workshop as before, but now, as a "graduate" apprentice, I was paid for each rice bowl or teacup I threw. I also had more liberty, even an obligation, to visit the other potters, all of whom protocol demanded be given a small omiyage. Chin Jukan's son was now back from traveling and studying in Italy and was at work in his family's pottery, as was Araki Mikijiro's son, who had been studying art in Tokyo. Two new apprentices sat behind the wheels in the Sataro workshop. Toriyama-san had built a barnlike new workshop on rented land in his hometown nearby, and Okada-san was looking for land to rent near Kushikino.

Old Kodama-san, who used to fire his noborigama once a year, was no longer making pottery, and the tataki builder Ikenoue-san had stopped working as well. The head pottery thrower at the Katsuragi pottery, a tall man in his early forties who had thrown pottery there for ten years, had opened a new kuromon workshop across the road from his teacher's huge production-line pottery. There had been a pottery festival that year and potters talked of making it a yearly event to attract tourists. But there seemed to be fewer young people than ever in the village. Even Kubo-san and his wife, who had come from Shigaraki in 1976, were planning to move.

I heard the same disputes about tradition, and about how the potters should keep their industry intact.

"Miyama needs young people to take over the old skills. It has to change, otherwise it won't survive. It'll just be a village of old people. What good is that?"

"There are too many potters in Miyama as it is. There's not enough business. Fewer is better. We don't need people coming in."

"Competition is good, from competition comes good work. But we don't need outsiders coming in, we want our own children to continue in the potteries."

Two days after its last firing, Reiko, Nagayoshi-san and I solemnly toasted the old kiln with cups of shōchū, and, after sprinkling some liquor on the bricks, began taking it apart, brick by brick.

A new double-lane road, complete with sidewalks, now connected the main street with the old road to the East China Sea, and truck traffic had increased. Just down from the Kirin store, a garden had been paved over and a large, ostentatious rectangular monument of rough-hewn gray granite had been erected in its place by the town hall. The monument, which commemorated the first Koreans' contribution of camphor-raising skills to the Satsuma domain, was almost directly across from the Jukan workshop and rumor had it that Chin Jukan had influenced the planning board. Still, no one complained.

When I stopped in at the Kirin store, the obāsan asked me what I thought of the new road. "Isn't it handsome?" she exclaimed proudly. "It'll be a while before takenoko finds a way to break through that concrete!"

I told her I supposed it was more convenient, and let the matter drop. But the speed at which Japan was paving itself over, leveling hills and bulldozing mountains, ripping down forests and farmhouses alike, erasing both its landscape and its history, depressed me.

Walking back that day, I followed the new road to the corner where it intersected with the pathway to Nagata-san's house. In the distance I saw a thin figure dressed in a white undershirt and slip leaning over the hedge to hand something to a woman on a red motorbike. It was Nagata-san.

"Ri-ra-san!" she called. When I approached, she slapped me hard on the back a few times, grinning widely. "You're well?"

"Yes, and you?"

"Oh, not so good—my back, it's a real nuisance." Her face took on its familiar scowl, then brightened. "But, there's good news—my son got a bride!"

I congratulated her, listened to her inevitable advice that I too should marry soon, and promised to come see the wedding pictures. Just as I turned to leave she fixed me with a hard stare.

"Ri-ra, you look different," she said quietly, looking me up and down.

"Just the same."

"No, you've changed," she insisted. "You look more American now."

"But, Nagata-san," I said, "I *am* American."

She stared at me for a moment, taking in my blue jeans and cotton T-shirt before speaking.

"I know," she began again, "it's your hair. Yes, it's different—much yellower now."

"Just the same," I answered, trying not to laugh.

"No, when you lived here your hair got dark. You stopped eating seaweed while you were away, didn't you? *Wakame* is what gives us Japanese black hair, you know."

"Is that so?"

"Certainly." She laughed, slapped me hard on the back once again, then, hugging her arms to her chest, hurried across the yard and disappeared into her house.

ABOUT THE AUTHOR

LEILA PHILIP divided her early years between Manhattan and her family's apple farm in upstate New York. She lived for a time in Oregon, where she worked on a sheep ranch and as a tree planter. She returned as a cheetah ranger during summers off from Princeton, where she graduated cum laude in Comparative Literature and East Asian Studies in 1986. From 1983 to 1985 she lived in the southern Japanese pottery village of Miyama as a pottery apprentice, an experience that formed the basis for *The Road Through Miyama*, which received P.E.N.'s Martha Albrand Citation for Nonfiction in 1990. A graduate of Columbia University's Masters Program in Creative Writing, Philip currently lives in New York City.

VINTAGE DEPARTURES

___ *Fast Company* by Jon Bradshaw	$6.95	394-75618-5
___ *Maple Leaf Rag* by Stephen Brook	$7.95	394-75833-1
___ *A Wolverine Is Eating My Leg* by Tim Cahill	$8.95	679-72026-X
___ *Coyotes* by Ted Conover	$6.95	394-75518-9
___ *In Xanadu* by William Dalrymple	$9.95	679-72853-8
___ *One for the Road* by Tony Horwitz	$6.95	394-75817-X
___ *Video Night in Kathmandu* by Pico Iyer	$9.95	679-72216-5
___ *Running the Amazon* by Joe Kane	$9.95	679-72902-X
___ *Navigations* by Ted Kerasote	$7.95	394-75993-1
___ *Making Hay* by Verlyn Klinkenborg	$5.95	394-75599-5
___ *In Bolivia* by Eric Lawlor	$8.95	394-75836-6
___ *The Panama Hat Trail* by Tom Miller	$6.95	394-75774-2
___ *All the Right Places* by Brad Newsham	$8.95	679-72713-2
___ *In Trouble Again* by Redmond O'Hanlon	$8.95	679-72714-0
___ *Into the Heart of Borneo* by Redmond O'Hanlon	$7.95	394-75540-5
___ *The Village of Waiting* by George Packer	$8.95	394-75754-8
___ *Iron & Silk* by Mark Salzman	$6.95	394-75511-1
___ *From Heaven Lake* by Vikram Seth	$5.95	394-75218-X
___ *In the Shadow of the Sacred Grove* by Carol Spindel	$8.95	679-72214-9
___ *Fool's Paradise* by Dale Walker	$7.95	394-75818-8

Now at your bookstore or call toll-free to order: 1-800-733-3000
(credit cards only).